D1416554

LOGIC PROGRAMMING

and its

APPLICATIONS

Jerry R. Hobbs, Editor

LOGIC PROGRAMMING
AND ITS
APPLICATIONS

edited by

Michel van Caneghem

and

David H.D. Warren

ABLEX SERIES IN ARTIFICIAL INTELLIGENCE

ABLEX PUBLISHING CORPORATION
NORWOOD, NEW JERSEY

Copyright © 1986 by Ablex Publishing Corporation

Printed in the United States of America.

Library of Congress Cataloging in Publication Data
Main entry under title:

Logic programming and its applications.

(Ablex Series in Artificial Intelligence)
Bibliography: p.
Includes index.
1. Electronic digital computers—Programming—
Addresses, essays, lectures. 2. Logic, Symbolic and
mathematical—Addresses, essays, lectures. 3. Programming
language (Electronic computers)—Addresses, essays,
lectures. I. van Caneghem, Michel. II. Warren, David
H. D.
QA76.6.L588 1985   001.64′2   85–6214
ISBN 0–89391–232–8

Ablex Publishing Corporation
355 Chestnut Street
Norwood, New Jersey 07648

Contents

Preface

Logic programming is an emerging approach to computer science in which computation is viewed as controlled deduction. The approach currently finds practical realization in the programming language Prolog. This book brings together some of the latest research in the field and places a special emphasis on applications. It can be considered to be a sequel to the book *Logic Programming*, edited by Clark and Tarnlund, published by Academic Press.

The original impetus for the book was the First International Logic Programming Conference, held in Marseille, France in September 1982. This conference drew participants from all over the world to the place where logic programming was born. The thirty-six papers presented came from Belgium, Canada, Czechoslovakia, Denmark, France, Hungary, Israel, Italy, Japan, Portugal, Sweden, the United Kingdom, and the United States.

We invited the authors of these papers and other people working in the field of logic programming to submit papers for possible inclusion in this book. The eighteen papers that we finally selected include eight that were originally presented at Marseille.

We should like to thank all the referees for the invaluable help they gave us in deciding which papers to include in the book, and for the many improvements they suggested to the authors of the papers. The referees were Harvey Abramson, Harry Barrow, Peter Borgwardt, Ken Bowen, Lawrence Byrd, Maarten van Emden, Richard Ennals, Kave Eshghi, Lynette Hirschman, Luis Jenkins, Jan Komorowski, Bill Kornfeld, David Maier, Michael McCord, Sanjai Narain, Roger Nasr, Richard O'Keefe, Fernando Pereira, Luis Pereira, Antonio Porto, Alan Robinson, Ehud Shapiro, Mark Stickel, Adrian Walker, Jim Weiner, Walter Wilson, and Bill Zaumen. In all, twenty-five papers were refereed, each by at least two referees. The final selection was of course the responsibility of us, the editors.

December 1983
The Editors

Introduction

It is now more than 12 years since Alain Colmerauer and his team at Marseille first created Prolog for the purpose of building a natural language question–answering system. The language has spread little by little throughout the world, particularly as a result of the DEC-10 Prolog implementation produced at Edinburgh. In parallel, thanks largely to Robert Kowalski's efforts, the field of logic programming has come into being. This field has recently started to come of age, spurred in part by the interest created by Japan's Fifth Generation Computer Systems project, and helped by such people as Alan Robinson, who can be said to be the grandfather of the subject and who has recently founded the *Journal of Logic Programming*. The time therefore seems appropriate for a book covering the latest research in the field of logic programming and the diverse applications which it is now finding.

The book comprises eighteen papers, which have been grouped into six sections, each having a common theme.

The first section, LANGUAGES AND FORMALISMS, contains three papers. The first paper is by Alain Colmerauer, the originator of Prolog. Colmerauer presents a novel theoretical model of Prolog, which is independent of its origins in logic, and which provides a coherent treatment of infinite data structures and formal inequality. The next paper, by Adrian Walker, describes a language, Syllog, based on Prolog, which assists nonprogrammers in setting up and using knowledge bases. Unlike Prolog, Syllog does not require the user to understand programming concepts. The third paper, by Ehud Shapiro, describes an elegant approach to concurrent processing within the logic programming paradigm, called Concurrent Prolog, and shows how it can be applied to implement various functions of an operating system. Concurrent Prolog and standard Prolog can be viewed as different special cases of the general logic programming concept.

The second section, IMPLEMENTATION, contains two papers. David Warren discusses an important technique from the influential DEC-10 Prolog implementation, called tail recursion optimization, and shows how it enables Prolog implementations to achieve a space and time efficiency comparable with more machine-oriented languages. The second paper, by Furukawa, Nitta and Matsumoto, describes a model for exploiting or-parallelism in Prolog programs, in which multiple processes perform an "eager" search of the Prolog search space, generating alternative results more quickly than would be achieved by standard backtracking.

The third section, TOOLS, contains papers on two rather different systems to assist in the development of logic programs. The first paper, by Farkas, Szeredi and Santane-Toth, describes LDM, a tool to support all stages of the development of Prolog programs, from the original specification through to the final implementation. It has been incorporated in the M-Prolog system developed by the Institute for Coordination of Computer Techniques (SZKI) in Hungary. The other paper is by Eriksson, Johansson and Tarnlund, and describes a derivation editor for proofs in a natural deduction system. The purpose of this editor is to assist in the interactive construction of proofs, and to help the user convert informal reasoning into a formal proof.

The next section, APPLICATIONS, is the largest in the book, and contains seven papers. The first paper, by Richard Ennals, concerns an application area of logic programming that promises to be of great importance in the future, namely its use as an aid to teaching in schools. Ennals describes a pilot project where Prolog was used as a vehicle for teaching logic to schoolchildren aged 10 to 13. In the second paper, John Roach and Theodore Fuller demonstrate how logic programming can be applied in the social sciences to create novel, nonstatistical, models of social phenomena. They describe a Prolog program which provides a simple model of how villagers in Thailand decide where to live and work. The third paper, by Luis Pereira and Antonio Porto, concerns an application in the field of political science, implemented on a microcomputer (an LSI-11). They describe a natural language question–answering system to aid the planning of research investment in Portugal, and discuss the techniques which enabled such an application to run on a small computer. The fourth paper is by Sanjai Narain, and describes an implementation of the expert system MYCIN in the logic programming language LogLisp. MYCIN is a well-known expert system, whose original implementation was based on Lisp, that advises on the diagnosis of microbial infection. Narain discusses the advantages of the logic programming approach to implementing such expert systems.

The fifth applications paper is by Fernando Pereira, and concerns a new approach to graphics databases based on logic programming. Pereira argues that current graphics database tools provide too low-level a view to the user, and describes a method for relating objects in a design database to their graphical representations, which has been implemented in the form of a graphics front-end to Prolog and applied to the area of computer-aided architectural design. In the sixth paper, Norihisa Suzuki describes how he used Ehud Shapiro's Concurrent Prolog to simulate the complex memory caching mechanism of the Dorado, a high performance personal computer. He discusses the importance of doing preliminary simulations of complex hardware designs, and compares his logic programming approach with other methods. In the final paper in this section, Kave Eshgi describes a Prolog program for diagnosing faults in digital circuits. To find the fault, the program reasons at the meta-level about the logical axioms which define the circuit.

The fifth section, NATURAL LANGUAGE, covers an application area which provided much of the original impetus for the development of Prolog and logic programming, and which continues to have great importance. There are three papers in this section, the first being by Michael McCord. McCord describes a system for semantic interpretation of natural language within a logic programming framework. The central concern of the paper is the problem of determining the scopes of certain grammatical items called "focalizers," which include quantificational determiners and certain adverbs. The second paper is by Lynette Hirschman and Karl Puder. It describes a Prolog implementation of Restriction Grammar, a formalism for writing natural language grammars. The paper discusses the techniques for implementing such grammar formalisms in Prolog, and the advantages of doing so. The last paper in this section is by Matsumoto, Tanaka and Kiyono. It describes techniques for implementing bottom-up parsers in Prolog. Bottom-up parsing is particularly appropriate for languages such as Japanese, and has not previously received much attention in the context of logic-based grammar formalisms.

The final section, FUTURE DIRECTIONS, contains just one paper, by Kazuhiro Fuchi, the director of research at Japan's Institute for New Generation Computer Technology. Fuchi discusses the thinking which underlies Japan's Fifth Generation Computer Systems project, and describes the central role that he envisages logic programming will play in the computer systems of the 1990s.

PART I
LANGUAGES AND FORMALISMS

CHAPTER 1

Theoretical Model of Prolog II

Alain Colmerauer

GIA - Case 901
Faculté des Sciences de Luminy
13288 Marseille Cedex 9
France

1   Introduction

Ten years have elapsed since Prolog's first words (Colmerauer, Kanoui, Pasero, and Roussel, 1973). Needless to say, the language has indeed developed, spreading to every country where computer science is known: Europe (France, Belgium, Poland, Czechoslovakia, Denmark, Germany, Portugal, Sweden, the United Kindom, Hungary, Spain), Canada, the USA, South America (Venezuela, Argentina), Japan, Australia, New Zealand etc. It seems destined to play an important role in the development of computer science, as can be seen in the reports describing the gigantic effort the Japanese scientific community will make in the next decade to develop fifth generation computers.

Facing this development and having taken account of accumulated experience, the research center where Prolog was born has been led to rethink it and to propose a new system, free from infantile maladies. Three people initiated this effort: Michel van Caneghem, Henry Kanoui, and myself. This was a long and difficult task and I must congratulate my two partners for their extraordinary tenacity, a tenacity which has made possible the creation of the Prolog II system, which in spite of its huge size, has been implemented on a microcomputer. The documentation of this system can be found in three manuals (Colmerauer, 1982b; Kanoui, 1982; van Caneghem, 1982). This paper is an extract of the first one. It describes, explains and justifies the theoretical model of Prolog II.

In the beginning, Prolog (Battani and Meloni, 1973; Roussel, 1975) was fundamentally a theorem-prover based on A. Robinson's resolution principle (Robinson, 1965) with draconian restrictions to shrink the search space: linear proofs and access only to the first literal of each clause. R. Kowalski and M. Van Emden (1976) deserve credit for diagnosing that our restrictions were equivalent to using clauses having at most one positive literal (Horn clauses) and for proposing the first theoretical model of what Prolog really computes. We adopted this model in Colmerauer (1978) to systematize the use of grammars formed from rule schemas and create a formalism as powerful for the treatment of natural languages as the Q-Systems described in Colmerauer (1970). These Q-Systems can moreover be considered as the ancestors of Prolog: general rewriting rules plus a first type of unification.

Paradoxically, the success of Prolog in the community of computer scientists is due to a certain number of additions, horrible from a theoretical point of view, but indispensable to the programming of substantial applications. The famous and much contested operator "/" is the most striking example, but it was necessary to have a means of preventing the interpreter from exploring too many paths. Another affront to the theory is the unification algorithm used in the majority of interpreters: it allows the unification of a variable "x" with a formula already containing "x"; preventing this would mean bringing in tests which would transform many programs, which now work in linear time, into programs which would work in quadratic time, i.e. in a time proportional to the number of data items squared.

We propose to reconcile theory and practice. First, there is a deep reason for constantly using the operator "/": because it is impossible to express that two objects are and must remain different, some conditions, which would reduce the search space, cannot be expressed. We have thus introduced the notion of inequality into Prolog with all the implied consequences both for the theoretical model and for the implementation. We mention that P. Roussel (1972) was already interested in inequations in the context of automatic theorem-proving and had introduced them in his very first interpreter, an interpreter which, by contrast, still did not provide the operator "/" in its current form.

The solution of the problem of the unification of a variable against a formula already containing it, consists in extending the domain of the data items manipulated in Prolog: from the Herbrand universe (finite trees) we pass to the domain of finite and infinite trees. All this leads to replacing the notion of unifying by that of solving a system of equations and inequations in the domain of finite and infinite trees. A large part of this report is aimed at making readers familiar with these systems.

As shown in Colmerauer (1982a), infinite trees add to the richness of Prolog: we have at last a data structure for representing graphs with circuits. However, in certain applications, it is necessary to work only on finite trees. The program that checks whether or not a completely or partially unknown tree will ever be infinite is written in a few lines in Colmerauer (1982b). It is worthwhile to point out that this little program needs infinite trees and inequalities. It needs also the notion of postponed evaluation, made possible by the introduction of the concept of "freeze(x.p)" which means: postpone "p" as long as the variable "x" is free. This concept has other names in others skies: coroutines, processes attached to objects, demons, etc.

Finally, the global theoretical model of Prolog has been completely reworked.

The goal was not only to introduce infinite trees but also to uncover the minimal set of concepts necessary to give Prolog an autonomous existence independent of lengthy considerations about first-order logic and inference rules. Mágic has been sacrificed to clarity. The reader must therefore expect to encounter a new terminology. Everything rests on two equivalent definitions of what is meant by a set of "assertions." This ambivalence permits us to consider a program simultaneously as a rewrite system and as a set of implications. The difficulty of programming well in Prolog consists in acquiring a mechanism of "double consciousness" which takes advantage of this ambivalence. Once you have this mechanism, you've got the message!

2   Finite and Infinite Trees

2.1   Intuitive notions

All data items manipulated in Prolog are trees which in some cases may be infinite. We first give an informal description. These trees are formed from nodes which are labeled:

- either by a *constant*, in which case there are no sons,
- or by the character *period* in which case there are exactly two sons,
- or by ⟨⟩ or ⟨-⟩ or ⟨--⟩ or ⟨---⟩ or . . . where the number of dashes corresponds to the number of sons.

The set of *constants* includes, among others, the identifiers starting with at least two letters, the nonnegative integers and the sequences of characters between quotation marks. Here are two examples of finite trees:

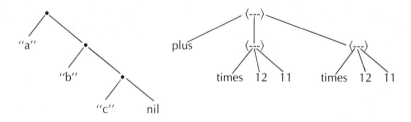

and at the top of the next page is an example of an infinite tree. The notion of an infinite tree is sufficiently unfamiliar that we need to spend some time clarifying this concept. Intuitively, a tree is infinite if it possesses an infinite branch. We are especially interested in those infinite trees which together with the finite trees form the *rational* trees.

Definition: A tree is *rational* if the set of its subtrees is finite.

We use an intuitive notion of subtree, just as we have used so far an intuitive notion of tree. Reconsidering the last two tree examples, we can see that the set of their subtrees is respectively, as shown on the next page. These sets being finite, they are thus rational trees. The fact that a rational tree contains a finite set of subtrees gives an immediate method of representing it by a finite diagram: by merging all the nodes from which the same subtrees descend. From our two examples, we obtain:

2.2   The first two characteristic properties

It is now time to give a more formal definition of trees. Finite trees can be viewed as formulas with parentheses. Difficulties crop up when a tree is infinite: the sequence of characters, constituting the formula which represents it, might become infinite in its interior, and in mathematics a sequence can only be infinite at one end! To escape this problem, people define trees in a relatively complex fashion, making use of sequences of integers to designate the nodes. One such definition can be found in chapter five of the thesis of G. Huet (1976). This

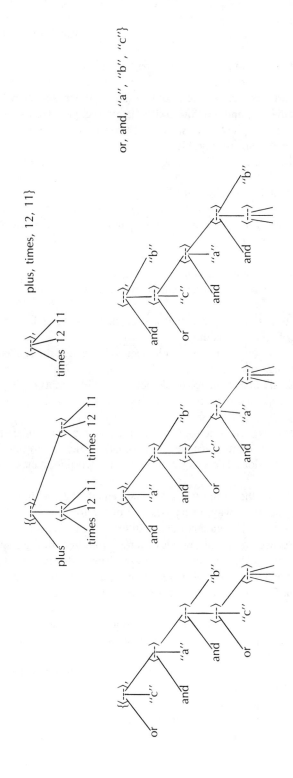

plus, times, 12, 11}

or, and, "a", "b", "c"}

definition, which has the advantage of being a truly formal one, seems to us ultimately more obscure than the intuitive notion of tree. For our part, all we demand of the set R of trees is that it satisfies three properties. We will define the first two immediately, and the third a little later. We qualify these properties as *characteristic* because they seem sufficiently constraining, so that all the sets R to which they apply are isomorphic.

Characteristic property 1 (composition): We have the three subproperties:

1. each constant k is an element of R.
2. if r_1 and r_2 are elements of R, then the object written $(r_1.r_2)$ is also;
3. if $r_1,r_2,...,r_n$ is a sequence (possibly empty) of elements of R, then the object written $\langle r_1,r_2,,r_n \rangle$ is an element of R.

Characteristic property 2 (unique decomposition): If r is an element of R, then exactly one of the three propositions which follow is true:

1. there exists exactly one constant k such that $r = k$, and we say that the sequence of *sons* of r is empty;
2. there is exactly one pair r_1,r_2 of elements of R, called the sequence of *sons* of r, such that $r=(r_1.r_2)$;
3. there is exactly one sequence of elements (possibly empty) $r_1,r_2,...,r_n$ of R, called the sequence of *sons* of r, such that $r = \langle r_1,r_2,...,r_n \rangle$.

The first property gives a way to construct a tree from other trees. This property will lead us to introduce the notion of *term* which is a formula representing such a construction. The second property has two important consequences:

*   every equality of the form $(r_1.r_2) = (s_1.s_2)$ entails the equalities $r_1 = s_1$ and $r_2 = s_2$; in the same way, every equality of the form: $\langle r_1,...,r_n \rangle = \langle s_1,...,s_n \rangle$ entails the equalities $r_1 = s_1$ ... and $r_n = s_n$;
*   every tree reduced to a constant k is different from trees of the form $(r_1.r_2)$ or $\langle r_1,...,r_m \rangle$; all trees of the form $(r_1.r_2)$ are different from trees of the form $\langle r_1,...,r_n \rangle$; moreover, if m and n are different, all trees of the form $\langle r_1,...,r_m \rangle$ are different from trees of the form $\langle s_1,...,s_n \rangle$.

Also note that property 2 introduces the notion of *son* in a formal manner. Therefore, it is now possible to define formally both an infinite tree and the set of subtrees of a given tree.

Definition: A tree r_0 is infinite if and only if an infinite sequence of trees $r_0,r_1,r_2,...$ exists such that each r_{i+1} is a son of r_i.

Definition: The set of subtrees of a tree r is the smallest set of trees which contains r and which contains the sons of the trees it contains.

The definition of a rational tree still remains the same: "a tree which has a finite set of subtrees."

2.3   Terms and systems of equations and inequations

In order to represent trees we will use formulas called *terms*. We first introduce
the notion of a *strict term:*

⟨strict term⟩
     ::= ⟨variable⟩
     ::= ⟨constant⟩
     ::= (⟨strict term⟩ . ⟨strict term⟩)
     ::= ⟨ ⟩
     ::= ⟨ ⟨strict term⟩ ⟩
     ::= ⟨ ⟨strict term⟩ , ⟨strict term⟩ ⟩
     ::= ⟨ ⟨strict term⟩ , ⟨strict term⟩ , ⟨strict term⟩ ⟩

....

The set of *variables* includes, among others, the one-letter identifier possibly
followed by apostrophes. The strict terms are the true terms. However, for
reasons of convenience, we will extend the syntax of strict terms (without alter-
ing their meaning) by permitting:

* the addition and removal of parentheses, but with the convention that:
  $t_1.t_2.$———$.t_n$ represents $(t_1.(t_2.(———.t_n)-)))$;
* the writing of:
  $id(t_1,t_2,...,t_n)$ in place of $⟨id,t_1,t_2,...,t_n⟩$,
  on the condition that *id* be an identifier and *n* be different from 0.

To transform a term into a tree, it is necessary to assign trees to the term's
variables:
Definition: We will call a *tree assignment* any set X of the form:

$$X = \{x_1:=r_1,\ x_2:=r_2,\ ...\}$$

where the x_i are distinct variables and the r_i trees.
   The tree associated to a term t is written $t(X)$ and is defined as follows:
Definition: If t is a strict term containing a subset of the set of variables of the
tree assignment $X = \{x_1:=r_1,x_2:=r_2,...\}$ then the expression $t(X)$ will denote tree
t obtained by replacing the variables x_i by the corresponding trees r_i. More
precisely:

$$t(X) = r_i \text{ if } t = x_i$$
$$t(X) = k \text{ if } t \text{ is the constant } k$$
$$t(X) = (t_1(X).t_2(X)) \text{ if } t = (t_1.t_2)$$
$$t(X) = ⟨t_1(X),...,t_n (X)⟩ \text{ if } t = ⟨t_1,...,t_n⟩$$

If t contains no variables, $t(X)$ is written as 't'.

If t_1 and t_2 are terms then the formulas $t_1 = t_2$ and $t_1 \neq t_2$ are respectively an *equation* and an *inequation*. A set of such formulas is a *system* (of equations and inequations). Unless there is a note to the contrary, we use the word system to denote a finite system.

We mention now a particular type of system which has caused us a great deal of difficulty: *circuits of variables:*

Definition: A *circuit of variables* is a nonempty system of the form:

$$\{x_1 = x_2,\ x_2 = x_3,\ ...,\ x_n = x_1\}$$

the x_i being distinct variables and n being possibly equal to 1.

The idea of system evokes that of solutions of a system. This notion of solution must be precisely defined and in such a way that, paradoxically, the variables occurring in a solution do not depend on those occurring in the system. This is fundamental if we want to be able to reason about the solution of the union of several systems.

Definition: The tree assignment X is called a *tree solution* of the following system (possibly infinite):

$$\{p_1 = q_1,\ p_2 = q_2,\ ...\}\ \cup \{s_1 \neq t_1,\ s_2 \neq t_2,\ ...\}$$

if X is a subset of a tree assignment Y such that the $p_i(Y)$ are respectively equal to the $q_i(Y)$ and that the $s_i(Y)$ are respectively different from the $t_i(Y)$.

Notice that any system (possibly infinite) which admits at least one tree solution admits also the empty tree solution $\{\}$.

2.4   The third characteristic property

We now have all the elements we need to state the third characteristic property of the set R of trees.

Characteristic property 3 (unique solution): Let S be a system of equations (possibly infinite) of the form:

$$S = \{x_1 = t_1,\ x_2 = t_2,\ ...\}$$

the x_i being distinct variables and the t_i being terms not reduced to variables and not containing any variables other than the x_i. Then there exists exactly one sequence of trees $r_1, r_2, ...$ such that the tree assignment:

$$\{x_1 := r_1,\ x_2 := r_2,\ ...\}$$

is a solution of S.

Consider for example the system:

$$\{x_1 = ll(x_1,x_2), \ x_2 = rr(x_1,x_2)\}$$

We can pass immediately to the diagram:

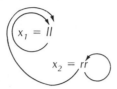

with the unique solution:

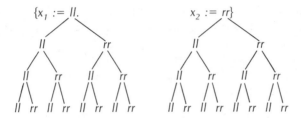

Let $\{r_1,r_2,...\}$ be the set of subtrees of a given set of trees. If we associate a variable x_i to each tree r_i, and notice that the sons of each r_i are also r_i, then we can associate an equation to each r_i and obtain thus a system of equations of which $\{x_1:=r_1,x_2:=r_2,...\}$ is a solution. We conclude:

Associated system property: For any set of subtrees $\{r_1,r_2,...\}$ of a given tree, there exists a system (possibly infinite) S:

$$S = \{x_1=t_1, \ x_2=t_2, \ ...\}$$

admitting

$$\{x_1:=r_1, \ x_2:=r_2, \ ...\}$$

as a tree solution. The x_i are distinct variables and the t_i are not variables and do not contain variables other than the x_i.

3　Solving Systems of Equations and Inequations

3.1　Systems in reduced form

The problem which interests us here is to determine whether or not a system admits a tree solution. If it does, we call it *solvable*, if not, *unsolvable*. We introduce first a particular type of system, a system in *reduced* form.

Definition: A system S for which E represents the set of equations and I the set of inequations is in *reduced* form if it is in one of the two forms:

1. I is empty and E, which may be empty, contains no circuit of variables and is of the form:

$$\{x_1 = t_1, \ldots, x_n = t_n\}$$

   the x_i being distinct variables, the t_i being any terms;

2. I is not empty, and each of its inequations is of the form:

$$\langle y_1, \ldots, y_m \rangle \neq \langle t_1, \ldots, t_m \rangle$$

   where the number m is different from 0, the y_1 are variables each different from any of the x_i, the t_i are any terms, and the associated system:

$$E \cup \{y_1 = t_1, \ldots, y_m = t_m\}$$

   is in reduced form.

Here is the first fundamental property of systems in reduced form:
   Solvability property: All systems in reduced form are solvable.
   The proof is given in Colmerauer (1982b). We give now some examples of systems in reduced form:

$$\{x = 1, \ y = 2\}$$
$$\{x = \langle x, u \rangle, \ y = \langle x, v \rangle, \ \langle u, v \rangle \neq \langle x, y \rangle, \ \langle v, u \rangle \neq \langle u, 1 \rangle\}$$

and some examples of systems which are not in reduced form:

$$\{u = 1, \ v = x, \ \langle x, y, z \rangle \neq \langle y, z, x \rangle\}$$
$$\{x = 1, \ \langle u, v \rangle \neq \langle x, u \rangle, \ \langle x \rangle \neq \langle 1 \rangle\}$$

3.2   Equivalent systems

Systems in reduced form have a second fundamental property tied to the notion of equivalent systems.
   Definition: Two systems are *equivalent* if they have the same set of tree solutions.
   If we refer to the definition of a tree solution, we notice that in order to show that two systems are equivalent, we only need to consider solutions which contain the variables in the union of the two systems. Let us mention four interesting and useful cases of equivalence:

Equivalence 1: For any terms t_i and s_i, the systems:

$$\{(s_1.s_2)=(t_1.t_2)\} \text{ and } \{s_1=t_1,\ s_2=t_2\}$$

are equivalent, as are the systems:

$$\{(s_1,...,s_n)=(t_1,...,t_n)\} \text{ and } \{s_1=t_1,\ ...,\ s_n=t_n\}$$

Equivalence 2: Let S and T be two systems in reduced form and of the form:

$$S = \{x_1=t_1,...,x_n=t_n\} \text{ and } T = \{x_1=t_1',....x_n=t_n'\}$$

If every tree solution of S is a tree solution of T then S and T are equivalent.

Equivalence 3: Let S be a system and let s and t be two terms, if the system $S \cup \{s=t\}$ is unsolvable, then the systems:

$$S \cup \{s \neq t\} \text{ and } S$$

are equivalent.

Equivalence 4: Let S be a system, let s and t be terms, and let $s_1,...,s_n$ and $t_1,...,t_n$ be sequences of terms (possibly empty). If the systems:

$$E \cup \{s=t\} \text{ and } E \cup \{s_1=t_1,...,s_n=t_n\}$$

are equivalent then the systems:

$$E \cup \{s \neq t\} \text{ and } E \cup \{(s_1,...,s_n) \neq (t_1,...,t_n)\}$$

are also.

Equivalence 1 is a direct consequence of the second characteristic property (unique decomposition). The proof of Equivalence 2 is given in Colmerauer (1982b). Equivalence 3 is trivial, and Equivalence 4 is also, if we notice that no solution of the system $\{s_1=t_1,...,s_n=t_n\}$, which includes all the variables of the system, is also a solution of $\{(s_1,...,s_n) \neq (t_1,...,t_n)\}$ and vice versa.

After this prelude, we can give the second fundamental property of systems in reduced form:

Normal form property: Every solvable system is equivalent to a system in reduced form.

To prove this, it suffices to exhibit a formal algorithm, of *reduction*, which transforms any finite system into an equivalent system which is either reduced or trivially unsolvable. At the same time, we solve our initial problem: to decide if a given system S is or is not solvable. For, it suffices to apply the reduction algorithm to S and, depending on whether the resulting system is or is not in reduced form, S is or is not solvable.

3.3   Reduction of equations

We first present a partial algorithm which only reduces the set of equations of a system. Since the goal is to establish an existence property, we have chosen a simple, pedagogical algorithm. In no way can this algorithm be considered as any sort of efficient algorithm which we would consider programming! It consists of the following:

Partial reduction algorithm: Let S be a system. The algorithm consists of applying to S, as long as possible, transformations chosen from among T1, T2, T3, T4, and T5:

T1 absorption: Delete all equations of the form $x=x$ or $k=k$, x being a variable and k being a constant.

T2 variable elimination: If the equation $x=y$ appears in the system, x and y being distinct variables, and if x has other occurrences, replace these other occurrences by y.

T3 variable anteposition: Replace the equation $t=x$ by the equation $x=t$, when x is a variable and when t is not.

T4 confrontation: Replace the subsystem $\{x=t_1, x=t_2\}$ by the subsystem $\{ x=t_1, t_1=t_2\}$, on the condition that, in contrast to t_1 and t_2, x is a variable and that the *size* of the term t_1 is less than or equal to the *size* of the term t_2. By *the size* of a term, we understand the total number of occurrences of variables, constants, periods and signs "$<$" in the term.

T5 splitting: Replace the subsystem $\{(s_1.s_2)=(t_1.t_2)\}$ by $\{s_1=t_1, s_2=t_2\}$. In the same way, replace $\{\langle s_1,\ldots,s_n\rangle=\langle t_1,\ldots,t_n\rangle\}$ by $\{s_1=t_1,\ldots,s_n=t_n\}$.

Because of the following property (proof in Colmerauer, 1982b), this algorithm always terminates.

Termination property: If S_1 is a system, then there is no infinite sequence $S_1, S_2, S_3,\ldots$ of systems such that each S_{i+1} is obtained by applying one of the transformations T1, T2, T3, T4 or T5 to S_i.

This alogrithm indeed reduces equations for two reasons:

1.   Each transformation produces a system equivalent to the one to which it is applied. This is due to the properties of equality in the case of the transformations T1,T2,T3,T4 and to equivalence 1 in the case of T5.
2.   When no more transformations can be applied, the final subsystem of equations, if it is not in reduced form, contains necessarily an equation of one of the five forms:
1. $k_1=k_2$, k_1 and k_2 different constants,
2. $k=(t_1.t_2)$ or $(t_1.t_2)=k$, k constant,

3. $k = \langle t_1, \ldots, t_n \rangle$ or $\langle t_1, \ldots, t_n \rangle = k$, k constant,
4. $(s_1.s_2) = \langle t_1, \ldots, t_n \rangle$ or $\langle t_1, \ldots, t_n \rangle = (s_1.s_2)$,
5. $\langle s_1, \ldots, s_m \rangle = \langle t_1, \ldots, t_n \rangle$, with m different from n.

It is thus trivially unsolvable because of the second characteristic property of trees (unique decomposition).

Here are three examples of the use of this reduction algorithm.

Example 1

$\{\langle\langle x, jean\rangle, y\rangle = \langle y, \langle paul, jean\rangle\rangle\}$ is solvable because:

$\{\langle\langle x, jean\rangle, y\rangle = \langle y, \langle paul, jean\rangle\rangle\}$	by splitting,
$\{\langle x, jean\rangle = y, \ y = \langle paul, jean\rangle\}$	by anteposition
$\{y = \langle x, jean\rangle, \ y = \langle paul, jean\rangle\}$	by confrontation,
$\{y = \langle x, jean\rangle, \ \langle x, jean\rangle = \langle paul, jean\rangle\}$	by splitting,
$\{y = \langle x, jean\rangle, \ x = paul, \ jean = jean\}$	by absorption,
$\{y = \langle x, jean\rangle, \ x = paul\}$	which is reduced.

Example 2

$\{x = \langle\langle x\rangle\rangle, \ \langle\langle bob\rangle\rangle = x\}$ is an unsolvable system because:

$\{x = \langle\langle x\rangle\rangle, \ \langle\langle bob\rangle\rangle = x\}$	by variable anteposition,
$\{x = \langle\langle x\rangle\rangle, \ x = \langle\langle bob\rangle\rangle\}$	by confrontation,
$\{x = \langle\langle x\rangle\rangle, \ \langle\langle x\rangle\rangle = \langle\langle bob\rangle\rangle\}$	by splitting,
$\{x = \langle\langle x\rangle\rangle, \ \langle x\rangle = \langle bob\rangle\}$	by splitting,
$\{x = \langle\langle x\rangle\rangle, \ x = bob\}$	by confrontation,
$\{bob = \langle\langle x\rangle\rangle, \ x = bob\}$	which is trivially unsolvable.

Example 3

$\{x = y, \ x = \langle\langle x\rangle\rangle, \ y = \langle\langle\langle y\rangle\rangle\rangle\}$ is solvable because:

$\{x = y, \ x = \langle\langle x\rangle\rangle, \ y = \langle\langle\langle y\rangle\rangle\rangle\}$	by variable elimination,
$\{x = y, \ y = \langle\langle y\rangle\rangle, \ y = \langle\langle\langle y\rangle\rangle\rangle\}$	by confrontation
$\{x = y, \ y = \langle\langle y\rangle\rangle, \ \langle\langle y\rangle\rangle = \langle\langle\langle y\rangle\rangle\rangle\}$	by splitting,
$\{x = y, \ y = \langle\langle y\rangle\rangle, \ \langle y\rangle = \langle\langle y\rangle\rangle\}$	by splitting,
$\{x = y, \ y = \langle\langle y\rangle\rangle, \ y = \langle y\rangle\}$	by confrontation,
$\{x = y, \ \langle y\rangle = \langle\langle y\rangle\rangle, \ y = \langle y\rangle\}$	by splitting,
$\{x = y, \ y = \langle y\rangle\}$	which is in reduced form.

In the last example, an infinite loop can result if the test for the size of terms is not made in the second confrontation transformation:

$\{x=y,\ y=\langle\langle y\rangle\rangle,\ y=\langle y\rangle\}$ by confrontation without test,
$\{x=y,\ y=\langle\langle y\rangle\rangle,\ \langle\langle y\rangle\rangle=\langle y\rangle\}$ by splitting,
$\{x=y,\ y=\langle\langle y\rangle\rangle,\ \langle y\rangle=y\}$ by variable anteposition,
$\{x=y,\ y=\langle\langle y\rangle\rangle,\ y=\langle y\rangle\}$ same as three lines above.

If we are given a system of equations S, containing an already reduced subsystem E, it is interesting, if S is solvable, to calculate a reduced form of S still containing the same reduced subsystem E. The following fact makes this possible.

Conservation property: Let S_I be a solvable system without inequations and of the form: $S_I = E_I \cup F_I$ where E_I is in reduced form:

$$E_I = \{x_1 = t_1, ..., x_n = t_n\}$$

with the restriction that each x_i, whose corresponding t_i is a variable, occurs only once in the system $E_I \cup F_I$. If we apply the partial reduction algorithm to S_I, we obtain a reduced system S_2 of the form $S_2 = E_2 \cup F_2$, with E_2 and F_2 disjoint and E_2 in the form:

$$E_2 = \{x_1 = t_1', ..., x_n = t_n'\}$$

Moreover, the system $E_I \cup F_2$ is in reduced form and is equivalent to the initial system $E_I \cup F_I$.

The proof in Colmerauer (1982b) of this property makes use of equivalence 2. Consider, for example, the partially reduced system:

$$\{x=\langle x,u\rangle,\ y=\langle y,v\rangle,\ v=u\}\ \cup\{\langle x,z\rangle=\langle y,5\rangle\}$$

Notice that the variable v has only one occurrence in the system. Applying the partial reduction algorithm, we obtain successively:

$$\{x=\langle x,u\rangle,\ y=\langle y,v\rangle,\ v=u,\ \langle x,z\rangle=\langle y,5\rangle\}$$
$$\{x=\langle x,u\rangle,\ y=\langle y,v\rangle,\ v=u,\ x=y,\ z=5\}$$
$$\{x=\langle x,u\rangle,\ y=\langle y,u\rangle,\ v=u,\ x=y,\ z=5\}$$
$$\{y=\langle y,u\rangle,\ v=u,\ x=y,\ z=5\}$$

and thus, the initial system admits, as a reduced form, both the system:

$$\{x=y,\ y=\langle y,u\rangle,\ v=u\}\ \cup\ \{z=5\}$$

and the system which conserves the reduced subsystem:

$$\{x=\langle x,u\rangle,\ y=\langle y,v\rangle,\ v=u\}\ \cup\ \{z=5\}$$

3.4 Reduction of equations and inequations

In order to reduce a system containing inequations, it is necessary to set up transformations which modify them and always yield equivalent systems. The equivalences 3 and 4 furnish two of them. Using in addition the conservation property of the partial algorithm, we can construct a general reduction algorithm which will also deal with inequations:

Reduction algorithm: Let S be the system to be reduced. First, we apply the partial reduction algorithm to S and obtain a system formed from a set E of equations and a set I of inequations. If E is not in reduced form, S is unsolvable; if not, let:

$$E = \{x_1 = t_1, \ldots, x_n = t_n\}$$

We now consider each inequation $s \neq t$ of I and apply the partial reduction algorithm to the system $E \cup \{s = t\}$. Each time, two cases occur:

1. the system $E \cup \{s = t\}$ is not solvable; we then eliminate the inequation $s \neq t$
2. the system $E \cup \{s = t\}$ is solvable and its reduced form is:

$$\{x_1 = t_1', \ldots, x_n = t_n', y_1 = s_1, \ldots, y_m = s_m\}$$

with possibly m equal to zero; then we keep the inequation:

$$\langle y_1, \ldots, y_m \rangle \neq \langle s_1, \ldots, s_m \rangle$$

We designate by J the set of inequations which are kept. If J contains the inequation $\langle \rangle \neq \langle \rangle$, then the initial system S is unsolvable; if not, its reduced form is $E \cup J$ and, of course, S is solvable.

Here are some examples to illustrate all this:

Example 1. The system to be reduced is:

$$\{(u,v) = \langle\langle x\rangle, w\rangle,\ (v.w) = (w.v),\ u \neq 1,\ \langle x,y,z\rangle \neq \langle y,z,x\rangle\}$$

We apply the partial algorithm:

$$\{(u,v) = \langle\langle x\rangle, w\rangle,\ (v.w) = (w.v),\ u \neq 1,\ \langle x,y,z\rangle \neq \langle y,z,x\rangle\}$$
$$\{u = \langle x\rangle,\ v = w,\ (v.w) = (w.v),\ u \neq 1,\ \langle x,y,z\rangle \neq \langle y,z,x\rangle\}$$
$$\{u = \langle x\rangle,\ v = w,\ w = v,\ u \neq 1,\ \langle x,y,z\rangle \neq \langle y,z,x\rangle\}$$
$$\{u = \langle x\rangle,\ v = w,\ w = w,\ u \neq 1,\ \langle x,y,z\rangle \neq \langle y,z,x\rangle\}$$
$$\{u = \langle x\rangle,\ v = w,\ u \neq 1,\ \langle x,y,z\rangle \neq \langle y,z,x\rangle\}$$

The initial system is thus equivalent to:

$$\{u=\langle x\rangle,\ v=w\}\ \cup\{u\neq 1,\ \langle x,y,z\rangle\cup\langle y,z,x\rangle\}$$

We treat the first inequation; replacing it by an equation we obtain:

$$\{u=\langle x\rangle,\ v=w,\ u=1\}$$
$$\{1=\langle x\rangle,\ v=w,\ u=1\}$$

The last system being unsolvable, we can delete the inequation $u\neq 1$ and thus it only remains to reduce:

$$\{u=\langle x\rangle,\ v=w\}\ \cup\{\langle x,y,z\rangle\neq\langle y,z,x\rangle\}$$

The treatment of the inequation gives:

$$\{u=\langle x\rangle,\ v=w,\ \langle x,y,z\rangle=\langle y,z,x\rangle\}$$
$$\{u=\langle x\rangle,\ v=w,\ x=y,\ y=z,\ z=x\}$$
$$\{u=\langle y\rangle,\ v=w,\ x=y,\ y=z,\ z=y\}$$
$$\{u=\langle z\rangle,\ v=w,\ x=z,\ y=z,\ z=z\}$$
$$\{u=\langle z\rangle,\ v=w,\ x=z,\ y=z\}$$

The initial system is thus equivalent to the following system in reduced form:

$$\{u=\langle x\rangle,\ v=w,\ \langle x,y\rangle\neq\langle z,z\rangle\}$$

It is thus solvable.

Example 2. Consider the system:

$$\{x=\langle x\rangle,\ y=\langle\langle y\rangle\rangle,\ x\neq y\}$$

The partial algorithm does not modify this system. The inequation is thus transformed into an equation yielding:

$$\{x=\langle x\rangle,\ y=\langle\langle y\rangle\rangle,\ x=y\}$$
$$\{x=y,\ y=\langle y\rangle,\ y=\langle\langle y\rangle\rangle\}$$
$$\{x=y,\ y=\langle y\rangle,\ \langle y\rangle=\langle\langle y\rangle\rangle\}$$
$$\{x=y,\ y=\langle y\rangle\}$$

The initial system with the inequation is thus equivalent to the system:

$$\{x=\langle x\rangle,\ y=\langle\langle y\rangle\rangle,\ \langle\rangle\neq\langle\rangle\}$$

and thus not solvable because it is impossible to satisfy the inequation

$$\langle\rangle\neq\langle\rangle$$

Example 3. Consider the system:

$$\{x = \langle z, x \rangle, \ y = \langle y, z \rangle, \ x \neq y\}$$

The treatment of the inequation gives:

$$\{x = \langle z, x \rangle, \ y = \langle y, z \rangle, \ x = y\}$$
$$\{x = y, \ y = \langle z, y \rangle, \ y = \langle y, z \rangle\}$$
$$\{x = y, \ y = \langle z, y \rangle, \ \langle z, y \rangle = \langle y, z \rangle\}$$
$$\{x = y, \ y = \langle z, y \rangle, \ z = y, \ y = z\}$$
$$\{x = z, \ z = \langle z, z \rangle, \ z = z, \ y = z\}$$
$$\{x = z, \ y = z, \ z = \langle z, z \rangle\}$$

The initial system with the inequation is thus equivalent to the following system in reduced form:

$$\{x = \langle z, x \rangle, \ y = \langle y, z \rangle, \ z \neq \langle z, z \rangle\}$$

It is thus solvable.

4   Assertions

4.1   The double definition

From a theoretical point of view, a Prolog program defines a subset A of the set R of trees. The elements of A are called *assertions* and, in general, we can associate a declarative sentence with each of them. Here are some examples of such associations:

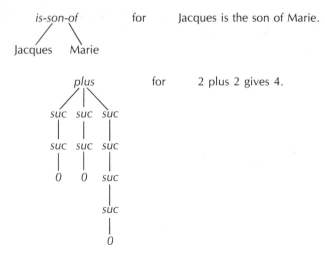

infinite-sequence   for   1 1 1 . . . is an infinite sequence.

The set A of assertions is generally infinite and constitutes somehow an immense database. We will see later that the execution of a program can be seen as a search through a fraction of this database. Of course this database cannot be stored in explicit form. It must be represented by a finite amount of information which suffices to deduce the totality of information contained in the database.

For this purpose, the definition of the set A of assertions consists of a finite set of rules, each of the form:

$$t_0 \rightarrow t_1 ... t_n, \; S$$

where n can be zero, where the t_i are terms and where S is a system of equations and inequations which may be missing. In this latter case, the system is the empty system $\{\}$.

The rules generate a set (in general infinite) of particular rules which deal with trees:

$$t_0(X) =\rangle t_1(X)...t_n(X)$$

obtained by considering all the possible tree assignments:

$$X = \{x_1 := s_1,...,x_m := s_m\}$$

which are solutions of S and which contain the variables of the generating rule.

Each of these particular rules:

$$r_0 =\rangle r_1...r_n$$

can be interpreted in two ways:

1.   as a *rewrite rule:*

r_0 can be rewritten as the sequence $r_1...r_n$,

and thus, when $n=0$, as:

r_0 can be deleted.

2. as a *logical implication* ranging over the subset of trees A:

$$r_1, r_2, \ldots \text{ and } r_n \text{ elements of } A, \text{ implies}$$
$$r_0 \text{ an element of } A.$$

In this case, when $n=0$, the implication reduces to:

$$r_0 \text{ an element of } A.$$

Depending on which of these interpretations we take, the *assertions* are defined by:

Definition 1: The assertions are the trees that can be *deleted* in one or several steps by means of the rewrite rules.

Definition 2: The set of assertions is the smallest subset A of trees which satisfy the logical implications.

These two definitions are equivalent. To justify this and also to show the existence of the smallest subset of definition 2, we must introduce some notation:

The word *empty* will denote any empty sequence, and $u \Rightarrow_i v$ will mean: the sequence of trees u is rewritten in i steps to the sequence v by means of the particular rewrite rules. More precisely:

Definition: If u and v are two sequences, possibly empty, of trees then $\Rightarrow_i$ is defined by:

$$u \Rightarrow_{i+1} v \text{ iff:}$$
$$\text{there is a particular rule } r_0 \Rightarrow r_1 \ldots r_m \text{ and a}$$
$$\text{possibly empty sequence of trees } s_1 \ldots s_n \text{ such that:}$$
$$u = r_0 s_1 \ldots s_n \text{ and } r_1 \ldots r_m s_1 \ldots s_n \Rightarrow_i v$$
$$u \Rightarrow_0 v \text{ iff } u = v$$

We can see immediately that the statement $u \Rightarrow_n v$ corresponds to the existence of a sequence of u_i such that:

$$u = u_0 \Rightarrow_1 u_1 \Rightarrow_1 u_2 \Rightarrow_1 \ldots \Rightarrow_1 u_n = v.$$

The double definition of the set of assertions can now be justified by the following property:

Double definition property: If we assume that: $A = $ the set of trees r such that there exists an i with $r \Rightarrow_i empty$, then A is the smallest subset of trees which satisfies the logical implications associated with the particular rules.

The proof is given in Colmerauer (1982b). It rests primarily on the principle of *the independence of deletions* which is easily proved by induction on k:

Principle of the independence of deletions: For any tree $r_1, r_2, \ldots$ and r_n:

$r_1...r_n =\rangle_k$ *empty* iff:
k is a sum of n integers $k = k_1 +...+k_n$ with:
$r_1 =\rangle_{k_1}$ *empty, $r_2 =\rangle_{k_2}$ empty, ... and $r_n =\rangle_{k_n}$ empty*

It follows that to delete a sequence of trees, their order can be permuted at any time, and thus the restriction, in the definition of $=\rangle_i$, of always rewriting the first tree can be ignored.

4.2   Examples

Example 1. Consider the following rules:

plus(0,x,x) -⟩ ;
plus(suc(x),y,suc(z)) -⟩ plus(x,y,z);

Among other particular rules, these rules will generate:

'plus(0,suc(suc(0)),suc(suc(0)))' =⟩ empty
......
'plus(suc(0),suc(suc(0)),suc(suc(0))))' =⟩
                                        'plus(0,suc(suc(0)),suc(suc(0)))'
'plus(suc(suc(0)),suc(suc(0)),suc(suc(suc(0))))' =⟩
                                        'plus(suc(0),suc(suc(0)),suc(suc(suc(0))))'
......

We have:

'plus(suc(suc(0)),suc(suc(0)),suc(suc(suc(0))))' =⟩$_1$

'plus(suc(0),suc(suc(0)),suc(suc(suc(0))))' =⟩$_1$

'plus(0,suc(suc(0)),suc(suc(0)))' =⟩$_1$ empty

and therefore:

'plus(suc(suc(0)),suc(suc(0)),suc(suc(suc(0))))' =⟩$_3$ empty

from which we derive the assertion:

'plus(suc(suc(0)),suc(suc(0)),suc(suc(suc(0))))

It seems as if all the assertions of this example must be of the form *plus(x,y,z)* with $x+y = z$, the natural number being represented by *suc* of *suc* of ... 0. This is not, in fact, the case because the two rules generate also the particular rules giving rise to infinite trees like:

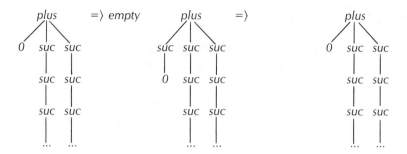

From these rules, the following assertion can be deduced:

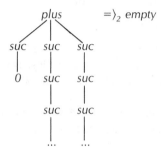

Which could be interpreted as *1* plus *infinity* always gives *infinity*. If we really want *plus(x,y,z)* to correspond to addition of natural numbers, we must modify the two original rules and write:

> *plus(0,x,x) -⟩ integer(x);*
> *plus(suc(x),y,suc(z)) -⟩ plus(x,y,z);*

> *integer(0) -⟩ ;*
> *integer(suc(x)) -⟩ integer(x);*

Example 2. Here is an example which includes an inequation

> *out-of(x,nil) -⟩ ;*
> *out-of-(x,y,l) -⟩ out-of(x,l), {x≠y};*

These rules generate among others the particular rules:

'out-of("d",nil)'=⟩ empty

....

'out-of("d","c".nil)' =⟩ 'out-of("d",nil)'
'out-of("d","b","c".nil)' =⟩ 'out-of("d","c".nil)'
'out-of("d","a"."b"."c".nil)' =⟩
                    'out-of("d","b"."c"."d".nil)'

....

which allow the derivation:

$$'out\text{-}of("d","a"."b"."c".nil)' =\rangle_1$$
$$'out\text{-}of("d","b"."c".nil)' =\rangle_1$$
$$'out\text{-}of("d","c".nil)' =\rangle_1$$
$$'out\text{-}of("d",nil)' =\rangle_1 \ empty$$

In general, all the assertions of this example are of the form $out\text{-}of(x,l)$, where l is a list of elements all different from x.

5 Calculation of Subsets of Assertions

5.1 The window problem

We have just discussed the implicit information a Prolog program defines, but we have not shown how a Prolog program executes. This execution aims to solve the following problem, called the *window problem:*

> given a program which is a recursive definition of a set A of assertions,
> given a *window*, that is to say a term t and the set of its variables $\{x_1, ...,x_n\}$,
> find all the assertions that can be *seen* through this *window*, that is to say, calculate all the tree assignments $X = \{x_1:=r_1,...,x_n:=r_n\}$ for which $t(X)$ becomes an assertion.

The solution of this problem proceeds by introducing the binary relation $-\rangle_i$ between pairs of the form (u,S) where u is a sequence of terms, possibly empty, and S is a system of equations and inequations.

Definition: If u and v are two sequences of terms, possibly empty, and S and T are two systems, then the relation $-\rangle_i$ is defined by:

$$(u,S) -\rangle_{i+1} (v,T) \ iff:$$

there is a rule $s_0 -\rangle s_1...s_m$, U, whose variables have been renamed so that none are in common with those of (u,S), and if we assume that $u = t_0 \ t_1...t_n$, the t_i being terms, then we get:

$$(s_1...s_m \ t_1...t_n, \ S \cup U \cup \{t_0=s_0\}) -\rangle_i (u,T);$$
$$(u,S) -\rangle_0 (v,T) \ iff \ u = v, \ S = T, \ and \ S \ is \ solvable.$$

The relation $-\rangle_i$ has several properties analogous to those of the relation $=\rangle_i$:

First of all, it falls out immediately from the definition that the expression $(u,S) -\rangle_n (v,T)$ corresponds to the existence of a sequence of (u_i,S_i) such that:

$$(u,S) = (u_0,S_0) \text{ -} \rangle_1 \ (u_1,S_1) \text{ -} \rangle_1 \ ... \text{ -} \rangle_1 \ (u_n,S_n) = (v,T).$$

Moreover, the principle of the independence of deletions is rediscovered in a slightly different form which is given below and which can be proved by induction on k:

Generalized principle of the independence of deletions: For all terms $t_1,...,t_n$ and systems S and T:

$$(t_1...t_n,S) \text{ -} \rangle k \ (empty,T) \ \text{iff:}$$

k is a sum of n integers $k_1 + ... + k_n = k$ and T is a union of n systems $T_1 \cup ... \cup T_n = T$, which pairwise have no variables in common other than those contained in $(t_1...t_n,S)$, with:

$$(t_1,S) \text{ -} \rangle_{k_1} \ (empty,T_1) \ ... \ \text{and} \ (t_n,S) \text{ -} \rangle_{k_n} \ (empty,T_n).$$

It follows that to *delete* (by means of $\text{-} \rangle_i$) a sequence u of terms occurring in a pair (u,S), the terms in the sequence can be permuted at any time. Here is the final analogous property. It allows us to conclude that $\text{-} \rangle_i$ is a *generalization of* $= \rangle_i$.

Principle of generalization: Let i be a nonnegative integer, and let $t_1...t_n$ be a sequence of terms, possibly empty, let S be a system and let X be a tree assignment of the variables contained in $(t_1...t_n,S)$, then:

> X is a tree solution of S, and $t_1(X)...t_n(X) = \rangle_i$ empty
> iff:
>> there exists a system T with:
>> $(t_1...t_n,S) \text{ -} \rangle_i \ (empty,T)$ and X a tree solution of T.

We give a proof of this property in Colmerauer (1982b). In restricting this principle to $n = 1$, $S = \{\}$ and by using the first definition of the set of assertions, we obtain:

Principle of the window: For any term t and any tree assignment X of its variables:

> $t(X)$ is an assertion iff:
>> there is an integer i and a system S with:
>> $(t,\{\}) \text{ -} \rangle_i \ (empty,S)$ and X a tree solution of S.

In order to solve our initial problem, it will suffice, therefore, to enumerate all the sequences:

$$(t,\{\}) = (u_0,S_0) \text{ -} \rangle_1 \ (u_1,S_1) \text{ -} \rangle_1 \ (u_2,S_2) \text{ -} \rangle_1 \ ...$$

and to try to reach every S_i whose corresponding u_i is empty. Each tree assignment X of the variables of the window t which makes $t(X)$ an assertion will then be a solution of such an S_i. Of course, from an algorithmic point of view, there will be a problem because some of these sequences can be infinite.

To illustrate all this, we reconsider the two examples from the preceding chapter:

5.2   Examples

Example 1. The rules are:

$$plus(0,x,x) \text{ -}\text{)};$$
$$plus(suc(x),y,suc(z)) \text{ -}\text{)} \; plus \; (x,y,z);$$

To show our ability to handle infinite trees, let us calculate the assertions that can be seen through the window:

$$t = plus(suc(0),x,x)$$

that is to say, to find the tree assignments:

$$X = \{x:=r\}$$

such that $t(X)$ is an assertion.

We have successively:

$$u_0 = plus(suc(0),x,x)$$
$$S_0 = \{\}$$
$$S_0' = \{\}$$

$$u_1 = plus(x,y,z)$$
$$S_1 = S_0 \; \cup \; \{plus(suc(0),x,x)=plus(suc(x'),y',suc(z'))\}$$
$$S_1' = \{x=y', \; x'=0, \; y'=suc(z')\}$$

$$u_2 = empty$$
$$S_2 = S_1 \; \cup \; \{plus(x',y',z')=plus(0,x'',x'')\}$$
$$S_2' = \{x=x'', \; x'=0, \; x''=suc(x''), \; y'=x'', \; z'=x''\}$$

The only solution is thus:

$$X = \{x := suc\}$$
$$\mid$$
$$suc$$
$$\mid$$
$$suc$$
$$\mid$$
$$...$$

Example 2. The rules are:

$$out\text{-}of(x,nil) \rightarrow\rangle \ ;$$
$$out\text{-}of(x,y.l) \rightarrow\rangle \ out\text{-}of(x,l), \ \{x\neq y\};$$

The window is:

$$t = out\text{-}of("c","a"."b".nil)$$

It must be verified that $t(\{\})$ is an assertion.
This is true because we have successively:

$$u_0 = out\text{-}of("c","a"."b".nil)$$
$$S_0 = \{\}$$
$$S_0' = \{\}$$

$$u_1 = out\text{-}of(x,l)$$
$$S_1 = S_0 \ \cup \ \{out\text{-}of("c","a"."b".nil)=out\text{-}of(x,y.l), \ x\neq y\}$$
$$S_1' = \{x="c", \ l="b".nil, \ y="a"\}$$

$$u_2 = out\text{-}of(x',l')$$
$$S_2 = S_1 \ \cup \ \{out\text{-}of(x,l)=out\text{-}of(x',y'.l'), \ x'\neq y'\}$$
$$S_2' = \{x=x', \ x'="c", \ l=y'.l', \ l'=nil, \ y="a", \ y'="b"\}$$

$$u_3 = empty$$
$$S_3 = S_2 \ \cup \ \{out\text{-}of(x',l')=out\text{-}of(x'',nil)\}$$
$$S_3' = \{x=x',x'=x'', \ x''="c", \ l=y'.l', \ l'=nil, \ y="a", \ y'="b"\}$$

6   The Prolog Time Machine

As we have seen, the programming language Prolog allows us, on the one hand, to define indirectly infinite sets of assertions, and on the other, to select and to calculate some of these assertions. This calculation is made by enumerating sequences of pairs:

$$(u_0,S_0) \rightarrow\rangle_1 \ (u_1,S_1) \rightarrow\rangle_1 \ (u_2,S_2) \rightarrow\rangle_1 \ ....$$

Up until now, we have always considered that u_0 was reduced to a single term t and that the system S_0 was the empty set $\{\}$. If we reconsider the principle of generalization, and simultaneously what is meant by both the first definition of assertions and the principle of the independence of deletions by $\rightarrow\rangle_i$, we can reformulate the window principle in a more general form where u_0 will be some sequence $t_1...t_n$ of terms and S_0 some system S of equations and inequations:

Enlarged window principle: Let $\{t_1,...,t_n\}$ be a set of terms, let S be a system, let $\{x_1,...,x_m\}$ be the set of variables that occur in them, and let X be a tree assignment of the form $X = \{x_1:=r_1,...,x_m:=r_m\}$, then:
X is a solution of S and $\{t_1(X),...,t_n(X)\}$ is contained in the set of assertions iff:

there is an integer i and a system T with:
$(t_1...t_n,S)$ -$\rangle_i$ (empty,T) and X a solution of T

The enumeration of sequences of pairs (u_i,S_i) can be done in many different ways, for instance, by changing the order of the enumeration. To make all this more precise, as well as to give access to an interface with external subprograms, we now describe the operational semantics of Prolog by means of an abstract machine called the *time machine*.

The machine is composed of:

1. A cell *sequence-of-rules* containing the sequence of rules which constitutes the Prolog program.
2. A cell t containing the time. This time is in fact the index i of the current pair (u_i,S_i);
3. Three infinite sequences of cells, each cell indexed by a nonnegative integer i:
    a. *goals$_i$* contains the sequence of terms u_i,
    b. *system$_i$* contains the system S_i,
    c. *rules$_i$* contains the sequence of rules which are *active* at time t.

Only the cell *sequence-of-rules* is given an initial value which provides the programmer with an initial environment. The machine reads the commands on its input unit, executes them one after another and prints out the results as they become available. Here is the syntax of a command:

⟨command⟩
    ::= ⟨sequence of term⟩ ;
    ::= ⟨sequence of terms⟩, ⟨system⟩;

Of course, the absence of ⟨system⟩ in a command corresponds to the empty system $\{\}$. The operation of the machine is schematized as in Figure 1.1.

head[x]: represents the first element of the sequence x, or the left member of the rule x.

tail[x]: represents either the sequence x cut off from its first element or the right member (without the system) of the rule x.

conditions[r]: represents the system of equalities and inequalities of the rule r.

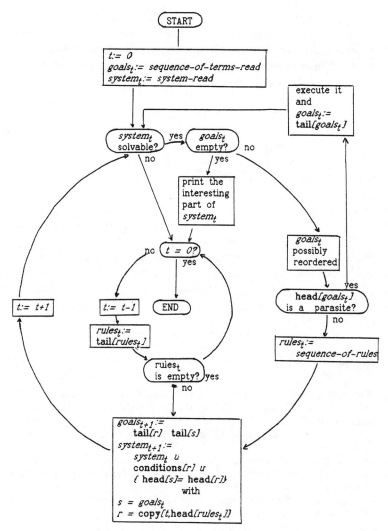

Figure 1.1 Operation of the Prolog Time Machine

copy[*t,r*]: represents a *t*-th copy of the rule *r*. This copy has variables in common neither with the value of *goals_t* nor with the value of *system_t*.

Parasites are the names of subprograms which perform different tasks.

⟨parasite⟩
::= /
::= ⟨syntax unknown, but different from that of a term⟩

Only the parasite "/", whose effect we describe subsequently, is directly accessible to the programmer. The other parasites occur inside the large set of predefined rules assigned at initialization to the cell *sequence-of-rules*. This set of predefined rules constitutes a complete programming environment described in Colmerauer (1982b) and van Caneghem (1982). It permits us:

1. to control and to modify program execution;
2. to modify the current set of rules contained in *sequence-of-rules* and thus to input and to update programs;
3. to access the classical arithmetic and string functions;
4. to manage input and output.

The time machine simulates a nondeterministic machine. As can be seen from the schema, this simulation is done by backtracking on the accumulated choice points. This accumulation of information has limits, and it is necessary to be able to delete all the choice points accumulated between the time t-k and the present time t. The execution of the parasite "/" has the effect of assigning *empty* to all the cells $rules_i$ whose index i is an element of $\{t$-$k,\ldots,t$-$1,t\}$ The integer t-k is the last moment such that $goals_{t-k}$ did not contain that occurrence of "/".

References

Battani, G., and H. Meloni. (1973). *Interpréteur de langage de programmation Prolog*. Internal Report, Groupe Intelligence Artificielle, Université Aix-Marseille II, September.

Colmerauer, A. (1970). *Les systèmes-q ou un formalisme pour analyser et synthétiser des phrases sur ordinateur*. Internal Report 43. Départment d'Informatique, Université de Montréal, September.

Colmerauer, A. (1978). "Metamorphosis Grammars, Natural Language Communication with Computers." Edited by L. Bolc, *Lectures Notes in Computer Science* 63, pp. 133–189, Springer Verlag, May.

Colmerauer, A. (1982a). "Prolog and infinite trees." In *Logic programming*, Edited by K. L. Clark and S. A. Tarnlund, Academic Press.

Colmerauer, A. (1982b). *Prolog II Reference Manual and Theoretical Model*. Internal Report, Groupe Intelligence Artificielle, Université Aix-Marseille II, October.

Colmerauer, A., H. Kanoui, R. Pasero, and P. Roussel. (1973). *Un système de communication homme-machine en francais*. Research Report CRI 72-18, Groupe Intelligence Artificelle, Université Aix-Marseille II, June.

Huet G. (1976). *Résolution d'équations dans des langages d'ordre 1,2,...,oméga*. Thèse d'ëtat, Université Paris VII, September.

Kanoui H. (1982). *PROLOG II, Manual of Examples*, Internal Report, Groupe Intelligence Artificielle, Université Aix-Marseille II, October.

Kowalski, R., and M. Van Emden. (1976). "The Semantics of Predicate Logic as Programming Language." *JACM*, 23, no. 4, pp. 733–743, October.

Robinson, J. A. (1965). "A Machine-oriented Logic Based on the Resolution Principle." *JACM*, 12, no. 1, pp. 227–234, December.

Roussel, P. (1972). *Définition et traitement de l'égalite formelle en démonstration automatique.* Thèse de 3ème cycle, Groupe Intelligence Artificielle, Université Aix-Marseille II.

Roussel P. (1975). *Prolog: manuel de reference et d'utilisation.* Rapport de recherche CNRS, Groupe Intelligence Artificielle, Université Aix-Marseille II, October.

van Caneghem, M. (1982). *Prolog II User's Manual.* Internal Report, Groupe Intelligence Artificielle, Université Aix-Marseille II, October.

CHAPTER 2

Syllog: An Approach to Prolog for Nonprogrammers

Adrian Walker

IBM Thomas J. Watson Research Center
P.O. Box 218
Yorktown Heights, New York 10598

1   Introduction

It is widely thought that the potential for new applications of computers far outstrips what can be supplied using presently known programming techniques. For example, Michie (1983) indicates that over three decades, hardware performance for fixed cost has increased by about a million times, while programmer productivity has increased by a factor of about four.

Logic programming (Kowalski, 1979) promises to ease this software bottleneck, to the extent that it allows a programmer to write a specification, and then to run it as a program (Walker, 1984). Prolog (Clocksin & Mellish, 1982; Pereira et al., 1978; Roberts, 1977), the main current logic programming language, is a delight for many programmers to work in. However, it is definitely a programming language, hence it is rarely used directly by nonprogrammers for writing substantial applications. Rather, specific systems, e.g., for querying a knowledge base in English (Warren & Pereira, 1981; McCord, 1982; Walker & Porto, 1983) are written by programmers in Prolog, and can then be used by anyone who can type at a terminal.

However, full natural language access to knowledge bases is still a research area, particularly when the goal is to use natural language to construct a knowledge base, as well as to query it conce it has been constructed. There are many different human languages and jargons, and there are many different subject areas in which knowledge bases could be useful. It appears expensive to write and maintain robust practical natural language packages and their supporting dictionaries for all of these languages and subjects. In particular, keeping the built-in expertise of such packages up to date could be costly.

To complement work on natural language packages, we can try to see if the services needed by a nonprogrammer in setting up, querying, and changing a knowledge base, can be provided in a different, but still adequate way. Syllog is designed for just this purpose. During normal use, Syllog gradually accumulates knowledge about an application in the form of English-like syllogisms. Syllog automatically prompts with sentences that it has been told about. Provided that certain simple conventions are followed, these sentences can be in English, or in any other language or specialized dialect that uses the same letters as English. Typically, a question is posed by choosing a sentence on the screen, and then modifying it if necessary. A question can be about facts, or about rules for using the facts. Both facts and rules can be modified on the screen. Since Syllog's prompt consists of the sentences it has been told about, with the most recently used sentences appearing first, one can see at a glance what a knowledge base is about.

Other approaches to extending Prolog so that it can be used by people with little programming experience include Simple Prolog (Clark et al., 1981), and the related Query-the-User program (Sergot, 1982). These differ in purpose from Syllog in that they are designed to teach the user their own notation (Ennals, 1985), which is similar to mathematical logic, rather than to approximate the user's natural language. At the time of writing, they do not provide a full-screen interface for the user, and explanations of 'no' answers are not available.

A major problem for novice users of Prolog is that a recursive program can loop in an unbounded fashion without returning any answer. One needs experience in the language to change a program to avoid this behavior. Hence some versions of Prolog contain a limited means of detecting such recursions. However, in such Prologs, the order of the clauses matters, and it is not known whether the prevention of recursions could cause the interpreter to miss solutions that follow logically from the clauses of a program. The problem of detecting and correcting recursive looping has been widely studied (see for example Henschen & Naqvi, 1984; Walker, 1981; Walker, 1983). It is possible that it is unsolvable in general, as it could amount to a 'solution' to the well-known halting problem (Rogers, 1967). However, it seems clear that some interpreters are able to deal correctly with a wider class of recursions than others, and hence are easier to use in practice. The Syllog interpreter handles cases that cannot be computed by other methods, and is not known to miss any solutions. It has the property that the order in which syllogisms are made known to the system has no effect on the answers to questions, hence the language is, to this extent, even more declarative than Prolog. Further, when the answer to a question is just 'yes' or 'no' (rather than a table), Syllog automatically provides an explanation of the answer. As has been pointed out by Michie (1982), it is very important that any system be able to provide an explanation of its reasoning.

Section 2 of this chapter describes the use of Syllog by means of an extended example. Section 3 gives an example of a set of syllogisms which could be written by a nonprogrammer, but which would have to be rewritten by a programmer to run correctly in conventional Prologs. The section also sketches the implementation of Syllog. Finally, Section 4 consists of conclusions.

2   The Syllog Language

This section describes the Syllog language, from the user's point of view, by means of a simple example of setting up and using a knowledge base.

Suppose we are interested in knowledge and data about airports, and about flights from one airport to another. Then we might want to know about facts such as "american has flight 183 from jfk to chi," and about rules such as "if american has flight 183 from jfk to chi, then one can fly from jfk to chi."

In Syllog, one says that a new knowledge base will be concerned with such facts by typing in

       eg_airline has flight eg_number from eg_place to eg_place2
       ----
       one can fly from eg_place1 to eg_place2

and we call this a syllogism. A syllogism states that, if the sentence (or sentences) above the line are true, then so is the sentence below the line. The eg_'s in front of words indicate example items (Zloof, 1977). Thus the sentence

       eg_airline has flight eg_number from eg_place1 to eg_place2

can be read as "the knowledge base will be concerned, amongst other things, with airline names, flight numbers, and places between which there are flights." The whole syllogism is read as "if some airline has a flight with some number from some place called place1 to another place called place2, then one can fly from place1 to place2." This corresponds to a nonstop flight. To give the system some knowledge about journeys with a change of plane one can type in another syllogism

       eg_airline has flight eg_number from eg_place1 to eg_place2
       one can fly from eg_place2 to eg_place3
       ----
       one can fly from eg_place1 to eg_place3

This can be read as "if there is a flight from place1 to place2, and one can fly from place2 to place3, then one can fly from place1 to place3."

At this stage, the system contains no facts, just the statement that it will be about two kinds of facts: airlines having flights with numbers, departure points and destinations; and places between which one can fly.

One could now type in some data like this.

```
eg_airline has flight eg_number from eg_place1 to eg_place2
-----------------------------------------------------------------------------

american        183          jfk          chi
eastern         223          jfk          bos
eastern         131          bos          chi
eastern         132          jfk          chi
american        65           chi          sfo
aircal          2            sfo          jfk
```

However, it is not necessary to type the first sentence. The standard Syllog prompt to the user is of the form
   Make a command using these and other sentences:

   eg_airline has flight eg_number from eg_place1 to eg_place2
   one can fly from eg_place1 to eg_place2

Thus, to make the above command to add some facts, one selects the sentence "eg_airline has flight eg_number from eg_place1 to eg_place2" on the screen, then types in an underline followed by the facts. (If the facts are in a file they could simply be loaded.)

At this point, the system contains some facts, and some elementary knowledge about how to use the facts. Suppose we want a list of american airline flights. The Syllog prompt places the sentences

   eg_airline has flight eg_number from eg_place1 to eg_place2
   one can fly from eg_place1 to eg_place2

on the screen. We then pick the first sentence, and underline it giving

   eg_airline has flight eg_number from eg_place1 to eg_place2

The underline is an instruction to Syllog to give a table of facts with this heading. This is a question to find all flights by all airlines, so before asking it we change eg_airline to american so that the screen reads

   american has flight eg_number from eg_place1 to eg_place2

If we now ask the question, the flights appear on the screen below the heading like this

```
american has flight eg_number from eg_place1 to eg_place2
------------------------------------------------------------------------
            183              jfk            chi
            65               chi            sfo
```

and the system has answered the question "what are the american airline flights?"

   We could also ask the question "between what places does american flight 183 travel?"

```
american has flight 183 from eg_place1 to eg_place2
--------------------------------------------------------------------
```

and get the answer

```
american has flight 183 from eg_place1 to eg_place2
--------------------------------------------------------------------
                              jfk            chi
```

Or we could ask the question "is it true that american flight 183 flies from jfk to chi?"

```
american has flight 183 from jfk to chi
--------------------------------------------------
```

and get the answer

```
american has flight 183 from jfk to chi
--------------------------------------------------
          Yes, that's true
```

On the other hand, the question "is it true that american flight 183 flies from jfk to sfo?"

```
american has flight 183 from jfk to sfo
--------------------------------------------------
```

yields the answer

```
american has flight 183 from jfk to sfo
--------------------------------------------------
          Sorry, no
```

So far, the questions have just been about facts in the knowledge base.

Suppose we are interested in journeys with connections. As usual, Syllog prompts with the sentences

> eg_airline has flight eg_number from eg_place1 to eg_place2
> one can fly from eg_place1 to eg_place2

One can select the second sentence, and use it to ask the question "where can one fly to from jfk?"; that is

> one can fly from jfk to eg_place2
> --

which gives the answer

> one can fly from jfk to eg_place2
> --
>   chi
>   bos
>   sfo
>   jfk

This answer includes a round trip from jfk to jfk, for which an explanation might be of interest. Syllog explains its answers to yes-no questions, so one can get an explanation of the round trip by asking "can one fly from jfk to jfk?"; that is

> one can fly from jfk to jfk
> ---------------------------------

This gives the answer:

> one can fly from jfk to jfk
> ----------------------------------
>   Yes, that's true
>   Because. . . .
>
> american has flight 183 from jfk to chi
> one can fly from chi to jfk
> ---
> one can fly from jfk to jfk
>
> american has flight 65 from chi to sfo
> one can fly from sfo to jfk
> ---
> one can fly from chi to jfk

aircal has flight 2 from sfo to jfk

----

one can fly from sfo to jfk

The explanation consists of the instances of the syllogisms that have been used in getting the 'yes' answer. In general, explanations given by Syllog are top-down, in that a sentence may appear first in a premise (e.g. the first "one can fly from chi to jfk" above) and then be justified later (as in the second syllogism above).

The knowledge base only contains information about flights within the USA. If we ask "can one fly from jfk to lhr?", that is

one can fly from jfk to lhr

----

the answer is

one can fly from jfk to lhr

    Sorry, no
    Because. . . .

eg_airline has flight eg_number from eg_place1 to lhr?

----

one can fly from jfk to lhr

The explanation can be read as saying that the answer to the question is 'no' because, in trying to show that the answer might be 'yes', it was discovered that no airline has any flight to lhr. The first sentence of the explanation syllogism has a question mark to indicate this.

So far, we have set up a knowledge base, and have questioned it about facts, and about inferences that can be made from the facts using the syllogisms. One can update facts by getting a table on the screen and changing it. For example, we could get this table on the screen:

eg_airline	has flight eg_number	from eg_place1	to eg_place2
american	183	jfk	chi
eastern	223	jfk	bos
eastern	131	bos	chi
eastern	132	jfk	chi
american	65	chi	sfo
aircal	2	sfo	jfk

To delete american flight 183, change the aircal flight to panam, and add a new twa flight, we simply edit the table, on the screen, to

eg_airline	has flight eg_number	from eg_place1	to eg_place2
eastern	223	jfk	bos
eastern	131	bos	chi
eastern	132	jfk	chi
american	65	chi	sfo
panam	2	sfo	jfk
twa	55	chi	jfk

So it is straightforward to make changes to facts that have been loaded as such. However, Syllog does not allow changes to deduced statements. For example, suppose we get

one can fly from jfk to eg_place 2
chi
bos
sfo
jfk

on the screen, and try to change it to

one can fly from jfk to eg_place2
lhr
bos
sfo
jfk

This asserts that there is some way of flying from jfk to lhr, without giving airlines or flight numbers. Syllog replies that

> Deduced facts may not be changed, update not processed:
> one can fly from jfk to chi.

We have now asked questions about facts, and about statements that can be deduced, and we have seen that facts can be updated while deduced statements cannot be changed. One can also ask questions about the syllogisms. If we get the prompt

> eg_airline has flight eg_number from eg_place1 to eg_place2
> one can fly from eg_place1 to eg_place2

we can select just the sentence

> one can fly from eg_place1 to eg_place2

and leave it on the screen without underlining it. This is understood as the question ''which syllogisms conclude about flying from place1 to place2?'' The answer is

> eg_airline has flight eg_number from eg_place1 to eg_place2
> ---
> one can fly from eg_place1 to eg_place2
>
> eg_airline has flight eg_number from eg_place1 to eg_place2
> one can fly from eg_place2 to eg_place3
> ---
> one can fly from eg_place1 to eg_place3

Thus, one can not only ask questions about facts, but also about the syllogisms. This equal treatment of facts and syllogisms extends to update operations. Suppose we wish to distinguish between flying nonstop, and flying with a change of plane. We can get the above two syllogisms on the screen and add two more syllogisms as follows:

> eg_airline has flight eg_number from eg_place1 to eg_place2
> ---
> one can fly from eg_place1 to eg_place2
>
> eg_airline has flight eg_number from eg_place1 to eg_place2
> one can fly from eg_place2 to eg_place3
> ---
> one can fly from eg_place1 to eg_place3
>
> eg_airline has flight eg_number from eg_place1 to eg_place2
> ---
> one can fly nonstop from eg_place1 to eg_place2
>
> eg_airline has flight eg_number from eg_place1 to eg_place2
> one can fly from eg_place2 to eg_place3
> ---
> one can fly from eg_place1 via eg_place2 to eg_place3

The next Syllog prompt then has two new sentences in it:

> eg_airline has flight eg_number from eg_place1 to eg_place2
> one can fly from eg_place1 to eg_place2
> one can fly nonstop from eg_place1 to eg_place2
> one can fly from eg_place1 via eg_place2 to eg_place3

and one can now ask questions such as "between which pairs of places can one fly nonstop?"

> one can fly nonstop from eg_place1 to eg_place2
> --

which gives the answer

> one can fly nonstop from eg_place1 to eg_place2
> --
> jfk   chi
> jfk   bos
> bos   chi
> chi   sfo
> sfo   jfk

and "what are the possible places to change planes on a journey from jfk to sfo?"

> one can fly from jfk via eg_place2 to sfo
> ---

which gives the answer

> one can fly from jfk via eg_place2 to sfo
> ---
> chi
> bos

This section has described the Syllog language from the user's point of view, by means of a simple example. If the example were further simplified to omit sequences of flights that make up round trip journeys, it could be programmed in Prolog and run under a standard interpreter. However, even the presence of one round trip would cause unbounded recursion problems (Walker, 1983). The next section describes an example that is also beyond the capability of a standard Prolog interpreter, and sketches the implementation of Syllog.

3   Query Evaluation by Backchain-Iteration

The last section described Syllog from the point of view of a user. This section outlines how a query is processed in Syllog, by means of an example knowledge base of parts and subparts used in assembling a car.

Syllogisms are stored internally in Syllog in the form of Prolog rules; however, they are interpreted not as in Prolog, but by a different process. The process is based on an algorithm called backchain-iteration (Walker, 1981). The following syllogism begins our example. It links parts to subparts in a manufactured assembly, such as a car. (For simplicity, we shall assume in the rest of the example that no part is mentioned twice in a subpart tree.)

> eg_assembly has eg_4 of the part eg_subpart at level eg_1
> eg_subpart has eg_6 of the part eg_subsubpart at level eg_2
> eg_4 * eg_6 = eg_24
> eg_1 + eg_2 = eg_3
> --
> eg_assembly has eg_24 of the part eg_subsubpart at level eg_3

In Prolog notation, this can be written as the rule

> r(A, N24, SSP, L3) <-
>   r(A, N4, SP, L1) & r(SP, N6, SSP, L2) &
>   prod(N4, N6, N24) & sum(L1, L2, L3)

However, the rule does not have a procedural meaning under standard Prolog because it is left-recursive; Prolog's depth-first search yields an unbounded chain of goals if one tries to execute it.

Suppose we have the above rule, the syllogism

> eg_assembly has eg_24 of the immediate part eg_subpart
> --
> eg_assembly has eg_24 of the part eg_subpart at level 1

and the facts

> eg_assembly has eg_24 of the immediate part eg_subpart
> --

car	1	gearbox
car	2	headlight
headlight	4	clamp
headlight	1	lens
clamp	3	washer

These are held internally in Syllog as the rule

$$r(A, N24, SP, 1) \langle- f(A, N24, SP)$$

and as the facts

> f(car, 1, gearbox)
> f(car, 2, headlight)
> f(headlight, 4, clamp)
> f(headlight, 1, lens)
> f(clamp, 3, washer)

If we now ask "does a car have 24 of the part washer at level 3?", we get on the screen the answer

> car has 24 of the part washer at level 3
> --
>   Yes, that's true.
>   Because. . . .
>
> car has 8 of the part clamp at level 2
> clamp has 3 of the part washer at level 1
> 8 * 3 = 24
> 2 + 1 = 3
> --
> car has 24 of the part washer at level 3
>
> car has 2 of the part headlight at level 1
> headlight has 4 of the part clamp at level 1
> 2 * 4 = 8
> 1 + 1 = 2
> ---
> car has 8 of the part clamp at level 2
>
> clamp has 3 of the immediate part washer
> --
> clamp has 3 of the part washer at level 1

The answer is found by a version of the backchain-iteration method (Walker, 1981). In simplified outline, the method is as follows:

First the question is mapped to r(car, 24, washer, 3). A family of finite trees starting with

> r(car, 24, washer, 3) ⟨-
> (r(car, N4, SP, L1) ⟨- . . .⟩ &
> (r(SP, N6, washer, L2) ⟨- . . .⟩ &
> prod(N4, N6, 24) & sum(L1, L2, 3)

is generated by chaining backward through the rules, stopping a branch if a rule instance is about to be repeated.

For each tree generated by backward chaining, the leaf nodes are matched to assertions, and the lowest level non-leaf nodes are evaluated by temporarily asserting the items that may be deduced from the leaf nodes. This process is iterated to see if the items just asserted can be used to compute further temporary assertions. The iteration ceases when no new assertions can be found for the lowest level non-leaf nodes.

Then, the nodes at the next levels up in the tree are evaluated successively, in the same way. The entire process of evaluating a tree stops when no new items that match the root can be asserted. Finally, the answer to the original question is saved, and the temporary assertions used in computing the answer are erased.

In our example, backchain-iteration is combined with explanation extraction (Walker, 1983) to produce the internal explanation tree

> r(car,24,washer,3)
> r(car,8,clamp,2)
> r(car,2,headlight,1)
> f(car,2,headlight)
> r(headlight,4,clamp,1)
> f(headlight,4,clamp)
> prod(2,4,8)
> sum(1,1,2)
> r(clamp,3,washer,1)
> f(clamp,3,washer)
> prod(8,3,24)
> sum(2,1,3)

which is then mapped back into the explanation syllogisms shown above.

An explanation of a 'yes' answer, such as the one above, is produced by a reasonably straightforward technique in which the instances of the rules that are used to make a deduction are stored as the deduction proceeds. Explaining a 'no' answer satisfactorily is more complicated. The method used by Syllog is described near the end of this section.

The parts and subparts example can be continued to show the handling of negation and left recursion together. Suppose we add the facts

```
                we have eg_5 of eg_item in stock
        ---------------------------------------------
             20      gearbox
             27      clamp
             71      washer
             12      lens
```

and the rule

```
        car has eg_4 of the part eg_item at level eg_2
        we have eg_22 of eg_ item in stock
        eg_22 / eg_4 = eg_5
        --------------------------------------------------------------------
        we have just enough of the part eg_item to make eg_5 cars
```

Then we can ask how each item limits the number of cars that could be made

```
        we have just enough of the part eg_item to make eg_5 cars
        --------------------------------------------------------------------
```

and get the answer

```
        we have just enough of the part eg_item to make eg_5 cars
        --------------------------------------------------------------------
                        gearbox         20
                        clamp           3
                        lens            6
                        washer          2
```

However, in a real situation with many items, we might want just the lowest limit (2), and the name of the part (washer) that causes it. To be able to ask directly about this, we can add the syllogisms

```
        we have just enough of the part eg_item to make eg_3 cars
        eg_3 less than eg_5
        -------------------------------------------------------------------
        there is a lower limit than eg_5 on the cars we can make

        we have eg_level of eg_item in stock
        we have just enough of the part eg_item to make eg_number cars
        there is not a lower limit than eg_number on the cars we can make
        -------------------------------------------------------------------
        can make at most eg_number cars, because stock of eg_item is eg_level
```

The last line of the first syllogism appears negated as the third line of the second syllogism, and both syllogisms make use of left recursion to compute the number of subparts of a part. If we now ask about the lowest limit on the number of cars,

    can make at most eg_number cars, because stock of eg_item is eg_level
    ----

the answer is

    can make at most eg_number cars, because stock of eg_item is eg_level
    ----
              2   washer   71

If one now asks for an explanation of the statement that only 2 cars can be made because there are 71 washers in stock, one gets on the screen:

        can make at most 2 cars, because stock of washer is 71

          Yes, that's true
          Because . . .

        we have 71 of washer in stock
        we have just enough of the part washer to make 2 cars
        not: there is a lower limit than 2 on the cars we can make
        ----
        can make at most 2 cars, because stock of washer is 71

        car has 24 of the part washer at level 3
        we have 71 of washer in stock
        71 / 24 = 2
        ----
        we have just enough of the part washer to make 2 cars

One can then ask for further explanation if needed.

As mentioned above, Syllog uses a reasonably straightforward technique to produce an explanation of a 'yes' answer. Essentially, a proof is accumulated during backchain-iteration, and a top-down presentation of the proof, in the form of instances of syllogisms, provides the explanation. Finding an explanation of a 'no' answer is less direct, since such an answer arises when there is no deduction leading to a 'yes'.

To explain both 'yes' and 'no' answers, Syllog proceeds as follows. First, it checks to see if the answer is yes, using the straightforward technique in which an explanation is accumulated as the deduction proceeds. If a 'yes' answer is not found then, instead of failing, Syllog proceeds to explore possible partial proofs in which certain steps are assumed to succeed (even though in fact they fail). These steps are marked as conditional, and are later printed with a question mark in an explanation, to indicate where the failures occur.

In finding explanations, Syllog follows several guidelines about what kind of explanation is likely to be a help. For a 'yes' answer, it finds a shortest explanation. For a 'no' answer, it finds a conditional explanation in which the first assumption is as deep as possible. Also, for a 'no' answer, if there is a constant in the question, it makes sure that the constant is in the knowledge base and is reachable from the question; otherwise it generalizes the question by changing all other constants to distinct variables. This last technique produces, for instance, the explanation that no airline has a flight from any place to lhr, in response to the question "can one fly from jfk to lhr?", in the example in Section 2 above. (In the example, the flights are all internal to the USA.)

Thus Syllog is implemented with two techniques that help to make it easy to use. The techniques are explanation generation, and backchain-iteration. Explanation of both 'yes' and 'no' answers is important if a user is held responsible for actions based on answers given by a knowledge base. Explanation of a 'no' answer is helpful in deciding to add new syllogisms. Backchain-iteration directly executes some sets of syllogisms that would otherwise have to be transformed by an experienced programmer in order to run correctly, in which case it would be more difficult to generate explanations in terms of the original syllogisms.

4   Conclusions

The Syllog system provides a simple, English-like language in which a non-programmer can set up and use a knowledge base. The system prompts the user by showing the currently known sentences on the screen, and the user can make a command by choosing one of these sentences and modifying it, or by combining these sentences and new ones into a syllogism. The sentences need not be in English, but can be in any language or technical dialect using the same letters as English. There is no need to build or maintain dictionaries for these languages. When the system is in use, the most recently used sentences migrate to the top of the prompt.

The sentences are grouped into syllogisms, which function as a way of encoding knowledge about a particular domain, e.g. travel, manufacturing, etc. A question is a single sentence. If underlined, it is taken as a request for the facts for which it forms a heading. Otherwise, it is taken as a request to show the syllogisms that conclude about it. Facts that have been brought on to the screen can be updated by changing them in place, and so can syllogisms. When syllogisms are changed, the system watches the changes, and alerts the user to certain events, such as the addition of a rule that is a special case of another rule.

Syllog can accumulate knowledge, in the form of syllogisms, during normal use. If a syllogism is intended by a user, but is not in the knowledge base of the system, an explanation of a 'no' answer can prompt the user to formulate the syllogism and type it in.

The order in which syllogisms are made known to Syllog has no effect on the result of a query. In this respect, and in the handling of recursion, Syllog is less procedural than Prolog, which is itself a remarkably declarative language.

The Syllog language has been described in this chapter by examples of deductive retrieval over knowledge bases. In its role as a retrieval language, Syllog is strictly more powerful than the relational algebra (Codd, 1971). Each operation of the relational algebra can be expressed in Syllog (Walker, 1981), but transitive closure operations of the kind used in our Syllog examples above cannot be expressed in the relational algebra (Aho & Ullman, 1979). Syllog correctly executes a number of programs that have clear declarative meanings, but do not run on a standard Prolog interpreter. It is unlikely that this fact provides more theoretical power, but it does make Syllog easier to use in practice, particularly for nonprogrammers.

While the Syllog language naturally supports the construction and use of knowledge bases by nonprogrammers, it is also a programming language. It is quite straightforward to code some normal programming exercises in Syllog, while for others, the notation must be extended to support structured terms. If the language is used in the way indicated in this chapter, then the resulting programs are self-documenting when read by a person, and self-explaining when executed.

Acknowledgments

It is a pleasure to acknowledge discussions with many people about various aspects of Syllog. In particular Damaris Ayuso, Chin Chang, Se June Hong, Clayton Lewis, Michel McCord, Donald Michie, Antonio Porto, Ross Quinlan, Phyllis Reisner, Ehud Shapiro, Jack Schwartz, David Sheilds, and David H. D. Warren have kindly taken time for this. Of course, debit for any lapse of judgment or accuracy belongs to the author.

References

Aho, A. V., and J. D. Ullman. (1979). "Universality of data retrieval languages." *Proc. 6th Annual Symp. Princ. Prog. Lang.*, pp. 110–119.

Clark, K. L., J. R. Ennals, and F. G. McCabe. (1981). *A micro-Prolog Primer*. Logic Programming Associates Ltd., 10 Burntwood Close, London, England.

Clocksin, W. F., and C. S. Mellish. (1982). *Programming in Prolog*. Springer-Verlag.

Codd, E. F. (1971). "Relational completeness of data base sublanguages." *Courant Computer*

Science Symposium 6: Data Base Systems. Prentice-Hall, Englewood Cliffs, New Jersey, pp. 65–98.

Ennals, R. (1985). Teaching logic as a computer language in schools. This volume.

Henschen L. J., and S. A. Naqvi. (1984). "On compiling queries in recursive first-order databases." *JACM.*

Kowalski, R. (1979). *Logic for Problem Solving.* North-Holland Publishing Co.

McCord, M. (1982). "Using slots and modifiers in logic grammars for natural language." *Artificial Intelligence* 18, pp. 327–367.

Michie, D. (1982). "Game playing programs and the conceptual interface." *ACM Sigart Newsletter* No 80, pp. 64–70.

Michie, D. (1983). *Expert systems: old problems, new opportunities.* Manuscript, Machine Intelligence Research Unit, University of Edinburgh.

Pereira, L. M., F. C. N. Pereira, and D. H. D. Warren. (1978). *User's guide to Decsystem-10 Prolog.* Occasional Paper No. 15, Department of Artificial Intelligence, University of Edinburgh.

Roberts, G. M. (1977). *An implementation of Prolog.* M.S. thesis, Department of Computer Science, University of Waterloo.

Rogers, H. (1967). *Theory of Recursive Functions and Effective Computability.* McGraw-Hill.

Sergot, M. (1982). *A query-the-user facility for logic programming.* Report DOC 82/18, Department of Computing, Imperial College, London.

Walker, A. (1981). *Syllog: A knowledge based data management system.* Report No. 034, Computer Science Department, New York University.

Walker, A. (1983). *Prolog/EX1: An inference engine which explains both yes and no answers.* Report RJ 3771, IBM Research Laboratory, San Jose, California. Also Proc. Eighth Int. Joint Conf. on Artificial Intelligence, Karlsruhe.

Walker, A. (1984). "Data Bases, Expert Systems, and Prolog." *In: Artificial Intelligence Applications for Business,* W. Reitman (Ed.), Ablex.

Walker, A., and A. Porto. (1983). *Kbo1, A knowledge based garden store assistant.* Report RJ 3928, IBM Research Laboratory, San Jose, CA.

Warren, D. H. D., and F. C. N. Pereira. (1981). *An efficient easily adaptable system for interpreting natural language queries.* DAI Research Paper No. 155, Department of Artificial Intelligence, University of Edinburgh.

Zloof, M. M. (1977). "Query-by-Example: a data base language." *IBM Systems Journal,* 16:4, pp. 324–343.

CHAPTER 3

Systems Programming in Concurrent Prolog

Ehud Shapiro

Department of Applied Mathematics
The Weizmann Institute of Science
Rehovot 76100, Israel

1 Introduction

The process of turning a bare von Neumann machine into a usable computer is well understood. One of the more elegant techniques to do so is to implement a cross-compiler for a systems programming language (say C) on a usable computer. Then implement in that language an operating system kernel (say Unix), device drivers, a file system, and a programming environment. Then boot the operating system on the target computer. From that stage on the computer is usable, and application programs, compilers and interpreters for higher-level languages (say Franz Lisp and CProlog) can be developed on it.

This paper addresses the question of turning a bare computer into a usable one, but for a machine of a different type, namely, a parallel logic programming machine. In particular, it explores the suitability of Concurrent Prolog (Shapiro, 1983b) as the kernel programming language[1] of such a computer, by asking the question:

1. Will a machine that implements Concurrent Prolog in hardware or firmware be usable as a general-purpose, multiuser, interactive computer?

or, stated slightly differently,

2. Is Concurrent Prolog expressive enough to be a kernel language of a general-purpose computer?

---

[1] The term *Kernel Language* denotes a hybrid between a machine language and a systems programming language, implemented by hardware or firmware. As far as I know it was introduced by the Fifth Generation Project (Moto-Oka et al., 1981).

We investigate these questions only from the software, not from the hardware, side. Our concern with efficiency is limited by the assumption that the machine will execute at least as many Megalips[2] as today's computers execute Mips.

These questions are far-reaching, but not purely speculative, given the Fifth Generation Computers Project's plans to design and build a parallel logic programming machine, and to use Concurrent Prolog as the basis for the machine's kernel language (Kunifuji et al., 1983).

The paper attempts to give some evidence towards affirmative answers to these questions. To do so, we assume a computer that behaves like a virtual Concurrent Prolog machine, but has no other (lower-level or otherwise) programming constructs, special instructions, hardware interrupts, etc. We also assume that basic drivers for I/O devices are provided, which make each device understand Concurrent Prolog streams. This assumption is elaborated further below.

We then develop a collection of Concurrent Prolog programs that can run on such a machine, including:

• A Concurrent Prolog interpreter/debugger.
• A top-level crash/reboot loop, that reboots the operating system automatically upon a software (and perhaps also a hardware) crash.
• A Unix-like shell, that handles foreground and background processes, pipelining, and an abort ("Control-C") interrupt for foreground processes.
• A multiple-process manager *a la* MUF (Ellis, Mishkin, and Wood, 1982), that manages the creation of, and communication with, multiple interactive processes.
• Programs for merging streams, using various scheduling strategies.
• A solution to the readers-and-writers problem, based on the concept of monitors (Hoare, 1974).
• Shared queues, and their application to implementing managers of shared resources, such as a disk scheduler.

The programs have been developed and tested using a Concurrent Prolog interpreter, written in Prolog (Shapiro, 1983b). They show Concurrent Prolog's ability to express process creation, termination, communication, synchronization, and indeterminacy. They suggest that a "pure" Concurrent Prolog machine is self-contained, and that it will be be usable "as is," without too many extraneous features.

Even if such a machine is usable, it is not necessarily useful. For Concurrent Prolog to be a general purpose programming language, it has to solve conven-

---

[2] LIPS: Logical Inferences Per Second. In the context of Concurrent Prolog, it means process reductions per second.

iently a broad range of "real-life" problems. However, determining what is a real-life problem depends upon one's point of view. One may suggest implementing the algorithms in Aho, Hopcroft, and Ullman's book (1974) as such a problem. Concurrent Prolog will exhibit a grand failure if such an implementation is attempted, and for a reason. The algorithms in that book (and, most other sequential algorithms) are deeply rooted in the von Neumann computer. One of the basic operations they use is destructive assignment of values to variables (including destructive pointer manipulation). This operation is cheap on a von Neumann machine, but is not available directly in the logic programming computation model, is prohibitively expensive to simulate, and thinking in terms of it results in an awkward programming style.

On the other hand the operations that are cheap in Concurrent Prolog—process creation and communication—are not used on conventional sequential algorithms, almost by definition. Hence Concurrent Prolog (or any other logic programming language) is not adequate for implementing most von Neumann algorithms. One may ask: Is there anything else to implement (besides payroll programs)? Or: What is Concurrent Prolog good for, then?

Our experience to date suggests that, in contrast to von Neumann languages and algorithms, Concurrent Prolog exhibits strong affiliation with four other "trends" in computer science: object-oriented programming, dataflow and graph-reduction languages, distributed algorithms, and systolic algorithms.

A. Takeuchi and the author (Shapiro and Takeuchi, 1983) show that Concurrent Prolog lends itself very naturally to the programming style and idioms of object-oriented programming languages such as Smalltalk (Ingalls, 1976) and Actors (Hewitt, 1973). Many applications are easier to implement in this framework.

The synchronization mechanism of Concurrent Prolog—read-only variables—is a natural generalization of dataflow synchronization from functional to relational languages. The basic operation of a Concurrent Prolog program—process reduction—is basically a graph reduction operation, since a process is a directed acyclic graph (DAG), and a clause can be viewed as specifying how to replace one DAG by a (possibly empty) collection of other DAGS. It is interesting to observe that the synthesis of dataflow and graph reduction mechanisms has been attempted by hardware researchers, independently of logic programming (Keller, Lindstrom, and Organic, 1983).

We have some experience with implementing distributed algorithms in Concurrent Prolog. The implementation of the "Lord of the Ring" algorithm (Dolev, Klawe, and Rodek, 1982) in Concurrent Prolog, described in Shafrir and Shapiro (1983), exhibits a striking similarity to the English description of the algorithm, where every rule of process behavior corresponds to one Concurrent Prolog clause. That paper also reports on an implementation of a complicated minimum spanning tree algorithm.

An implementation of Shiloach and Vishkin's (1982) MAXFLOW algorithm demonstrates the ability of Concurrent Prolog to implement complex parallel algorithms without loss of efficiency (Hellerstein and Shapiro, 1983).

Numerical computations are quite remote from artificial intelligence, the original ecological niche of logic programming. Nevertheless, we find that the natural Concurrent Prolog solutions to numerical problems have a "systolic touch" to them, and vice-versa: that implementing systolic algorithms (Kung, 1979) in Concurrent Prolog is easy. A forthcoming paper (Shapiro, 1984) will include Concurrent Prolog implementations of several systolic algorithms, including the hexagonal band-matrix multiplication algorithm (Kung, 1979).

Other recent applications of Concurrent Prolog include the implementation of a parallel parsing algorithm (Hirakawa, 1983), an or-parallel Prolog interpreter (Hirakawa et al., 1983), a hardware specification and debugging system (Suzuki, forthcoming), and a LOOPS-like (Bobrow and Stefik, 1983) object-oriented knowledge representation language (Furukawa, Takeuchi, and Kunifuji, 1983).

2   Concurrent Prolog

Concurrent Prolog is a logic programming language, in that a program is a collection of universally quantified Horn-clause axioms, and a computation is an attempt to prove a goal—an existentially quantified conjunctive statement—from the axioms in the program. The goal statement describes an input/output relation for which the input is known; a successful (constructive) proof provides a corresponding output.

The difference between Concurrent Prolog and other logic programming languages (e.g. pure Prolog) is in the mechanism they provide for controlling the construction of the proof. Prolog uses the order of clauses in the program and the order of goals in a clause to guide a sequential search for a proof, and uses the cut operator to prune undesired portions of the search space. Concurrent Prolog searches for a proof in parallel. To control the search, Concurrent Prolog embodies two familiar concepts: guarded-command indeterminacy, and dataflow synchronization. They are implemented using two constructs: the commit operator "|" and the read-only annotation "?".

The commit operator is similar to Dijkstra's (1976) guarded command, and was first introduced to logic programming by Clark and Gregory (1981). It allows a process to make preliminary computations (specific in the guard of a clause), before choosing which action to take, i.e., which clause to use for reduction. Read-only annotations on occurrences of variables are the basic (and only) mechanism for process synchronization. Roughly spekaing, a process that attempts to instantiate a variable through a read-only occurrence of it suspends until the variable is instantiated by another process. The other components of concurrent programming: process creation, termination, and communication, are already available in the abstract computation model of logic programming. A unit goal corresponds to a process, and a conjunctive goal to a system of processes. A process is created via goal reduction, and terminated by being reduced to the empty (true) goal. Conjunctive goals may share variables, which are used as communication channels between processes.

More precisely, a *Concurrent Prolog program* is a finite set of guarded-clauses. A *guarded-clause* is a universally quantified axiom of the form

$$A \leftarrow G_1, G_2, ..., G_m | B_1, B_2, ..., B_n. \quad m,n \geq 0$$

where the G's and the B's are atomic formulas, also called unit goals. A is called the clause's head, the G's are called its guard, and the B's its body. When the guard is empty the commit operator ''|'' is omitted. Clauses may contain variables marked read-only, such as ''X?''. The Edinburgh Prolog syntactic conventions are followed: constants begin with a lower-case letter, and variables with an upper-case letter. The special binary term $[X|Y]$ is used to denote the list whose head (car) is X and tail (cdr) is Y. The constant [] denotes the empty list.

Concerning the declarative semantics of a guarded clause, the commit operator reads like a conjunction: A is implied by the G's and the B's. The read-only annotations can be ignored in the declarative reading.

Procedurally, a guarded-clause specifies a behavior similar to an alternative in a guarded-command. To reduce a process A using a clause

$$A1 \leftarrow G|B$$

unify A with $A1$, and, if successful, recursively reduce G to the empty system, and, if successful, commit to that clause, and, if successful, reduce A to B.

The unification of a process against the head of a clause serves several functions: passing parameters, assigning values to variables, selecting and constructing data-structures, and sending and receiving messages. The example programs below demonstrate all these uses of unification.

The reduction of a process may suspend or fail during almost any of the steps described above. The unification of the process against the head of a clause suspends if it requires the instantiation of variables occurring as read-only in A or $A1$. It fails if A and $A1$ are not unifiable. The computation of the guard system G suspends if any of the processes in it suspends, and fails if any of them fails. As in guarded-commands, at most one of the process's or-parallel guard-systems may commit.

Prior to commitment, partial results computed by the first two steps of the reduction—unifying the process against the head of the clause and solving the guard—are not accessible to other processes in A's system. This prevents interference between brother or-parallel computations, and eliminates the need for distributed backtracking.

This completes the informal description of Concurrent Prolog. The simplicity of the language is an asset when attempting a hardware or firmware implementation of it.

3   A Meta-Interpreter for Concurrent Prolog

One of the simpler ways to implement a programming environment for a programming language L is augmenting L's interpreter. Among the program development tools that can be implemented in this way are sophisticated debuggers (Shapiro, 1983a), runtime-statistics packages, extensions to the language, and new embedded languages. The difficulty of implementing these tools grows with the complexity of that interpreter.

For reasons of bootstrapping and elegance, the preferred implementation language for L's programming environment is L itself, as argued eloquently by Sandewall (1978). *Hence the ease in which an L interpreter can be implemented in L is of clear practical importance, as well as a useful criteria for evaluating the expressiveness and completeness of the language,* as argued by Steele and Sussman (1978).

Designing an expressive language with a simple meta-interpreter[3] is like solving a fixpoint equation. If the language L is too weak, then L's datastructures may not be rich enough to represent L programs conveniently. If the control constructs of L are incomplete they cannot be used to simulate themselves conveniently.

On the other hand, if the control structures of L are awkward and unrestricted and the data-structures are too baroque, then its interpreter becomes very large and unintelligible (e.g. *goto* cannot be used in a simple way to simulate unrestricted *goto*, but the easiest way to simulate a *while* statement is using a *while* statement in the interpreter).

A meta-interpreter for pure sequential Prolog can be written in three Prolog clauses, and, indeed, implementing software tools and embedded languages via extending this interpreter is a common activity for Prolog programmers.

A meta-interpreter for Concurrent Prolog is described below. It assumes the existence of a built-in system predicate *clauses(A,Cs)*, that returns in Cs the list of all clauses in the interpreted program whose head is potentially unifiable with A.[4] The constant *true* signifies an empty guard or an empty body.

---

[3] Called a meta-circular interpreter in Steele and Sussman (1978).

[4] In our current implementation Cs is the list of all clauses with the same head predicate as A. Better indexing mechanisms can make the predicate more selective. Another possible optimization is to use the bounded-buffer technique of Takeuchi and Furukawa (1983), to generate clauses on a demand-driven basis.

Program 3.1: A Meta-interpreter for Concurrent Prolog

```
reduce(true).
reduce((A,B) ←
        reduce(A?), reduce(B?).
reduce(A) ←
        clauses(A,Clauses) |
        resolve(A,Clauses,Body),
        reduce(Body?).

resolve(A,[(A←Guard|Body)|Cs],Body) ←
        reduce(Guard) | true.
resolve(A,[C|Clauses],Body)←
        resolve(A,Clauses,Body) | true.
```

Like any other Concurrent Prolog program, Program 3.1 can be read both declaratively, i.e. as a set of axioms, and operationally, i.e. as a set of rules defining the behavior of processes. Declaratively, *reduce(A)* states that A is true (provable) with respect to the axioms defined in the predicate *clauses*. Operationally, the process *reduce(A)* attempts to reduce the system of processes A to the empty (halting) system *true*.

Declaratively, the axioms of *reduce* read: *true* is true. The conjunction A,B is true if A is true and B is true. The goal A is true if there are clauses Cs with the same head predicate of A, resolving A with Cs gives B, and B is true. The predicate *resolve(A,[C/Cs],B)* reads, declaratively, that resolving A with the axioms [C|Cs] gives B if the clause C has head A, guard G and body B, and the guard G is true, or if recursively resolving A with Cs gives B.

Operationally, the clauses of *reduce* say that the process *true* halts. The process *A, B* reduces itself to the processes A and B, and the process A, with clauses Cs, reduces itself to B if the result of resolving A with Cs is B.

The reader not familiar with logic programming may be puzzled by this interpreter. It seems to capture the control part of the computation, but does not seem to deal at all with unification, the data component. The answer to the puzzle is that the call to the first clause of *resolve* is doing the work, by unifying the process with the head of the clause. Their unification is achieved by calling them with the same name, A.

This interpreter assumes one global program, whose axioms are accessible via the system predicate *clauses*, as in conventional Prolog implementations. In a real implementation of Concurrent Prolog, programs would be objects that can be passed as arguments, and *reduce* and *clauses* would have an additional argument, the program being simulated.

This interpreter cannot execute Concurrent Prolog programs that use built-in system predicates, such as itself (it uses the predicate *clauses*). The current implementation of Concurrent Prolog contains several (13) system predicates: metalogical predicates (*clauses* and *system*), control predicates (*otherwise* and =), interface to the underlying prolog, I/O (*read* and *write*), and arithmetic predicates (the lazy evaluator := and 5 arithmetic test predicates). To handle system predicates, the interpreter can be augmented with the clause

$$\text{reduce(A)} \leftarrow$$
$$\text{system(A)} \mid \text{A.}$$

system(X) is a system predicate that succeeds if X is a Concurrent Prolog system predicate, and fails otherwise. For example, the call *system(system(X))* succeeds. The clause demonstrates the use of the *meta-variable*, a facility also available in Prolog, which allows the passing of processes to other processes as data-structures. It is used extensively in the shell programs below.

One may suggest that using the meta-variable facility, a Concurrent Prolog meta-interpreter can be implemented via the clause

$$\text{reduce(A)} \leftarrow \text{A.}$$

This claim is true, except that it will be rather difficult to implement the software tools mentioned earlier as an extensions to this interpreter, whereas implementing a Concurrent Prolog single-stepper by extending Program 3.1 is a trivial matter.

The interpreter in Program 3.1 is ten to twenty times slower than the underlying Concurrent Prolog implementation. We feel that it is reasonable to pay a ten fold slowdown during the program development phase for a good programming environment. Besides, a default to the underlying Concurrent Prolog can be incorporated easily, as in the case of system predicates, so that in developing large systems only the portion of the code that is under development needs the extra layer of simulation.

4   Streams

Concurrent Prolog processes communicate via shared logical variables. Logical variables are single-assignment: they can be either uninstantiated or instantiated, but, once instantiated, their value cannot be destructively modified. Hence the Concurrent Prolog computation model is indifferent to the distinction between the shared-memory computation model and the communication-based model. A shared logical variable can be viewed as a shared memory cell that can accept only one value, or a communication channel that can transmit only one message.

The distinction between the ''reader'' and ''writer'' of a shared variable (or the ''sender'' and ''receiver'' of the message) is done via read-only annotations.

A process *p(...X?...)* cannot instantiate X. Attempts of *p* to reduce itself to other processes using clauses that require the instantiation of X, such as

$$p(...f(a)...) \leftarrow ...$$

suspend, until *X* is instantiated by some other process. If *X* is instantiated to *f(Y)*, then the process *p* can unify with that clause, even though it instantiated *Y* to *a*, since the scope of a read-only annotation is only the main functor of a term, but not variables that occur inside the term. This property enables a powerful programming technique that uses *incomplete messages* (Shapiro, 1983b).

Even though logical variables are single-assignment, two processes can communicate with each other via a single shared variable, by instantiating a variable into a term that contains both the message and another variable, to be used in subsequent communications. This programming techniques gives the effect of streams.

The cleanest way to implement I/O functions in a Concurrent Prolog machine is for I/O devices to generate and/or consume Concurrent Prolog streams. The current implementation of Concurrent Prolog, which is an interpreter written in Prolog (Shapiro, 1983b), supports only terminal I/O (the rest is done by the underlying Prolog). It implements the stream abstraction for the user terminal via two predicates, *instream(X)*, which generated the stream X of terms typed in by the user, and *outstream(X)*, that outputs to the screen the stream *X*. They are implemented using the underlying Prolog *read* and *write* predicates.

Program 3.2: Implementing terminal I/O streams using *read* and *write*

```
instream([X|Xs]) ←
    read(X) | instream(Xs).

outstream([]).
outstream([X|Xs]) ←
    write(X), outstream(Xs?).
```

If we want *instream* to allow the user to signify the end of the stream, the program has to be complicated a little.

Using these programs, a "device-driver" that implements a stream interface to the terminal can be specified:

```
terminal(Keyboard,Screen) ←
    instream(KeyBoard), outstream(Screen?).
```

In a virtual Concurrent Prolog machine in which interfaces to I/O device drivers are implemented as streams, there will be no need for specialized I/O primitives. One possible exception is a screen-output primitive (*write* or *bitblt*), which may be needed for convenience and efficiency.

5   Booting an Operating System

Assume that device drivers for a terminal (screen, keyboard and a mouse), disk, and a local network have been defined for a personal workstation. Then the following program can be used to boot its operating system:[5]

Program 3.3: Booting an operating system

```
boot ←
        monitor(KeyBoard?,Mouse?,Screen,DiskIn?,DiskOut,NetIn?,Netout),
        terminal(KeyBoard,Mouse,Screen?),
        disk(DiskIn,DiskOut?),
        net(NetIn,NetOut?) |
        true.
boot ←
        otherwise |
        boot.
```

The first clause invokes the device drivers and the monitor. The second clause automatically reboots the system upon a software crash of either the monitor or the device drivers. *otherwise* is a Concurrent Prolog system predicate that succeeds if and when all of its brother or-parallel guards fail. Declaratively, it may read as the negation of the disjunction of the guards of the brother clauses.[6]

6   A Unix-like Shell

A shell is a process that receives a stream of commands from the terminal and executes them. In our context the commands are processes, and executing them means invoking them. A simple shell can be implemented using the meta-variable facility,

```
                shell([X|Xs]) ←
                        X, shell(Xs?).
                shell([]).
```

---

[5] We are aware of the fact that efficiency considerations may prevent the use of pure streams for devices that generate a lot of useless data, such as a mouse, and that some lower-level interface may be required.

[6] The predicate *otherwise* is not implemented correctly in the current Concurrent Prolog interpreter (Shapiro, 1983b). It may succeed when it has suspended brother or-parallel guards, instead of suspending, and succeeding only when all such guards fail. Hence programs using it are not fully debugged.

This shell is batch-oriented. It behaves like a Unix-shell that executes all commands in "background" mode, in the sense that it does not wait for the completion of the previous process before accepting the next command. As is, it achieves the effect of Unix-like pipes, using conjunctive goals with shared variables as commands. For example, the Unix command

$$p \mid q \mid r$$

can be simulated with the conjunctive system

$$p(X), \ q(X?,Y), \ r(Y?).$$

provided that the Unix command p does not read from its primary input and q does not write to its primary output. External I/O by user programs is handled below.

Note that since the process's I/O streams have explicit names, we are not confined to linear pipelining, and any desired I/O configuration of the processes can be specified.

One of this shell's drawbacks is that it will crash if the user process X crashes, since X and shell(Xs) are part of the same conjunctive system, which fails if one of its members fails. This can be remedied by calling *envelope(X)* instead of X.

envelope(X) ← X | write(halted(X)).
envelope(X) ← otherwise | write(failed(X)).

It is easy to augment the shell to distinguish between background and foreground processes, assuming that every command X is tagged *bg(X)* or *fg(X)*, as done in Program 3.4.

Program 3.4: A shell that handles foreground and background processes

(1) shell([]).
(2) shell([fg(x)|Xs]) ←
        envelope(X) | shell(Xs?).
(3) shell([bg(X)|Xs]) →
        envelope(X), shell(Xs?).

Note that foreground processes are executed in the shell's guard. This allows a simple extension to shell so it will handle an abort ("control-C" on decent computers) interrupt for foreground processes. Upon the reception of an *abort* command the currently running foreground process (if there is one) is aborted, and the content of the input stream past the abort command is flushed. This is achieved by the clauses in Program 3.4a.

Program 3.4a: An extension to the shell that handles an *abort* interrupt

```
(4) shell(Xs) ←
        seek(abort,Xs,Ys) | shell(Ys?).

    seek(X,[X|Xs],Xs).
    seek(X,[Y|Xs],Ys) ←
        X\==Y | seek(X,Xs?,Ys).
```

The program operates as follows. When an *fg(X)* command is received, the two guards, *envelope* and *seek* are spawned in parallel, and begin to race. The first to commit aborts the second, so if *envelope* terminates before *seek* found an *abort* command in the input stream (most probably because the user hasn't typed such a command yet) then the *envelope* commits, *seek* is aborted, and *shell* proceeds normally with the next command. On the other hand, if *seek* succeeds in finding an *abort* command before *envelope* terminates, then *envelope* is aborted, and *shell* proceeds with the input past the *abort* command, as returned by *seek*.

A more general interrupt, *grand_abort,* that aborts all processes spawned by *shell,* both foreground and background, can also be implemented quite easily:

```
        topshell(Xs) ←
            shell(Xs) | true.
        topshell(Xs) ←
            seek(grand_abort,Xs,Ys) | topshell(Ys?).
```

The distinction of the shell in Program 3.4 makes between background and foreground processing is not of much use, however, since foreground processes are not interactive, i.e., they do not have access to the shell's input stream. One problem with the shell giving a user program its input stream is that upon termination the user program has to return the remaining stream back, so that the shell can proceed. Since we cannot expect every interactive user program to obey a certain convention for halting (cf. quit, exit, halt, stop, bye, etc.) the shell has to implement a uniform command, say *exit,* to "softly" terminate an interactive session with a user program (in contrast to aborting it). A filter, called *switch,* monitors the input stream to the program. Upon the reception of an *exit* command it closes the output stream to the program, returns the rest of the input stream to the shell, and terminates. A reasonable interactive user program should terminate upon encountering the end of the input stream. If it is not reasonable, an *abort* interrupt will always do the job. The following code implements this idea. Commands to interactive foreground processes are of the form *fg(P,Pi),* where P is the process and Pi is its input stream. For example, a command to run the process *foo(X)* with input stream X will be given as *fg(foo(X?),X).*

Program 3.4b: An extension to the shell that handles interactive user programs

```
(5) shell([fg(X,Xi)|Xs]) ←
        envelope(X), switch(Xs?,Xi,Ys) |
        shell(Ys?).

switch([exit|Xs],[],Xs).
switch([X|Xs],[X|Ys],Zs) ←
        X\==exit | switch(Xs?,Ys,Zs).
```

7   A manager of Multiple Interactive Processes

The shell described above can handle only one interactive process at a time, like the DEC-supplied TOPS-20 EXEC. MUF (Multiple User Forks) is a popular DEC-20 program, developed at Yale university (Ellis, Mishkin, and Wood, 1982), which overcomes this limitation. It can handle multiple interactive processes, and has a mechanism for easy context switching. It cannot compete, of course, with the convenience of a system with a bitmap display and a pointing device.

MUF associates names with processes. It has commands for creating a new process, freezing or killing a process, resuming a frozen process, and others. Program 3.5 achieves some of this functionality.

Program 3.5: mini-MUF

```
(0) muf(X) ←
        muf(X,[]).
(1) muf([create(Pname,Process,Pin,Pout)|Input],Ps) ←
        Process,
        tag(Pname,Pout),
        muf([resume(Pname)|Input?],[(Pname,Pin)|Ps]).
(2) muf([resume(Pname)|Input],Ps) ←
        find_process(Pname,Ps,Pin,Ps1)|
        distribute(input?,Pin,Input1,Pin1),
        muf(Input1?,[(Pname,Pin1)|Ps1]).
(3) muf([exit|Input],[(Pname,[])|Ps]) ←
        muf(Input?,Ps).
(4) muf([],Ps) ←
        close_input(Ps).
(1) find_process(Pname,[(Pname,Pin)|Ps],Pin,Ps).
(2) find_process(Pname,[Pr|Ps],Pin,[Pr|Ps1])←
        otherwise |
        find_process(Pname,Ps,Pin,Ps1).
```

(1) distribute([],Pin,[],Pin).
(2) distribute([X|Input],Pin,[X| Input],Pin)←
   muf_command(X)| true.
(3) distribute([X|Input],[X|Pin],Input1,Pin1)←
   otherwise |
   distribute(Input?,Pin,Input1,Pin1).

(1) close_input([]).
(2) close_input([(Pname,[])|Ps])←
   close_input(Ps).

(1) muf_command(create(_,_,_,_)).
(2) muf_command(resume(_)).
(3) muf_command(exit).

The *muf* process is invoked with the call *muf(X?)* where X is its input stream. It first initializes itself with the empty process list, using Clause (0), then iterates, serving user commands.

On the command *create(Pname,Process,Pi,Po)* it creates a process *Process*, and a process *tag(Pname,Po)*, that tags the process's output stream elements with the process's name, and displays them on the screen. It also adds a record with the process's name, *Pname*, and input stream, *Pi*, to its process list, and sends itself the command *resume(Pname)*.

On the command *resume(Pname)*, *muf* uses Clause (3). It searches its process list for the input stream of the process *Pname*, and puts this process record first on the list. This is done by *find_process*. If successful, it invokes

   distribute (Input?,Pin,Input1,Pin1),

which copies the elements of the stream *Input* to the stream *Pi*(Clause 3) until it reaches the end of the stream (Clause 1), or encounters a command to *muf* (Clause 2). In that event it terminates, returning the updated streams in *Pi1* and *Input1*. *muf* itself is suspended on *Input1*.

On the command *exit, muf* closes the input stream of the current process, and removes it from the process list (Clause 3).

When encountering the end of its input stream, *muf* closes the input streams of all the processes in its list, and terminates (Clause 4).

Some of the frills of the real MUF can be easily incorporated in our mini-implementation. For example, the *freeze* command resumes the previously re-sumed process, without having to name it explicitly. This is implemented by the following clause:

   muf([freeze|Input],[Pr,(Pname,Pi)|Ps]).
   muf([resume(Prame)|Input?],[(Prame,Pi),Pr|Ps]).

which reverses the order of the first two process records on the process list, and sends itself a *resume* command with the name of the previously resumed process. A similar default for *exit* can be added likewise.

Note that if the length of the process list is less then two, this clause would not apply, since its head would not unify with the *muf* process. Similarly, if a *resume* command is given with a wrong argument, Clause (2) wouldn't apply, since the guard, *find_process*, would fail.

muf, as defined in Program 3.5, would crash upon receiving such erroneous commands. Adding the following clause would cause it to default, in such cases, to an error-message routine:

$$\text{muf}([X|\text{Input}],\text{Ps}) \leftarrow$$
$$\text{otherwise} \mid$$
$$\text{muf\_error}(X,\text{Ps}),$$
$$\text{muf}(\text{Input?},\text{Ps}).$$

muf_error analyzes the command with respect to the process list, and reports to the user the type of error it's made.

Similarly easy to implement are queries concerning the names of the processes in the process list, and the identity of the currently resumed process.

8   Merging streams

A Concurrent Prolog process can have several input and/or output streams, and use them to communicate with several other processes; but the number of these streams is fixed for any given process. It is sometimes convenient to determine or change at runtime the number of processes communicating with another process; this can be achieved by merging communication streams.

In some functional and dataflow languages *merge* is a built-in operator (Arvind and Brock, 1979; Henderson, 1982). Logic programs, on the other hand, can express it directly, as shown by Clark and Gregory (1981). Program 3.6 adapts their implementation to Concurrent Prolog. It implements the process *merge(X?,Y?,Z)*, which computes the relation "*Z* is the interleaving of *X* and *Y*."

Program 3.6: Merging two streams

```
merge([X|Xs], Ys, [X|Zs])← merge(Xs?, Ys, Zs).
merge(Xs, [Y|Ys], [Y|Zs])← merge(Xs, Ys?, Zs).
merge(Xs,[], Xs).
merge([], Ys, Ys).
```

Using stream-merge as the basic method of many-to-one communication poses three major problems:

1.   How to provide a fair access to the shared process?
2.   How to minimize communication delay?
3.   How to route a response back to the sender?

The building-block of a fair communication network is a fair merge operator. The abstract computation model of Concurrent Prolog is underspecified, and does not determine which of the first two clauses of Program 3.6 would be chosen for reduction if both input streams have elements ready. Dijkstra (1976, p. 204) has considered this underspecification a desirable property of the guarded-command, and recommended simulating a totally erratic demon when choosing between two applicable guards. Nevertheless, for reasons of efficiency and expressiveness, we prefer to work in a more stable environment, and allow the programmer to control the chosen clause in the special case in which there are several applicable clauses with empty guards.

A stable Concurrent Prolog machine always reduces a process using the first unifiable clause with an empty guard, if such a clause exists.

A stable implementation is a natural consequence of having a sequential dispatcher for the guards of a process. Such a dispatcher would perform the unification of the process against the clauses' heads sequentially, and dispatch the guard of a clause if the unification with its head succeeds. It would commit as soon as it succeeds in unifying the process with the head of a clause whose guard is empty.

The definition of a stable machine assumes that some order (say, text order) is imposed on the clauses of each procedure in the program. Note that a stable implementation guarantees nothing about the selection of clauses with nonempty guards.

On a stable machine, Program 3.6 above will always prefer the first stream over the second, if both streams have elements ready. Hence it does not guarantee bounded waiting (however, it may be used to implement a notion of interrupts with different relative priorities).

To achieve fairness, this program is modified slightly, so it switches the positions of the two streams on each reduction, as specified in Program 3.7. On a stable machine, this would ensure 2-bounded-waiting.

Program 3.7: Fairly merging two streams

```
merge([[X|Xs], Ys, [X|Zs])← merge(Ys, Xs?, Zs).
merge(Xs, [Y|Ys], [Y|Zs])← merge(Ys?, Xs, Zs).
merge(Xs,[], Xs).
merge([], Ys, Ys).
```

This program is a satisfactory solution to the problem of merging two streams. More than two streams can be merged by constructing a tree of merge operators. It is not difficult to see (cf. Shapiro & Mierowsky, 1984) that a balanced merge tree composed of fair binary merge operators ensures linear bounded-waiting, and has a logarithmic communication delay.

The construction of a static balanced merge tree is easy. To allow a dynamically changing set of processes a fair and efficient access to a shared resource, a more innovative solution is required. In Shapiro and Mierowsky (1984) we define self-balancing binary and ternary merge operators. These operators compose dynamically into a balanced merge-tree, using algorithms similar to 2-3-tree insertion and deletion. The algorithms require sending messages that contain communication channels, in order to reshape the tree. In other words, the algorithm uses incomplete messages. 2-3 merge trees also ensure linear bounded-waiting and logarithmic communication delay, hence we believe they provide an acceptable solution to the problem of dynamic many-to-one communication.

The problem of routing back the response to a message is solved, at the programming level, using incomplete messages. A message that requires a response typically contains an uninstantiated variable; the sender of the message suspends, looking at the variable in read-only mode. The recipient of the message responds to it by instantiating that variable. This technique is used in the monitor, queue, and disk scheduling programs below.

8.1   A note on abstract stream operations

A more abstract (but also longer and less efficient) implementation of *merge* can be obtained using the *send(X,S,S1)* and *receive(X,S,S1)* operations on streams. They define the relation ''the result of sending (receiving) X on stream S is the stream S1'' as follows:

$$send(X,[X|Xs],Xs).$$
$$receive(X,[X|Xs],Xs?).$$

Such an implementation hides the internal representation of the stream, and eliminates the need to use the read-only annotation almost entirely in the calling program, since the resulting stream of *receive* is already annotated as read-only. We find the use of *send* and *receive* explicitly, instead of achieving this effect implicitly via unification, essential for the readability of programs with complex communication patterns, such as the ones described in Hellerstein and Shapiro (1983), and Shafrir and Shapiro (1983).

The *send* and *receive* calls can be eliminated for the sake of efficiency using standard partial-evaluation and program-transformation techniques (Komorowski, 1982; Tamaki and Sato, 1983).

9   Monitors and the readers-and-writers problem

The Concurrent Prolog solution to the readers-and-writers problem uses this method of many-to-one communication. It is very similar, in spirit, to the idea of monitors (Hoare, 1974). A designated process (a 'monitor') holds the shared data in a local argument, and serves the merged input stream of 'read' and 'write' requests ('monitor calls'). It responds to a 'read' request through the uninstantiated response variable in it ('result argument').

A schematic implementation of a monitor is shown in Program 3.8. Note that it serves a sequence of *read* requests in parallel, since the recursive invocation of *monitor* in Clause (2) is not suspended on the result of *serve*, in contrast to Clause (1).

Program 3.8: A schematic implementation of a monitor

```
(1) monitor([write(Args)|S], Data)←
        serve(write(Args), Data, NewData), monitor(S?, NewData?).
(2) monitor([read(Args)|S], Data)←
        serve(read(Args), Data, _), monitor(S?, Data).
(3) monitor([],_).
```

In monitor-based programming languages, a procedure call and a monitor call are two basic, mutually irreducible operations. In Concurrent Prolog, on the other hand, there is one basic construct, a process invocation, whereas a monitor call is a secondary concept, or rather, a programming technique.

Concurrent Prolog monitors and merge operators can implement operating systems in a functional style without side-effects, using techniques similar to Henderson's (1982).

10 Queues

Merged streams allow many client processes to share one resource; but when several client processes want to share several resources effectively, a more complex buffering strategy is needed. Such buffering can be obtained with a simple first-in, first-out (FIFO) queue: a client who requires the service of a resource enqueues its request. When a resource becomes available it dequeues the next request from the queue and serves it.

The following implementation of shared queues is a canonical example of Concurrent Prolog programming style. It exploits two powerful logic programming techniques: incomplete messages, and difference-lists.

A shared queue manager is an instance of a monitor. *enqueue* is a "write' operation, and "dequeue" involves both "read" and "write". An abstract implementation of a queue monitor is shown in Program 3.9.

Program 3.9: A queue monitor

```
(0) queue_monitor(S)
        ←create_queue(Q),
        queue_monitor(S,Q).
```

(1) queue_monitor([Request|S],Q) ←
    serve(Request,Q,Q1),
    queue_monitor(S?,Q1?).
(2) queue_monitor([],Q).

Clause (0) creates an empty queue; Clause (1) iterates, serving queue requests; and Clause (2) halts the queue monitor upon reaching the end of the requests stream.

The implementation of the queue operations employs difference-lists (Clark and Tarnlund, 1977). A difference-list represents a list of elements (in this context, the queue's content) as the difference between two lists. or streams. For example, the difference between [1,2,3,4|X] and X is the list [1,2,3,4]. As a notational convention, we use the binary term $X \setminus Y$ (read "the difference between X and Y"), to denote the list that is the difference between the list X and the list Y. Note that this term has no special properties predefined, and any binary term will do, as long as it is used consistently.

Program 3.9a: Queue operations

create_queue($X \setminus X$).

serve(enqueue(X),Head$\setminus$[X|NewTail],Head$\setminus$NewTail).
serve(dequeue(X),[X|NewHead]$\setminus$Tail,NewHead$\setminus$Tail).

First, *create_queue(Q)* states that Q is an empty difference-list. The clauses for *serve* define the relation between the operation, the old queue, and the new queue. On an *enqueue(X)* message, X is unified with the first element of the Tail stream, and in the new queue NewTail is the rest of the stream. On a *dequeue(X)* message, X is unified with the first element of the Head stream, and in the new queue NewHead is the rest of the old Head stream.

Operationally, the program mimics the pointer-twiddling of a conventional queue program. One difference is the simplicity and uniformity of the way in which variables are transmitted into and from the queue, using unification, compared to any other method of parameter-passing and message-routing.

Another is the behavior of the program when more *dequeue* messages have arrived then *enqueue* messages. In this case the content of the difference-list becomes "negative." The Head runs ahead of the Tail, and the negative difference between them is a list of uninstantiated variables, each for an excessive dequeue message. Presumably, a process which sends such a message then suspends on its variables in a read-only mode. One consequence is that excessive dequeue requests are served exactly in the order in which they arrived.

The program can be condensed and simplified, using program transformation techniques (Komorowski, 1982; Tamaki and Sato, 1983). The resulting program is more efficient, and reveals more clearly the declarative semantics of the queue monitor. Its operational semantics, however, seems to become a bit more obscure, and its does not hide the internal representation of the queue, as Program 3.9 does.

Program 3.10: A simplified queue monitor

```
(0) queue_monitor(S) ←
      queue_monitor(S?, X\X).
(1) queue_monitor([dequeue(X)|S], [X|NewHead]\Tail)←
      queue_monitor(S?, NewHead\Tail).
(2) queue_monitor([enqueue(X)|S], Head\[X|NewTail])←
      queue_monitor(S?, Head\NewTail).
(3) queue_monitor([],_).
```

Declaratively, the queue_monitor program computes the relation *queue(S)*, which says that S is a legal stream of queue operations. It uses an auxiliary relation *queue_monitor(S,Dequeue\Enqueue)*, which says that *Dequeue* is the list of all elements X such that *dequeue(X)* occurs in S (Clause 1), and that *Enqueue* is the list of all elements X such that *enqueue(X)* occurs in S (Clause 2). The interface between these two relations (Clause 0), constrains the list of enqueued elements to be identical to the list of dequeued elements, by calling them with the same name.

11 Bounded-buffer communication

Bounded buffers were introduced into logic programming by Clark and Gregory (1981, 1983) as a primitive construct. Their principal use in logic programming is not to utilize a fixed memory-area for communication, but rather to enforce tighter synchronization between the producer and the consumer of a stream.

Takeuchi and Furukawa (1983) have shown how to implement bounded-buffers in Concurrent Prolog, hence it need not be considered a primitive. Their implementation represents the buffer using a difference-list, and uses incomplete messages to synchronize the producer and the consumer of the stream.

12 An implementation of the SCAN disk-arm scheduling algorithm

The goal of a disk-arm scheduler is to satisfy disk I/O requests with minimal arm movements. The simplest algorithm is to serve the next I/O request which refers to the track closest to the current arm position. The algorithm may result in unbounded waiting—a disk I/O request may be postponed indefinitely. The

SCAN algorithm tries to minimize the arm movement, while guaranteeing bounded waiting. The algorithm reads as follows:

> *"while there remain requests in the current direction, the disk arm continues to move in that direction, serving the request(s) at the nearest cylinder; if there are no pending requests in that direction (possibly because an edge of the disk surface has been encountered), the arm direction changes, and the disk arm begins its sweep across the surface in the opposite direction"* (Holt et al., 1978, p. 94).

Program 3.11: The SCAN disk-arm scheduler

(0) disk_scheduler(DiskS, UserS) ←
　　disk_scheduler(DiskS?, UserS?, ([], []), (0, up)).

(1) disk_scheduler([Request|DiskS], UserS, Queues, ArmState) ←
　　dequeue(Request, Queues, Queues1, ArmState, ArmState1) |
　　disk_scheduler(DiskS?, UserS, Queues1, ArmState1).
(2) disk_scheduler(DiskS, [Request|UserS], Queues, ArmState) ←
　　enqueue(Request, Queues, Queues1, ArmState) |
　　disk_scheduler(DiskS, UserS?, Queues1, ArmState).
(3) disk_scheduler([io(0, halt)| _], [], ([],[]), _).

(1) dequeue(io(T,X), ([io(T,X)|UpQ],[]), (UpQ,[]), _, (T,up)).
(2) dequeue(io(T,X), ([io(T,X)|UpQ],DownQ), (UpQ,DownQ), (_,up), (T,up)).
(3) dequeue(io(T,X), ([], [io(T,X)| DownQ]), ([],DownQ), _, (T,down)).
(4) dequeue(io(T,X), (UpQ,[io(T,X)|DownQ]), (UpQ,DownQ), (_,down), (T,down)).

(1) enqueue(io(T, Args), (UpQ, DownQ), ([io(T, Args)|UpQ], DownQ), (T, down)).
(2) enqueue(io(T, Args), (UpQ, DownQ), (UpQ, [io(T, Args)|DownQ]), (T, up)).
(3) enqueue(io(T, Args), (UpQ, DownQ), (UpQ1, DownQ), (T1, Dir)) ←
　　T>T1 | insert(io(T, Args), UpQ, UpQ1, up).
(4) enqueue(io(T, Args), (UpQ, DownQ), (UpQ, DownQ1), (T1, Dir)) ←
　　T<T1 | insert(io(T, Args), DownQ, DownQ1, down).

(1) insert(io(T, X), [], [io(T,X)],_).
(2) insert(io(T, X), [io(T1, X1)|Q], [io(T, X), io(T1, X1)|Q], up)←
　　T<T1 | true.
(3) insert(io(T, X), [io(T1, X1)|Q], [io(T, X), io(T1, X1)|Q], down)←
　　T>T1 | true.
(4) insert(io(T, X), [io(T1, X1)|Q], [io(T1, X1)|Q1], up) ←
　　T>=T1 | insert(io(T, X), Q, Q1, up).
(5) insert(io(T, X), [io(T1, X1)|Q], [io(T1, X1)|Q1], down) ←
　　T=<T1 | insert(io(T, X), Q, Q1, down).

The disk scheduler has two input streams—a stream of I/O requests from the user(s) of the disk, and a stream of incomplete messages from the disk itself. The scheduler has two priority queues, represented as lists: one for requests to be served at the upsweep of the arm, and one for the requests to be served at the downsweep. It represents the arm state with the pair *(Track, Direction)*, where *Track* is the current track number, and *Direction* is *up* or *down*.

The disk scheduler is invoked with the goal:

disk_scheduler(DiskS?, UserS?)

where *UserS* is a stream of I/O requests from the user(s) of the disk, and *DiskS* is a stream of partially determined (incomplete) messages from the disk controller. I/O requests are of the form *io(Track, Args)*, where *Track* is the track number and *Args* contain all other necessary information.

The first step of the scheduler is to initialize itself with two empty queues and the arm positioned on track 0, ready for an upsweep; this is done by Clause (0). Following the initialization, the scheduler proceeds using three clauses:

- Clause (1) handles requests from the disk. If such a request is ready in the disk stream, the scheduler tries to dequeue the next request from one of the queues. If successful, that request is unified with the disk request, and the scheduler iterates with the rest of the disk stream, the new queues, and the new arm state. The dequeue operation fails if both queues are empty.
- Clause (2) handles requests from the user. If an I/O request is received from the user it is enqueued in one of the queues, and the scheduler iterates with the rest of the user stream and the new queues.
- Clause (3) terminates the scheduler, if the end of the user stream is reached and if both queues are empty. Upon termination, the scheduler sends a 'halt' message to the disk controller.

The *dequeue* procedure has clauses for each of the following four cases:

- Clause (1): If *DownQ* is empty then it dequeues the first request in *UpQ*, and changes the new state to be upsweep, where the track number is the track of the I/O request.
- Clause (2): If the arm is on the upsweep and *UpQ* is nonempty then it dequeues the first request in *UpQ*. The new state is as in Clause (1).
- Clauses (3) and (4): are the symmetric clauses for *DownQ*.

Note that no clause applies if both queues are empty, hence in such a case the *dequeue* procedure fails. Since the disk scheduler invokes *dequeue* as a guard, it must wait in this case for the next user request, and use Clause (3) to enqueue it. If such a request is received and enqueued then in the next iteration the disk request can be served.

The *enqueue* procedure also handles four cases. If the I/O request refers to the current arm track, than according to the SCAN algorithm it must be postponed to the next sweep. Clauses (1) and (2) handle this situation for the upsweep and downsweep cases. If the request refers to a track number larger than the current track, then it is inserted to *UpQ* by Clause (3), otherwise it is inserted to *DownQ*, by Clause (4).

The insertion operation is a straightforward ordered-list insertion. More efficient data-structures, such as 2-3-trees, can be used if necessary.

To test the disk scheduler, we have implemented a simulator for a 10-track disk controller. The controller sends a stream of partially determined I/O requests, and, when the arguments of the previous request become determined, it serves it and sends the next request.

Program 3.12: A simulator of a 10-track disk controller

```
(0) disk_controller([io(Track, Args)|S]) ←
            disk_controller(Track?, Args?, S, [0, 0, 0, 0, 0, 0, 0, 0, 0, 0]).
(1) disk_controller(Track, Args,[io(Track1, Args1) |S],D) ←
            disk(Track, Args, D, D1) | disk_controller(Track1?, Args1?, S, D1).
(2) disk_controller(_, halt, [], _).
(1) disk(_, (_, false),[],[]).
(2) disk(0, (read(X), true), [X|D], [X|D]).
(3) disk(0, (write(X), true), [_|D], [X|D]).
(4) disk(N, IO, [X|D], [X|D1]) ←
            N>0 | N1:=N-1, disk(N1?, IO, D, D1).
```

When invoked with a stream S, the controller initializes the disk content and ,ends the first request using Clause (0). It then iterates with Clause (1), serving the previous I/O request and sending the next partially determined request, until a *halt* message is received, upon which it closes its output stream and terminates, using Clause (2).

The disk simulator assumes that the arguments of an I/O request are pairs *(Operation, ResultCode)*, where the operations are *read(X)* and *write(X)*. On *read(X)* Clause (2) unifies X with the content of the requested track number. On *write(X)* Clause (3) replaces the requested track content with X. The *ResultCode* is unified with *true* if the operation completed successfully (Clauses (2) and (3)), and with *false* otherwise (Clause (1)). An example of an unsuccessful completion is when the requested track number exceeds the size of the disk.

13   Conclusion

We have provided some evidence that a machine that implements Concurrent Prolog in hardware or firmware will be self-contained, usable, and useful, without much need to resort to reactionary concepts and techniques.

The next logical step is to build it.

Acknowledgments

This research is supported in part by IBM Poughkeepsie, Data Systems Division. Part of it was carried on while the author was visiting ICOT, the Institute for New Generation Computer Technology, Tokyo.

The paper benefited from a critical survey of an earlier paper of mine, written by David Gelenter (1983).

References

Aho, A. V., J. E. Hopcroft, and J. D. Ullman. (1974) The Design and Analysis of Computer Algorithms, Addison-Wesley.

Arvind, and J. D. Brock (1979). "Streams and Managers. In *Semantics of Concurrent Computations*, G. Kahn (Ed.) pp. 452–465, LNCS 70, Springer-Verlag.

Bobrow, D. G., and M. Stefik. (1983). *The LOOPS Manual (preliminary version)*, Memo KB-VLSI-81-13, Xerox PARC.

Clark, K. L., and S. Tarnlund. (1977). "A first-order theory of data and programs." In *Information Processing 77*, B. Gilechrist (Ed.), pp. 939–944, North-Holland.

Clark, K. L., and S. Gregory. (1981). "A relational language for parallel programming." in *Proceedings of the ACM Conference on Functional Languages and Computer Architecture*, October.

Clark, K. L., and S. Gregory. (1983). *PARLOG: A Parallel Logic Programming Language* Research report DOC 83/5, Department of Computing, Imperial College of Science and Technology, May.

Dolev, D., M. Klawe and M. Rodeh. (1982). "An O(n log n) Uni-directional distributed algorithm for extrema finding in a circle." *Journal of Algorithm* 3, pp. 245–260.

Ellis, J. R., N. Mishkin, and S. R. Wood. (1982). *Tools: an Environment for Timeshared Computing and Programming*, Research Report 232, Department of Computer Science, Yale University.

E. W. Dijkstra. (1976). *A Discipline of Programming*, Prentice-Hall.

Friedman, D. P., and D. S. Wise. (1980). "An Indeterminate Constructor for Applicative Programming." In *Conference Record of the Seventh Annual ACM Symposium on Principle of Programming Languages*, pp. 245–250.

Furukawa, K., A. Takeuchi, and S. Kunifuji. (1983). *Mandala: A Knowledge Programming Language on Concurrent Prolog*, ICOT Technical Memorandum TM-0028 (in Japanese).

Gelenter, D. (1983). "A note on systems programming in concurrent prolog." *Proceedings of LPS-84*.

Henderson, P. (1982). "Purely Functional Operating Systems." In *Functional Programming and its Applications*, P. Henderson and D. A. Turner (Eds.), Cambridge University Press.

Hirakawa, H. (1983). *Chart Parsing in Concurrent Prolog*, ICOT Technical Report TR-008.

Hirakawa, H. et al. (1983). *Implementing an Or-Parallel Optimizing Prolog System (POPS) in Concurrent Prolog*, ICOT Technical Report TR-020.

Hewitt, C. C. (1973). "A universal modular Actor formalism for artificial intelligence." In *Proceedings of the Third International Joint Conference on Artificial Intelligence*, IJCAI.

Hellerstein, L. and E. Shapiro. (1983). *Algorithmic Programming in Concurrent Prolog: the MAX-FLOW experience*. Technical Report CS83-12, Department of Applied Mathematics, The Weizmann Institute of Science. Also proceedings of LPS-84.

Hoare, C. A. R. (1974). "Monitors: an operating systems structuring concept." *Communications of the ACM*, 17(10), pp. 4549–557.

Holt, R. C., G. S. Graham, E. D. Lazowska, and M. A. Scott. (1978). *Structured Programming with Operating Systems Applications*. Addison Wesley.

Ingalls, D. H. (1976, January). "The SmallTalk-76 programming system: design and implementation." In *Conference records of the Fifth Annual ACM Symposium on Principles of Programming Languages*, pp. 9–16, ACM.

Keller, R. M., G. Lindstrom, and E. I. Organic. (1983). *Rediflow: a multiprocessing architecture combining reduction with data-flow*. Unpublished manuscript, Department of Computer Science, University of Utah.

Komorowski, H. J. (1982). "Partial evaluation as a means for inferencing data-structures in an applicative language: a theory and implementation in the case of Prolog." In *Conference Record of the Ninth Annual ACM Symposium on Principles of Programming Languages*, pp. 255–268, ACM.

Kunifuji, S. et al. (1983). *Conceptual Specification of the Fifth Generation Kernel Language Version 1 (preliminary draft)*. ICOT Technical Memorandum TM-0028.

Kung, H. T. *Let's Design Algorithms for VLSI Systems*. Technical Report CMU-CS-79-151, Department of Computer Science, Carnegie-Mellon University.

Moto-Oka, T. et al. (1981). "Challenge for knowledge information processing systems (preliminary report on fifth generation computer systems)." In *Proceedings of International Conference on Fifth Generation Computer Systems*, pp. 1–85, JIPDEC.

Sandewall, E. (1978). "Programming in an interactive environment: the Lisp experience." *Computing Surveys*, ACM, March.

Shafrir, A., and Shapiro E. (1983). *Distributed Programming in Concurrent Prolog*. Technical Report CS83-12, Department of Applied Mathematics, The Weizmann Institute of Science.

Shapiro, E. (1983a). *Algorithmic Program Debugging*. ACM Distinguished Dissertation Series, MIT Press.

Shapiro. E. (1983b). *A Subset of Concurrent Prolog and its Interpreter*. Technical Report TR-003, ICOT—Institute for New Generation Computer Technology. Also available as Technical Report CS83-06, Department of Applied Mathematics, The Weizmann Institute of Science.

Shapiro, E., and Mierowsky, C. (1984). "Fair, biased, and self-balancing merge operators: Their specification and implementation in concurrent prolog." *Journal of New Generation Computer Technology*, 2(3).

Shapiro, E. and A. Takeuchi. (1983). "Object Oriented Programming In Concurrent Prolog." *Journal of New Generation Computing* 1(1).

Shiloach, Y., and U. Vishkin. (1982). "An $O(n2\log n)$ parallel MAX-FLOW algorithm." *J. of Algorithms*, Vol. 3, #2, June 1982, pp. 128–147.

Steele, G. L., Jr. and G. J. Sussman (1978). *The Art of the Interpreter or, The Modularity, Complex* Technical Memorandum AIM-453, Artificial Intelligence Laboratory, MIT, May.

Suzuki, N. (this volume). "Experience with specification and verification of complex computer using Concurrent Prolog."

Takeuchi, A. and K. Furukawa. (1983). "Interprocess Communication in Concurrent Prolog." In *Proc. Logic Programming Workshop 83*, pp. 171–185, Albufeira, Portugal, June. Also ICOT Technical Report TR-006.

Tamaki, H. and T. Sato (1983). *A Transformation System for Logic Programs which Preserves Equivalence*. ICOT Technical Report TR-018.

Uchida, S. (1983). "Inference machine: from sequential to parallel." In *Proceedings of the 10th Annual International Symposium on Computer Architecture*, pp. 410–416, Stockholm. Also ICOT Technical Report TR-011.

PART II
IMPLEMENTATION

Chapter 4

Optimizing Tail Recursion in Prolog

David H. D. Warren

Quintus Computer Systems, Inc.
2345 Yale Street
Palo Alto, California 94306

1   Introduction

The purpose of this paper is to describe how a major improvement—**tail recursion optimization** (TRO)—was incorporated in DEC-10 Prolog (Pereira, Pereira, and Warren, 1978). Familiarity with the Prolog language (Roussel, 1975; Warren, 1979; Warren, Pereira, and Pereira, 1977) is assumed, and for a full understanding of the more technical parts of this paper, the reader should refer to an earlier research report (Warren, 1977a), or my dissertation (Warren, 1977b), for details of the original DEC-10 implementation. Other useful accounts of Prolog implementation include those by Bruynooghe (1976), Roberts (1977), and Colmerauer et al. (1979).

A preliminary report on TRO appeared previously (Warren, 1979). At that time I had designed and partially implemented a completely new Prolog implementation, incorporating TRO and other associated improvements. It later became obvious that it would take a lot of work to bring this implementation to practical fruition. In particular, it was not clear whether the associated improvements could be made compatible with the needs of garbage collection. As I shall argue below, the full potential of TRO is only realized in conjunction with a garbage collector. I therefore abandoned the idea of reimplementing from scratch, and instead pursued the less ambitious course of making the minimum changes to the existing DEC-10 system necessary to support TRO. This entailed much less work, but has meant that not all the potential of TRO has been realized, particularly as regards speed.

2   Overview of Tail Recursion Optimization

Like most high-level languages, Prolog requires a stack (called the **local stack**) to hold frames, one for each active procedure. Each frame contains bookkeeping information together with the value cells for local variables. For most languages, the stack frame can be discarded at the time the procedure returns its result. With Prolog, however, this is not in general possible, since procedures may be non-determinate, i.e., they can return several alternative results. The stack frame is therefore not generally reclaimed until backtracking occurs, after the procedure has generated all of its results.

However, if the Prolog system can detect that it is generating the *last* alternative result of a procedure, it is possible to reclaim the stack frame immediately on return from the procedure, as in a conventional language, and many Prolog systems (including DEC-10 Prolog) do this. For example, when executing the clause:

$$P :- Q, R, S.$$

the stack frame corresponding to this clause can be discarded as soon as execution of S is complete, *provided* there are no other clauses which could match the original call to P, and provided no backtrack points have been created by the execution of Q, R, and S.

Detection of the determinate situation is therefore quite important, and normally requires either that the procedure be appropriately **indexed,** yielding only one candidate clause for matching, or that determinacy be signaled or imposed by the programmer through Prolog's ''cut'' operator. (Hence much of the importance both of indexing and of cut.)

The additional improvement of tail recursion optimization rests on the observation that one does not need to wait until a determinate procedure returns in order to reclaim its stack frame. Instead it is possible to recover the stack frame at the time the last goal in the procedure is invoked. To be more precise, if the Prolog system has reached the last goal in a clause, and there are no remaining backtrack points within the procedure to which that clause belongs, then the current stack frame can be overwritten by the stack frame for the procedure about to be invoked. Thus in the previous example, the effect of TRO is that the clause's stack frame can be discarded as the point S is invoked (provided there are no backtrack points left within P at this point), rather than when S returns. Note that it is not necessary for the procedure S to be determinate; the stack frame for the calling clause is discarded even if there are several clauses that match the call to S. Note also that it is not necessary for the last goal to be a *recursive* call; a better name for the improvement would perhaps be ''last call'' optimization.

To get away with the rather underhand manuever that TRO entails, it is obviously essential to extract from the old stack frame all information that will be needed subsequently. In particular, it is vital not to leave behind any pointers to the old information. Hence the following departures from previous practice (Warren, 1977b) in Prolog implementation.

1. Instead of information about the caller, a procedure is now passed a **continuation,** consisting of a pointer to the actual goal to be executed next, together with its associated stack frame. Thus the continuation does not necessarily correspond to the immediate parent procedure, but in fact indicates the most recent ancestor with further goals left to execute.

2. A called procedure is no longer able to access its arguments merely by referring to the information about its caller (since the caller's stack frame may well have been discarded). Instead the arguments of a call have to be copied into registers, to be subsequently stored in the callee's stack frame as extra bookkeeping information looking exactly like ordinary (local) variable cells. This scheme has the incidental advantage that certain unification steps become null operations, namely those steps concerning unification with the first occurrence of a variable at the outermost level in the head of a clause where that variable is **local** (i.e., it does not occur in a compound term). The value cell for such a variable can be identified with the location for the corresponding procedure argument, and so unification does not need to initialize it.

3. A final pitfall which has to be avoided concerns the case where an argument to a procedure is (a reference to) an uninstantiated variable in the stack frame about to be discarded. Possible solutions to this problem, including the one actually adopted, are discussed in a later section.

As has already been mentioned, the form of TRO which we have described is applicable to the last procedure call in *every* clause. It does not require that the *called* procedure be determinate. The only requirement is that there be no backtrack points remaining in the *calling* procedure. In this respect it differs from a weaker form of TRO included in some other Prolog implementations. In the weaker form of TRO, the caller's stack frame is discarded only *after* the "tail-recursive" call has been matched against some clause; if more than one clause can potentially match (as is commonly the case), a backtrack point must be created and the caller's stack frame can *not* be discarded. Thus this weaker form of TRO is not nearly as effective as the version we describe.

So much for what the TRO *is,* what are its benefits?

The most obvious benefit is a saving of (local) stack space. For example, the procedure "quicksort" now only requires a stack size of order log N instead of order N. And a determinate, directly tail-recursive procedure, such as "concatenate," now never uses more than *one* stack frame. However this benefit alone is not as significant as it might seem. First, the TRO is only recovering earlier space which would be recovered later anyway. Second, we have ignored the fact that most Prolog procedures create new structures which cannot be stored on the local stack. So the effect on total working storage requirements (which is all the user is aware of) is unlikely to be dramatic.

For the space-saving to really pay off, it is necessary to have a garbage collector which can recover the space occupied by structures which are no longer accessible. Such a garbage collector was already included in DEC-10 Prolog. The real worth of the TRO is then that, not only does it recover local stack frames, but also it allows structures which are only accessible through such stack frames to be garbage collected. A determinate tail-recursive procedure can therefore potentially continue executing indefinitely, even though it creates new structures. A typical example would look like:

$$cycle(S) :- modify(S,S1), cycle(S1).$$

where 'modify' is a determinate procedure which transforms a structure S into a new structure S1. The structure might be a term representing the state of a database, or a term representing the conversation so far in a natural language question-answering system, for example.

This ability of the TRO in conjunction with garbage collection to make certain kinds of Prolog programs feasible for the first time is, I think, the main argument for introducing it.

A further benefit of the TRO, which particularly appeals to me, is that it also saves time, although it could be argued that the saving is not, by itself, of major significance in practice. The saving arises because certain bookkeeping operations can be coalesced (so fewer such actions occur during an execution), and, moreover, in certain cases much work can be saved in the process. In particular, when one stack frame overwrites another, part of the bookkeeping information can be retained intact, and where a clause contains no more than one goal in its body, bookkeeping information can be kept in registers without the need for saving and restoring. The net effect is to remove most of the efficiency overheads of recursive procedures with respect to corresponding iterative loops in a conventional language. There is also the saving, already mentioned, of certain unification steps, which can be particularly significant in procedures where many clauses have to be examined for a possible match.

The actual speed improvement achieved when the TRO was incorporated in our DEC-10 implementation ranges from 6% for examples of nondeterminate procedures to 56% for 'concatenate' and 68% for 'length' (of a list). Note that this makes the speed of Prolog 'concatenate' almost identical to that of the corresponding Lisp version compiled with the DEC-10 Stanford Lisp compiler (assuming no change in the latter speed since performance benchmarks were made in 1977). The important special case of a unit clause had effectively already been optimized in the original implementation, so the improvements achieved in the best cases were not as typical of the general situation as had been hoped for.

TRO is, of course, not a new idea (cf. for example SCHEME (Steele, 1978)), although it seems that it has seldom been incorporated in software in widespread use. The reason is probably that, because most languages include explicit iterative constructs, implementors feel the burden can be left on the programmer to recognize the iterative situation. However, this state of affairs seems hard to justify, since TRO is relatively easy to implement (see below).

It is important to notice that TRO is more widely applicable in Prolog than in other languages such as Lisp. For example the Prolog procedure for 'concatenate':

```
concatenate([],L,L).
concatenate([X|L1],L2,[X|L3]):- concatenate(L1,L2,L3).
```

is susceptible to TRO, giving essentially the following iterative version:

```
concatenate(L1,L2,L3) =
(while L1 is a nonempty list
do
        let List be a new record with 2 fields;
        head(List) := head(L1);
        L1 := tail(L1);
        field pointed to by L3 := List;
        L3 := a pointer to tail(List)
repeat;
field pointed to by L3 := L2;
return)
```

However for the Lisp version:

```
concatenate(L1,L2) =
(null(L1) → L2,
    T → cons(car(L1),concatenate(tail(L1),L2)))
```

straightforward TRO does not yield an iterative version, since the last function call to be executed is the call to 'cons', not the call to 'concatenate'. It will be seen that the iterative version requires the handling of partially completed structures and the passing around of pointers to the corresponding "holes." This is available as a matter of course in a Prolog implementation, since it is a feature of the language (the "logical variable"), but the same is not true of Lisp. Now because, in cases like this, the iterative version can only be programmed using the very low-level concepts of pointers and pointer assignments, it seems even more unreasonable for the job to be left to the programmer rather than the implementation.

The following section gives a detailed description of what is involved in implementing the TRO. The reader familiar with the standard implementation will see that TRO introduces very little extra complexity, provided it is designed in from the outset. For this reason, I think the TRO should be included as a matter of course in any new Prolog implementation, even if, without the inclusion of a garbage collector, the full potential is not realized.

3   Design Details for Tail Recursion Optimization

This account aims to be as self-contained as possible, but the reader should refer to the sources mentioned earlier (Warren, 1977a; 1977b) for certain details. Note that the version actually implemented differs slightly from the more ideal design given here, because of constraints imposed by adapting the existing implementation.

3.1   Data Areas

The main data areas are the **code area,** containing data representing the program itself, and three areas operated as stacks, the **local stack,** the **global stack** and the **trail.** Each procedure invocation leads to the creation of an **environment** comprising three stack **frames,** one on each stack. The **local frame** contains information that is only required during the execution of the procedure concerned, namely **bookkeeping** information and the value cells for **local** variables. The **global frame** contains information representing the new structures (complex terms) created by the procedure. For structure-sharing implementations, this will comprise just the value cells for **global** variables. The **trail** frame contains the addresses of variable cells which have been assigned to during unification and which must be reset to "unassigned" on backtracking.

3.2   Registers

The current state of a Prolog computation is defined by certain registers containing pointers into the main data areas. These registers are:

L	latest local frame	(V)
G	latest global frame	(V1)
TR	top of trail	(TR)
CP	continuation point	
	(goals to be executed next)	(A)
CL	continuation local frame	(X)
CG	continuation global frame	(X1)
BP	backtrack point (alternative clauses)	(FL)

BL   backtrack local frame   (VV)
BG   backtrack global frame   (VV1)

where the names in parentheses are those used previously (Warren, 1977a; 1977b) for roughly corresponding registers. In addition, there are registers:

$$A1, A2, \ldots$$

representing the arguments of a procedure call. These registers contain **constructed terms,** i.e., representations of atoms, compound terms or **references** to variable cells.

3.3   Bookkeeping Items

Each local frame contains space for six items of bookkeeping information, referred to as:

CP(l)
CL(l)
G(l)
TR(l)
BP(l)
BL(**l**)

where l is the address of the local frame. These items are the values of the corresponding registers at the time the procedure was invoked. The items TR, BP and BL are only needed if the procedure is a choice point.

3.4   Shadows

Certain registers are not strictly essential, since they merely "shadow" certain stack locations:

G = G(L)
CG = G(CL)
BG = G(BL)
CP = CP(L)
CL = CL(L)

However the use of these nonessential registers is likely to be more efficient. (Certainly this is the case in the DEC-10 implementation.) In particular, BG is involved in checking whether a variable assignment needs to be trailed.

3.5   Procedure Arguments

The local frame also contains **n** locations (where **n** is the arity [number of arguments] of the procedure) into which the procedure's arguments are stored. These locations are called:

$$A1(I), \quad A2(I), \quad \ldots$$

where **I** is the address of the local frame. These locations look just like ordinary variable cells, except that the value of the cell cannot be "unassigned."

3.6   Analysis of a Prolog Program into Basic Operations

Let us now analyze the procedural aspect of a Prolog program into some basic operations which allow for the tail recursion optimization. The detailed implementation of each basic operation will then be described later. The *naive* analysis of a general clause:

$$P :- Q, R, S.$$

would be:

                    match **P**
                    enter
                    call **Q**
                    call **R**
                    call **S**
                    exit

However to allow for the tail recursion optimization, the last call must be treated differently; the actual analysis is:

                    match **P**
                    enter
                    call **Q**
                    call **R**
                    depart **S**

Thus, in effect, "depart = call + exit".

Clauses with no goal in the body (**unit** clauses), or with just one goal in the body (**doublet** clauses), are treated as special cases:

            match **P**   match **P**
            return   proceed **Q**

One can summarize this as "return = enter + exit" and "proceed = enter + depart."

The operations corresponding to a procedure **P** comprising clauses **C1, C2, C3** are:

> arrive **P**
> choice
> try **C1**
> try **C2**
> nochoice
> trust **C3**

If there is just one clause, the operations reduce to merely:

> arrive **P**
> trust **C1**

Note that if the procedure is **indexed,** instead of just one sequence of candidate clauses, there will be a set of alternative sub-sequences, one for each different **key;** for keys with just one candidate (a common case), only a single **trust** action will be necessary, as in the second of the two alternatives above.

3.7   Description of the Basic Operations

The details of each basic operation, apart from the unification operation 'match', are now described. Two other basic operations are also covered. These are 'fail', the backtracking operation which occurs when unification fails, and 'cut', the operation corresponding to the Prolog control primitive.

call
{Load arguments and invoke procedure with new continuation.}
load A1,... with **arguments** from CL and CG;
CP := **remaining goals;**
goto **procedure**

enter
{Complete the current local and global frames.}
save CP, CL, G into L;
CL := L; CG := G;
L := L + **size of local frame;**
check L is not full;
G := G + **size of global frame;**
check G is not full

exit

{Resume at continuation, discarding the local frame if the current procedure is determinate.}
if BL < CL then L := CL;
restore CP, CL from CL;
CG := G(CL);
goto CP

depart

{cf. "call + exit". Load arguments, and invoke the new procedure with the old continuation, overwriting the local frame if current procedure is determinate.}
load A1,... with **arguments** from CL and CG;
if BL < CL then L := CL;
restore CP, CL from CL;
CG := G(CL);
goto **procedure**

proceed

{cf. "enter + depart". Load arguments, complete the local frame only if the current procedure is nondeterminate, complete the global frame, and invoke the new procedure with the existing continuation.}
load A1,... with **arguments** from L and G;
if BL = L
then
    (save CP, CL, G at L;
    L := L + **size of local frame;**
    check L is not full);
G := G + **size of global frame;**
check G is not full;
goto **procedure**

return

{cf. "enter + exit". Complete the local frame only if the procedure is nondeterminate, complete the global frame, and resume at the current continuation.}
if BL = L
then
    (save CP, CL, G at L;
    L := L + **size of local frame;**
    check L is not full);
G := G + **size of global frame;**
check G is not full;
goto CP

arrive
>   {Store the procedure's arguments.}
>   store A1,... into L

choice
>   {Create backtracking point.}
>   save BP, BL, TR at L;
>   BL := L; BG := G

try
>   {Select a clause with other alternatives.}
>   BP := **other clauses;**
>   goto **clause**

nochoice
>   {Remove the backtracking point.}
>   restore BP, BL from L;
>   BG := G(BL)

trust
>   {Select a clause with no other alternatives.}
>   goto **clause**

fail
>   {Restore the state corresponding to the latest backtracking point.}
>   if BL < L
>   then
>   (L := BL; G := BG;
>   restore CP, CL from L;
>   CG := G(CL));
>   undo TR as far as TR(L);
>   goto BP

cut
>   {Remove backtracking points created since the current procedure was
>   invoked, delete trail entries no longer relevant, and remove any local frames
>   which still remain after the current one.}
>   if not BL < CL
>   then
>   (until BL(BL) < CL do BL := BL(BL);
>   restore BP, BL, oldTR from BL;
>   BG := G(BL);
>   tidy TR as far as oldTR;
>   L := CL + **size of local frame**)

3.8   Design Considerations

There are certain points to notice in the above design.

1. As already mentioned, it is assumed that it is advantageous to maintain the shadow registers (CP, CL, CG, G, BG) distinct from the stack locations they shadow. In implementation environments where there is no point in this (e.g. machines with few fast registers), the shadow registers can be regarded as pseudonyms for the corresponding stack locations, and much of the saving and restoring of registers can be avoided.

2. For completely determinate procedures (i.e., procedure activations within which the action **choice** is not executed), there is absolutely no saving or restoring of the "backtracking registers" BP, BL and TR. Note that the cut operation therefore has to be slightly more expensive in the general case, since it has to trace back down the BL chain.

3. The saving of the other registers (CP, CL and G) is not performed at the beginning of the procedure, but is postponed as much as possible in the hope that it will not be necessary to preserve the local frame. It may appear that this approach is disadvantageous in the nondeterminate case, since there is then the overhead of repeatedly saving the same information for each clause entered. However, in experimental comparisons of the two approaches, I have not found any example, even among very nondeterminate programs, where "late saving" is slower. The reason, I think, is that the extra overhead mentioned is balanced by reduced overheads in calling a procedure where no clause matches.

4. Registers CP, CL and CG are restored by 'depart' since otherwise it would be necessary for 'return' to restore these registers. The reasoning behind this is that 'return's are more frequent than 'depart's, and again experimental evidence supports this decision.

5. In the operations 'enter', 'proceed' and 'return', if there is no global frame, then obviously there is no need either to increment the G register or to check it for global stack overflow.

3.9   Treatment of Procedure Arguments

Certain details concerning the handling of procedure arguments have not yet been discussed. In particular we have to be able to guarantee that no "dangling reference" is left to a variable cell in a discarded stack frame.

One way to do this would be to fully "dereference" all procedure arguments, and to forego discarding the stack frame if any of the dereferenced values were a dangling reference. This approach has the disadvantage that it involves quite a lot of extra work at runtime.

As an alternative, one can try to spot the possibility of a dangling reference entirely at "compile-time", and only permit the stack frame to be discarded where it can be guaranteed always safe to do so. A variation of this, the approach actually adopted, is to force any variables which might otherwise have given rise to a dangling reference to be stored in the global stack. Both these options involve little or no runtime overhead, but are less efficient at conserving stack space. I have adopted the second option because it was the simplest to incorporate in the existing implementation and because hopefully the garbage collector will be able eventually to reclaim the extra global variables.

In the implemented version, no attempt is made to fully dereference procedure arguments. If an argument is a variable, the argument register is loaded with a **reference** to that variable's cell, *unless* it can be guaranteed (at compile-time) that the variable is instantiated (to something other than a reference to its own local stack frame), in which case the *value* of the variable's cell is loaded. This guarantee can be made if the variable has an occurrence in the head of a clause and satisfies the normal conditions for being a local. To understand why this is so, consult my dissertation (Warren, 1977b). The TRO then requires that a variable be deemed global if a reference to that variable is passed as an argument to the last goal in the clause. Thus, the only variables made global which would otherwise have been local are those which (i) occur in the last goal, and (ii) only occur in the body. In practice, this is quite a small minority of variables.

Acknowledgments

The improvements described were implemented with the help and encouragement of Fernando Pereira and Lawrence Byrd. The work was supported by a British Science Research Council grant. I thank the referees of this paper for their helpful comments.

References

Bruynooghe M. (1976). *An interpreter for predicate logic programs : Part 1.* Applied Maths & Programming Division, Katholieke Univ Leuven, Belgium. Report CW 10.

Colmerauer, A., H. Kanoui, and M. van Caneghem. (1979). *Etude et realisation d'un systeme Prolog.* Groupe d'Intelligence Artificielle, U. E. R. de Luminy, Universite d'Aix-Marseille II.

Pereira, L. M., F. Pereira and D. H. D. Warren (1978). *User's Guide to DECsystem-10 Prolog.* Dept. of Artificial Intelligence, University of Edinburgh.

Roberts, G. M. (1977). *An implementation of Prolog.* Master Th., Dept of Computer Science, Univ of Waterloo, Canada.

Roussel, P. (1975). *Prolog : Manuel de Reference et d'Utilisation.* Groupe d'Intelligence Artificielle, U. E. R. de Luminy, Universite d'Aix-Marseille II.

Steele, G. L. (1978). *RABBIT: A Compiler for SCHEME.* Master Th., MIT. AI-TR-474.

Warren, D. H. D. (1977a). *Implementing Prolog—compiling predicate logic programs.* Dept of Artificial Intelligence, Univ. of Edinburgh. Research Reports 39 & 40.

Warren, D. H. D. (1977b). *Applied logic—its use and implementation as a programming tool.* Ph.D. Th., Edinburgh University. Available as Technical Note 290, Artificial Intelligence Center, SRI International.

Warren, D. H. D. (1979). "Prolog on the DECsystem-10." In Michie D, Ed., *Expert Systems in the Micro-Electronic Age,* Edinburgh University Press.

Warren, D. H. D., L. M. Pereira and F. Pereira. (1977, August). "Prolog—the language and its implementation compared with Lisp." *ACM Symposium on AI and Programming Languages.*

CHAPTER 5

A Backup Parallel Interpreter for Prolog Programs

Koichi Furukawa

Institute for New Generation Computer Technology
Tokyo, Japan, 108

Katsumi Nitta
Yuji Matsumoto

Electrotechnical Laboratory
Ibaraki, Japan, 305

1   Introduction

This paper presents a parallel execution model for Prolog (Kowalski, 1974; Roussel, 1975; Warren et al., 1977) programs. The sequential execution of a Prolog program can be seen as a depth-first traversal of an AND/OR tree defined by the program. Our parallel interpreter is an extension of the sequential one based on this point of view, and consists of two kinds of processes, AND-processes and OR-processes.

Our parallel execution model is called a backup parallel model. The backup parallelism means that there is one main process, and other processes take care of the backtracking. Although the main process is conceptually distinguished from the others, the sets of operations required by these processes are all the same. This means that all the processors have the same set of operations and can be allocated to any processes.

The next section outlines our Prolog sequential interpreter based on the AND/OR process model. The behavior of the interpreter is shown using a sample program. Data structures are also discussed.

Sections 3 and 4 present the backup parallelism. The procedural semantics of our parallelism is the same as that of the sequential one, but it is faster.

Section 5 discusses the simulation and experiments of our backup parallel model. A simulator is written in Simula with about 1000 lines running on a DECsystem 2060.

2   A Model of the Sequential Prolog Interpreter

Our model is more concrete than Conery's (1981) execution model, and consists of a control part and a unification part.

2.1   The Control Part

The execution of a Prolog program corresponds to a traversal of an AND/OR tree. For example, suppose the following program is given:

1. a(X) <- b(X,Y),c(X).
2. b(X,Y) <- d(X,Y).
3. b(X,Y) <- e(X,Y).
4. c(X) <- f(X).
5. d(aa,bb) <-.
6. e(aa,cc) <-.
7. f(XX) <-.

0. <-a(X).   ! initial clause;

When this program is executed, the interpreter works as if it traverses the AND/OR tree given in Figure 5.1, in a left-to-right, depth-first manner. Our interpreter consists of two parts, called AND-process and OR-process corresponding to the AND-nodes and the OR-nodes in the tree. Variables in a clause are instantiated by an OR-node through "unification."

When an initial clause is passed to the interpreter, an OR-process is created and activated. The OR-process creates an AND-process and passes the body of the initial clause as an argument. The body consists of a sequence of goals. First, for the leftmost goal of the sequence, the AND-process creates an OR-process as a son, passes the control to it and waits for the answer. The AND-process is reactivated when the son OR-process returns an answer (SUCCESS or FAILURE). If the answer is SUCCESS, the OR-process is pushed on the B-stack

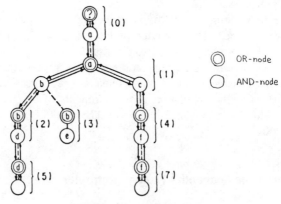

Figure 5.1. And/Or tree

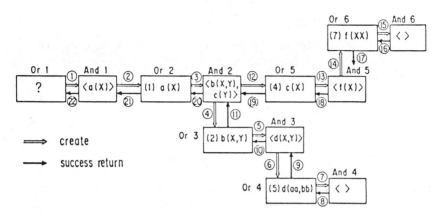

Figure 5.2. Flow of control

in the AND-process, and then the AND-process creates another OR-process for the next goal in the sequence and repeats the same behavior. When the OR-process for the last goal succeeds, the AND-process returns the answer SUCCESS to the parent process and suspends until its parent OR-process activates it. If the son OR-process fails to find an answer, the AND-process pops up the B-stack to get one OR-process, and reactivate it for another solution. When the B-stack becomes empty and the AND-process cannot pop up any OR-process, the AND-process returns FAILURE to its parent OR-process.

An OR-process is created by an AND-process, and is given a goal from it. The OR-process searches for a clause whose head has the identical predicate name as that of the goal, and executes the unification process. If they are unifiable, the OR-process creates an AND-process for the body of the selected clause, passes the control to it and waits for the answer. If the son AND-process returns SUCCESS, the OR-process is reactivated and returns SUCCESS to the parent AND-process and suspends until its parent AND-process activates it. When the unification fails or the son AND-process fails, the OR-process tries to find another unifiable clause and repeats the same behavior. If the OR-process tries out all candidate clauses and does not succeed, the OR-process fails.

The control transfers between son processes and parent processes, and only one process, called the main process, is active at a time. Therefore, each process behaves as a coroutine. When an AND-process or an OR-process returns SUCCESS, it is suspended and keeps its state, preparing for the backtracking. When it fails, it is deleted from the AND/OR tree.

Figure 5.2 shows the processes created through the execution of the previous example program. The flow of control is expressed by arrows with numbers. The number in each OR-process shows selected clause number, and the goal sequence in each AND-process is the body of selected clause.

2.2   The Unification Part

An OR-process has slots storing the values of the variables in the clause it selected. These slots are accessible from its son AND-process and its grandson OR-processes. When a unification is executed in an OR-process, the substitutions for the variables occur both in the OR-process itself and in its grandparent OR-process.

Unification is executed according to Robinson's algorithm (Chang and Lee, 1974). There are two major methods for data representation, Structure Sharing (Boyer and Moore, 1972) and Copying (see Bruynooghe, 1980 and Mellish, 1980). In the Structure Sharing method, the value of a variable is expressed by a pair of pointers ⟨⟨pointer to literal, pointer to environment for evaluating the literal⟩⟩. The first pointer indicates the structure of the value. If this structure includes variables, the second pointer indicates the list of the values of the variables, which is called the "environment."

In the Copy method, a copy of the structure is constructed in a copy stack when the structure includes variables. When the structure has no variable, the structure is not copied and the variable directly points to the structure. See Bruynooghe (1980) and Mellish (1980) for the details of this method.

Examples of both methods are shown in Figure 5.3. These figures show the snapshots of the execution of the following APPEND program. In these figures, "heap" is the area in which the structures of the source program are stored, and "copy" is the copy area.

1.   append(nil,X,X) <−.
2.   append(.(W,X),Y,.(W,Z)) <− append(X,Y,Z).

0.   <− append(.(a,.(b,nil)),.(c,.(d,nil)),P).

We adopted the Copy method for two reasons.

One is that this method nicely matches our process model. The lifetime of the information in the slots is the same as that of the OR-process itself. When an OR-process returns a SUCCESS message for the last candidate clause to its parent, this process can be deleted from the B-stack. In this case, the information in the slots of the process also disappears. But, if we adopt the Structure Sharing method, this process cannot be deleted, because the slots in this process might be referred to by other processes. On the contrary, in the case of Copying, this process can be deleted because the slots in a process only refer to the structures in the "heap" or "copy" area.

The other reason is the memory conflict of processors in the parallel interpreter. The Copy method helps by copying some structures into the copy area and thus scattering some of the memory accesses.

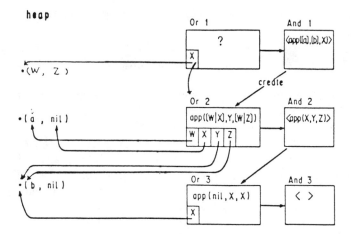

(a) Structure Sharing

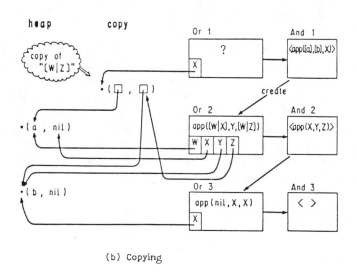

(b) Copying

Figure 5.3. Snapshot of unification

3   Parallel Realization of Prolog Interpreter

3.1   Parallelisms in Prolog

Since Prolog is a language based on predicate logic, the order to solve goals is not restricted intrinsically. Two basic types of parallel execution can be considered in a Prolog program: AND-parallelism and OR-parallelism. Suppose we have the clause

$$h(X,Y):-p(X,Y),q(X),r(Y).$$

When Prolog tries to solve a goal with a call to h and the head of this clause unifies with it, the body of this clause replaces h as the new goals. This clause is solved if and only if each of the goals in its body is solved.

The three goals in the body are connected by logical conjunction. From the viewpoint of declarative semantics, they can be solved in any order. AND-parallelism insists on the simultaneous execution of these goals. There is a difficulty inherent in AND-parallelism. A variable occurring in more than one goal in a clause body must have the same value throughout the computation. For example, p(X,Y) and q(X) in the body have the same variable X. If these are executed at the same time and one of them gives a value assignment to the variable X, this constrains the value of X in the other goals to have the same value. More precisely, each of the goals eventually gets the set of all combinations of variable assignments and the whole answer of the clause is to be the intersection of the sets for the goals in the body.

When p(X,Y) is called, there may be more than one clause whose head unifies with this call. OR-parallelism insists on the simultaneous execution of all the unifiable clause bodies. Since variables in different clauses are mutually independent, there is no difficulty of the variable intersection in OR-parallelism as in AND-parallelism. However, variables in the call may be assigned different values by different unifiable clauses. These assignments must be treated separately, since each of these values is used in a distinct environment. Moreover, assigning one processor to each OR-process leads to an explosion in the number of the processors.

3.2   Backup Parallelism in Prolog

This section shows a form of parallelism that we call ''backup parallel execution'' of Prolog programs.

In the preceding section, we have indicated some types of parallelism in Prolog. These forms of parallel execution ignore the order of the goals in a body or the order of the clauses in a program. When a given program has several answers, the programmer cannot predict the order of the answers obtained from these parallel executions. Users of Prolog always write their program in sequential order, and writing sequential programs is easier for them. And such programs run only in the sequential procedural semantics. Our parallel model aims at the faster execution of existing Prolog programs.

The backup parallel execution considered here is the natural extension of the AND/OR model of our Prolog interpreter. In our AND/OR model a parent

AND(OR)-process creates and activates an OR(AND)-process, and the son process answers with a solution when it finds one. In the sequential execution, the son process waits for reactivation from its parent after it sends an answer to the parent process. In the backup parallelism, when a process finds an answer, the process puts the answer into the message buffer in the process and tries to search for another solution without suspending. If the parent process needs another solution, the process does not reactivate the son process, but immediately gets the solution from the buffer of the son process. A process is suspended in only two cases. The first one is the case where it finds another answer though the buffer is full. The other is when the son process takes too much time to find another solution and the parent process cannot get another solution because the buffer is empty. A process which has failed to find an answer sends a failure message to the parent and can be deleted when all solutions in the buffer are used by the parent.

We have distinguished AND and OR processes in the preceding discussion. However, an OR-process deals with the head of a clause and its son process works with the body of the clause. Since variables are shared within a clause, it is reasonable to allocate a processor to the pair consisting of an OR-process and its son AND-process. Our simulator for the backup parallel model, shown in Section 5, has been constructed in this way.

Although an AND-process usually has several sons, it communicates with only one son process, which is on top of the B-stack in the AND-process. Suppose that a son OR-process whose corresponding goal is in the B-stack of its parent AND-process fails to find a solution. In the model stated above, the OR-process keeps the failure answer and waits for the parent's reactivation. However, if the preceding OR-process has already found a solution and this information can be sent to the OR-process, this OR-process can start to find solutions in this new environment. Such information transfer between son OR-processes leads to more efficient backup parallelism. Our simulator has not yet been equipped with this ability.

4   Data Structure for Backup Parallelism

As shown in Section 2.2, there are two major data representation methods in Prolog implementation. Of these methods, we adopted the Copy method for our Prolog interpreter. When unification occurs, a structure which includes undefined variables is copied in the copy stack.

In the backup parallel execution, each process works in its own environment. A variable in a Prolog program may have different value assignments in different processes. Therefore, a variable must be represented by a set of values, so that each process can access the proper value.

We represent a variable by the pair $\langle\langle$generation, value$\rangle\rangle$ in the backup parallel

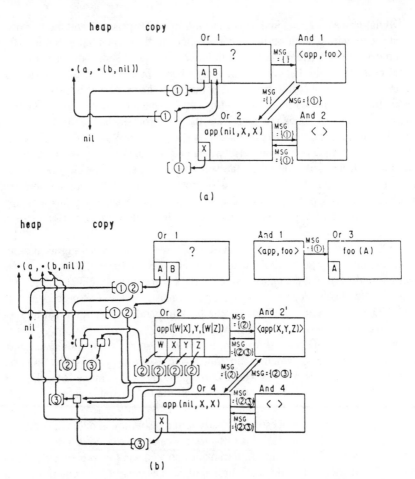

Figure 5.4. Snapshot of unification by back-up parallelism

model, where the "generation" part shows when this value is assigned to the variable. Hence a variable consists of a list of such pairs. In our parallel interpreter, each generation is represented by a number identifying a unification. A process has a set of numbers which is the history of the unifications of this process. This set is incremented and is passed the son process by the parent when the son process is created after the unification. Our parallel simulator directly uses this method of variable representation. We have mentioned in Section 2.2 that we adopt the Copy method for data representation. When this method is used in our parallel model, structures including undefined variables are copied. In the case of sequential execution, messages passed between the parent and son processes are only SUCCESS or FAILURE, for the solution can be obtained through the bindings to the variables made by the unification. In the parallel case, however, the set of generations is sent to the parent to construct the solution. Although copied structures are not shared by the variables in the same generation, they may be shared by the variables in the different generations.

Figure 5.4 is the snapshot of executing the following program:

$$\text{?:- app(A,B,.(a,.(b,nil))), foo(A).}$$

In figure 5.4(a), the OR-process "Or 2" finds a solution (A=nil,B=[a,b]) and sends the list of generation number {1} to the parent AND-process "And 1." In Figure 5.4(b), "And 1" creates the son OR-process "Or 3" and commits the calculation of foo(A), while "Or 2" selects another clause and finds the next solution (A=[a],B=[b]) which is expressed by the list {2,3} of generation number.

Unfortunately, we have not yet found an efficient realization of the above data representation. This is the key of the efficiency of our backup parallel model. At least the main process should be able to access its environment as fast as the sole process in the sequential model.

5   Simulation and Experiments

We implemented the Prolog interpreter shown in the previous section in the concurrent programming language Simula.

The interpreter works for two versions:
1. the sequential interpreter (SI) which is introduced in Section 2.
2. the parallel interpreter (PI) which is introduced in Section 3.

The parallel interpreter also achieves limited AND-parallelism.

Let the goal sequence $\langle p(X),q(X,Y)\rangle$ be given to an AND-process where $p(X)$ has two solutions for X and, for each X, $q(X,Y)$ has three solutions for Y, so that six pairs of (X,Y) are calculated. While executing it, the backup parallel interpreter creates OR-processes, once for $p(X)$ and twice for $q(X,Y)$. However, if goals p and q have no common variable, for example $\langle p(X),q(Y)\rangle$, and their solutions are independent, we don't have to execute the second goal twice. When two solutions of X and three solutions of Y are obtained, we can get six pairs of solutions by combining them.

If an unbounded number of processors are available, every pair of OR-process and its son AND-process is allocated to one processor and can communicate with its parent or its son process. However, in case the number of processors is limited, the number of processes often exceeds that of processors and some process must be suspended until some processor is released.

The allocation of processors is done as follows:

Each process corresponds to a node on the AND/OR tree, and a measure of priority is attached to the node. The priority is settled when the AND/OR tree is traversed in left-to-right and depth-first manner. The farther the node is from the root, the higher the priority that is attached. In our interpreter PI, a main process has the initiative and other processes work to back it up; this is a different point from AND-parallelism and OR-parallelism. Therefore, when there are not enough processors, the process whose priority is the lowest among active processes is forced into the waiting mode and pushed on the waiting process stack. When some processor is released, a process whose priority is the highest among processes in the stack is popped and allocated to this processor.

As an example, we use the following permutation program:

```
1.   perm(nil,nil) <-.
2.   perm(.(X,Y),.(U,V)) <- del(U,.(X,Y),W),perm(W,V).
3.   del(X,.(X,Y),Y) <-.
4.   del(U,.(X,Y),.(X,V)) <- del(U,Y,V).

0.   <- perm(.(1,.(2,nil))),P),perm(.(3,.(4,.(5,nil))),Q),app(P,Q,R).
```

This program has twelve solutions such as (1 2 3 4 5), (1 2 3 5 4), . . . , (2 1 5 4 3). The execution time of SI and PI are shown in Table 5.1. (It is assumed that the number of the processors is not limited.)

The time unit of this table is system time of Simula and is proportional to the

Table 5.1. Sequential and parallel execution times for the permutation program

	SI	PI
(1 2 3 4 5)	525	525
(1 2 3 5 4)	984	651
(1 2 4 3 5)	1590	852
(1 2 4 5 3)	2049	978
(1 2 5 3 4)	2669	1179
(1 2 5 4 3)	3128	1305
(2 1 3 4 5)	4110	1432
(2 1 3 5 4)	4539	1559
(2 1 4 3 5)	5175	1689
(2 1 4 5 3)	5634	1813
(2 1 5 3 4)	6254	1940
(2 1 5 4 3)	6713	2067
finish	7260	2082

Table 5.2. Percentage of the time a certain number of processors are active

Processors	1	2	3	4	5	6	7
(1 2 3 4 5)—(1 2 5 4 3)	16	41	23	12	4	2	0.5%
(2 1 3 4 5)—(2 1 5 4 3)	80	12	5				

real execution time. The time required to find the first solution (1 2 3 4 5) is the same, since backtrack does not occur. However, note that PI needs less time than SI to find the remaining solutions. In particular, it takes less time to compute (2 1 3 4 5) through (2 1 5 4 3), because P and Q are independent and the interpreter becomes AND-parallel mode after (1 2 5 4 3) is calculated. In the execution of PI, the number of allocated processors changes dynamically. The percentages of time for each number of processors is shown in Table 5.2.

6   Concluding Remarks

A Prolog interpreter and its extension to a parallel execution model are introduced. Our parallel model is called "backup parallel", which works on the AND/OR tree constructed by a Prolog program. This parallel model can run the original sequential Prolog program faster using several processors of the same type.

The sample program shown in Section 5 has achieved an execution speed which is only a few times faster than that of the sequential one. This is because there are at most four processes that are active at the same time. For larger programs, when there are more active processes, this model can save more execution time.

When backtracking occurs frequently, the backup parallel execution works effectively. Problems in artificial intelligence are often based on "searching." Such a program usually describes only the meaning of the problem (or relations between some objects). Prolog is just such a language. Therefore, we can say that our parallel model is suited for every problem that uses the essential property of Prolog.

There are some problems to be solved. One is the processor allocation and the other is the data representation.

When the number of processors is limited, processors should be allocated to the processes nearest to the main process. Difficulty lies not in determining which are the nearest processes, because processes can be ordered according to the time when they are created. In the parallel execution, processes are created dynamically not only by the main process. However, the order of the son process is determined by the order of the parent process and it can be merged into other processes, creating a total order among the processes. When a process enters into the waiting mode or the full mode, the processor is released from the process. A processor is allocated to such a process when it is activated by the son or parent process and there are free processors or there is a process not nearer to the main process.

We adopted the Copy method for our interpreter. It is also utilized in our parallel model. A variable in a Prolog program is represented by a pair consisting of its generation and its value. A variable is accessed by several processes which work under their own environments. They access the value of the variable by the generation it belongs to. It is the remaining and most important problem to find a way to realize a data representation which can be accessed efficiently by several processors.

References

Boyer, R. S. and J. S. Moore. (1972). "The Sharing of Structure in Theorem Proving Programs," in *Machine Intelligence 7*. Edinburgh UP.

Bruynooghe, M. (1980). *The Memory Management of Prolog Implementation*. Logic Programming Workshop, Hungary.

Chang, C. L. and R. C. Lee. (1974). *Symbolic Logic and Mechanical Theorem Proving*. Academic Press.

Conery, J. S. (1981). "Parallel Interpretation of Logic Programs," *ACM Conference on Functional Language*.

Kowalski, R. (1974). "Predicate Logic as Programming Language," *Information Processing 74*, 569–574.

Mellish, C. S. (1980). *An Alternative to Structure-Sharing in the Implementation of a Prolog Interpreter*. Logic Programming Workshop, Hungary.

Roussel, P. (1975). *Prolog: Manual de Reference et d'Utilisation*. Groupe d'Intelligence Artificielle, Marseille-Luminy.

Warren, D. H. D. et al. (1977). "Prolog—The Language and its Implementation Compared with Lisp." *Proc. Symposium on Artificial Intelligence and Programming Language*, pp. 109–115.

PART III
TOOLS

CHAPTER 6

LDM—A Program Specification Support System

Zs. Farkas
P. Szeredi
E. Santane-Toth

Institute for Co-ordination of Computer Techniques (SZKI)
Donati utca 35–45. H-1015 Budapest, Hungary

1   Introduction

The *Logic-based Development Method (LDM)* is a complex software technological tool supporting the whole program development cycle, from specification through design down to implementation. It is intended to have three components: a *language* and a *methodology* to be used during development, and an *interactive system* supporting their use. The concept of LDM and the formal specification of the language came into being in the years 1978–1980. Szeredi et al. (1980) gives an overview of the philosophy of LDM while Balogh et al. (1982) presents an outline of the LDM language with a number of detailed examples. In recent years we concentrated our efforts on development of the support system component. According to the original concepts, this system should help the *multilevel software development process,* supporting both the development of the individual levels, and the transition between them. Up to now, we have realized an experimental system with a smaller set of functions. The most important restriction is that it supports development of separate levels only. The language is, however, fully implemented; that is, LDM descriptions on any abstraction level can be executed. The possibility of *testing* is useful especially in the *specification* phase, because there are not too many other alternatives for checking the correspondence of the formal specification to the expectations of the user. This means that the system presented in this paper can be applied first of all as a program specification support system; therefore only the abstract, descriptive, applicative elements of the LDM language are presented.

2   LDM versus Prolog in program specification

It is reasonable to specify a program in a language making possible exact, concise and lucid formulation of the task to be programmed. A specification language also should not force the user to include implementation-specific information, e.g., algorithmic details. Mathematical logic is widely used as such a specification language. Prolog, as its sublanguage, can also be applied for this purpose, with the very advantageous extra feature of executability of these specifications (see e.g. Davis, 1982). However, viewed as a specification language Prolog lacks a number of features, e.g., tools for adequate handling of *data structures* or for expressing the systematic application of an operation to several objects. LDM is an extension of Prolog intended to be a more adequate specification language. The extra language elements are borrowed mainly from the Vienna Development Method (VDM) (Bjorner and Jones, 1978). The extension was performed preserving *constructivity,* i.e. specifications formulated in this extended language can still be executed.

The most important difference between LDM and Prolog is in data structure handling. On one hand, LDM allows finite sets and mappings as data structures, not only trees as in Prolog. On the other hand, the parameter-passing mechanism is different in the two languages: the *pattern-matching mechanism* is extended in LDM to cope with the new data structures introduced.

For example, one can use variables in "set-expressions" (throughout the paper capital letters denote variables): the expression

set(a,X)

denotes a set containing exactly the elements "a" and "X"; this becomes a one- or two-element set depending on whether "a" or some other object is substituted into X.

The extended pattern-matching of LDM can be combined with the possibility of functional notation. This means that some argument expressions—the so-called *implicit object expressions*—will be *evaluated* in LDM by some user-defined operations rather than considered to be data structures (as in Prolog). For example, as a Prolog call argument "2+3" denotes the binary tree:

In LDM, however, it is considered as an expression representing the object, which can be produced by executing the operation "+". From the logical point of view, "2+3" is a functional expression, i.e. the ternary relation "+" is used in functional form: "2+3" denotes the objects X for which +(2,3,X) holds.

Other forms of implicit object expressions are the conditional and case schemes and various versions of operation schemes based on bounded quantification. For example, the conditional scheme

$$r(X) \; --\rangle \;\; X;$$
$$\text{otherwise} \; --\rangle \; f(X)$$

represents X itself for any object X satisfying the relation r and the objects Y being in relation f(X,Y) for any other X (note, that there is exactly one such Y if f is a function, but one can use the functional form f(X) for any relation f). The quantification scheme

$$\text{list}(X \text{ forall } X \text{ elem } S \text{ suchthat } p(X))$$

represents the list consisting of the elements X of S satisfying the relation p for any set S. Similarly, the expression

$$\text{the } X \text{ elem } S \text{ suchthat } p(X)$$

represents the only element of S for which the relation p holds (it is defined only if there is exactly one such element).

As outlined above, in LDM, contrary to Prolog, any *evaluable* object expression may stand as an argument in operations, and relations can be used and defined also in functional form. Moreover, LDM contains operation shemes that allow systematic application of an operation to all elements of a set. This sort of operation can be described in Prolog using backtracking or recursion, while in LDM one can apply operation schemes based on bounded quantification. For example, using such a scheme it is simple to define a relation which holds on monotone increasing finite mappings on numbers (here "dom M", "<=" and "M[X]" are standard LDM operations, denoting the domain of a mapping, the usual less-or-equal relation on numbers and the value assigned by the mapping to a given object, respectively):

$$\text{monotone}(M) \text{ iff}$$
$$\text{forall } X,Y \text{ elem dom } M \text{ suchthat } X <= Y$$
$$\text{holds } M[X] <= M[Y].$$

As can be seen from the above discussion, all the extensions to Prolog remain within full first-order logic with equality. On the other hand, the LDM language is still reducible to Horn logic, mainly due to the boundedness of quantifiers. The reducibility means that one can retain the original semantics of this subset of first-order logic while executing it by translating to Prolog.

So far we have been speaking only about operation definitions. In LDM it is also possible to define *domains* (i.e. data types) as well as give *type specifications* for operations. These definitions make the description clearer and help in consistency-checking. For making the debugging of specifications more convenient, the use of *global variables* is allowed: complex test data can be stored in global variables instead of being given explicitly as an argument of the operation to be tested.

The above features will be illustrated by a simple example in section 4, together with an introduction to the use of the LDM Support System.

3   The LDM Support System

An adequate language can itself help the specification activity, but even a relatively simple support system makes this work much more efficient. The present section gives an overview of such a system—the first step towards a complex program development tool.

This system, called the *LDM Support System,* is an interactive program specification tool that supports development, editing and checking of specifications formulated in LDM. The most important and most useful function of the system is *execution of specifications,* which is realized by translating LDM definitions into Prolog.

The system is able to handle several descriptions (''levels'') at a time, making possible the elaboration of alternative solutions, though there are no tools yet for checking and supporting the transition between the levels.

The system accepts the following commands:

LEVEL	⟨level identifier⟩
ENTER	⟨LDM definition⟩
REPLACE	⟨LDM definition⟩
DELETE	⟨name⟩ | ⟨name⟩/⟨arity⟩
TYPE	⟨name⟩ | ⟨name⟩/⟨arity⟩
LIST	
EXECUTE	⟨LDM goal⟩ | = ⟨LDM object expression⟩

SOLUTIONS   ⟨LDM goal⟩ |
             = ⟨LDM object expression⟩

SAVE   ⟨filename⟩

LOAD   ⟨filename⟩

A LEVEL command serves for selecting a specific level, so that further commands concern this level. ENTER, REPLACE and DELETE serve for editing the specification; these commands work only for syntactically correct LDM definitions. An ENTER command adds the given definition to the current level, if the corresponding notion has not been defined yet. This notion can be a domain, a global variable, an operation or the type of an operation; domains and variables are identified by names, while operations and the specifications by their name and arity (number of arguments). Similarly, one can redefine (using a REPLACE command) and delete (by a DELETE command) definition(s) within the current level.

The TYPE and LIST commands serve for inquiring about the current state of the specification: a TYPE command displays a definition of the current level. Using the LIST command the names of currently defined notions of the level can be listed. The SAVE and LOAD commands can be used to store the definitions of the current level into a file and to read a full level description from a file.

The current level of the specification can be tested by the EXECUTE and SOLUTIONS commands. Their parameter can be either an LDM object expression to be evaluated, or an LDM goal, which, like a Prolog goal, is a question formulated in LDM and is to be answered on the base of the definitions. The difference between these two commands lies in that EXECUTE yields one solution while SOLUTIONS produces all the solutions, asking after each one whether to continue the search for further solutions or not.

4   An example

In the following dialog with the system, the specification of a program for creating cross-references of texts is developed, as an illustration of both the expressive power of the LDM language and the use of the system.

The dialog is started with a LEVEL command (1) followed by a sequence of ENTER commands (2-12). Output of the system is marked with an asterisk. The system answer to an ENTER command refers to the defined notion by displaying its name or name/arity (note that a relation defined in functional form with n arguments is considered as an $n+1$-ary relation).

In the sample specification "text" is defined to be a list of "line"'s (2), lines are lists of "word"'s (3). The type specification of the relation "cross_ref_of"

states that it is a total function between texts and "ref_table"'s (4). A "ref_ta-
ble" is defined as a mapping which assigns "descriptor"'s to words (5), where
descriptors are sets of "line_number"'s (6), which are positive "number"'s (7).
The relation "cross_ref_of" is defined in functional form: the "cross_ref_of" of
a given text is the finite mapping which assigns to each of the "key_words" in
the text its descriptor (8). Next, two type specifications follow: the relation
"key_words" is a total function from texts to sets of words (9), while "de-
scr_of" is a total function assigning a descriptor to a word and a text (10). The
"key_words" of a given text is defined as the set of all the objects W satisfying
the relation "is_key_word" and being elements of the lines which are elements
of the given text (11). Similarly, "descr_of" assigns to any word and text the set
of line numbers of all those lines which contain W as an element (12).

In the above specification the relation "is_key_word" remained undefined.
However, for the purposes of testing we define it to hold exactly on the given
objects (13). Moreover, a global variable "t" is defined (14), and its value is set
to the given "text" object by an EXECUTE command (15); in the following its
value can be referred to as "cont(t)". The next commands test the specification:
first the cross-reference of the text stored in the global variable "t" is presented
(16), and then it is asked whether or not there is a line in the given text which
does not contain any key word (17). Finally, the line numbers occurring in the set
assigned to "ldm" by the "cross_reference" of the given text are produced
using a SOLUTIONS command (18).

(1)   LEVEL cross_reference.
         * cross_reference started

(2)   ENTER text ::= list line.
         * text entered

(3)   ENTER line ::= list word.
         * line entered

(4)   ENTER type cross_ref_of: total fct
                          text −−) ref_table.
         * type of cross_ref_of/2 entered

(5)   ENTER ref_table ::= map(word,descriptor).
         * ref_table entered

(6)   ENTER descriptor ::= set line_number.
         * descriptor entered

(7)   ENTER line_number ::= number suchthat positive.
         * line_number entered

(8)   ENTER cross_ref_of (TEXT) =
          map(KW —⟩ descr_of (KW,TEXT)
              forall KW elem key_words(TEXT)).
          * cross_ref_of/2 entered

(9)   ENTER type key_words : total fct
                        text −−⟩ set word.
          * type of key_words/2 entered

(10)   ENTER type descr_of : total fct
                        (word,text) −−⟩ descriptor.
          * type of descr_of/3 entered

(11)   ENTER key_words(TEXT) = set(W forall
          W elem LINE,LINE elem TEXT suchthat
          is_key_word(W)).
          * key_words/2 entered

(12)   ENTER descr_of (W,TEXT) = set(I forall
          I elem ind(TEXT) suchthat W elem TEXT[I]).
          * descr_of/3 entered

(13)   ENTER is_key_word (W) iff W elem
          set (prolog,ldm,logic).
          * is_key_word/1 entered

(14)   ENTER variable t : text.
          * variable t entered

(15)   EXECUTE t := list(
          list(prolog,is,based,on,logic),
          list(prolog,is,a,very,high,level,language),
          list(ldm,is,based,on,prolog),
          list(ldm,is,in,experimental,phase)
).
          * yes

(16)   EXECUTE = cross_ref_of (cont(t)).
          * the result:
          * map(prolog —⟩ set(1,2,3),
          *   logic —⟩ set(1),
          *   ldm —⟩ set(3,4)).

(17)   EXECUTE exists LINE elem cont(t) suchthat
          forall W elem LINE holds not is_key_word(W).
          * no

(18)   SOLUTIONS L elem cross_ref_of(cont(t))[ldm].
            * L = 3
            * continue?
        yes
            * L = 4
            * continue?
        yes
            * no

5   Realization of the system

The LDM Support System is implemented in the Prolog using the MPROLOG
system (Bendl et al., 1980; Institute for Co-ordination of Computer Techniques,
1983). The main functions of the system are: analyzing commands, storing and
maintaining LDM definitions, input and output driven by the LDM syntax, and
translating of LDM operation definitions into Prolog.

The LDM definitions are stored in the database as facts of the following form:

    op_def   (⟨operation name⟩ / ⟨arity⟩,
               ⟨internal form of the definition⟩,
               ⟨level identifier⟩)

    type_def (⟨operation name⟩ / ⟨arity⟩,
               ⟨internal form of the specification⟩,
               ⟨level identifier⟩)

    dom_def   (⟨domain name⟩,
               ⟨internal form of the domain definition⟩,
               ⟨level identifier⟩)

    var_def   (⟨variable name⟩,
               ⟨internal form of the variable definition⟩,
               ⟨current value of the variable⟩,
               ⟨level identifier⟩)

Moreover, when an operation definition is entered, it is translated into a
Prolog procedure with the same name and arity and this procedure is added to the
database.

The ENTER, REPLACE and DELETE commands operate on the appropriate
". . ._def" clauses, and in the case of an operation definition the corresponding
Prolog procedure is modified as well. The TYPE and LIST commands use only
the ". . ._def" clauses, while testing is made on the basis of Prolog form of the
operation definitions: the given LDM goal or object expression is transformed to
a Prolog goal and executed.

In the following the *translation of the LDM operation definitions* is discussed in somewhat more detail. The main problem is argument handling: in the course of translating an LDM operation the implicit operation references must be unfolded, i.e. transformed into a sequence of explicit calls. For this *unfolding* a strategy of the execution order of the operations had to be chosen. Our strategy is based on the type specification of the operations: the calls are ordered in such a way that during execution the arguments declared as input would be evaluated before, and the output arguments after, the execution of the given operation. For example, an operation reference of the form

$$r(f(X), g(Y))$$

in the presence of a type specification (declaring both arguments input)

$$\text{type r : (number,number)} \dashrightarrow .$$

is transformed into the call sequence:

$$f(X,Z1), \ g(Y,Z2), \ r(Z1,Z2)$$

while having the type specification

$$\text{type r: number} \dashrightarrow \text{number.}$$

is translated into the call sequence

$$f(X,Z1), \ r(Z1,Z2), \ g(Y,Z2).$$

Besides unfolding there is another problem, namely, that we need a *unifying mechanism* more general than that of Prolog to handle arbitrary LDM data expressions; for example, the data expressions

$$set(5,X,Z) \text{ and } set(6,Y)$$

should be unified using, e.g., the substitution

$$X \mathrel{<--} 6, \ Y \mathrel{<--} 5, \ Z \mathrel{<--}5.$$

For this purpose a procedure "unify" is implemented in Prolog, and its call is generated into the translated form at any point where an LDM parameter-matching is necessary.

Finally, translation of *operation schemes* based on bounded quantification is introduced. The central notion of these schemes is that of "quantifier expression'' which describes a finite class of substitutions. For example, the following so-called simple quantifier expression

$$X,Y \text{ elem } S \text{ suchthat } X<=Y$$

describes the substitutions of the variables X and Y by pairs a,b which are elements of the set S such at a<=b.

For these quantifier expressions a Prolog procedure

$$subst\_of(QE)$$

is defined whose argument can be a quantifier expression, and it can succeed as many times as there are substitutions corresponding to QE; at any backtrack further substitutions are produced. All the quantification schemes are translated in a uniform way using this procedure (and therefore based on the backtracking mechanism of Prolog): moreover, we have some other procedures corresponding to the various versions of these schemes, e.g.

solvable(G)	the goal G succeeds
uniquely_solvable(G)	the goal G can succed exactly in one way
forall(G1,G2)	whenever the goal G1 succeeds G2 also does so
list_of_solutions(G1,G2,E,L)	L is unified with the list of the values assigned to the data expression E by executing the goal G2 for each solution of the goal G1
the_solution (G,E)	E is unified with the value assigned by the only solution of the goal G to the data expression E (if G is uniquely solvable).

As an illustration, the translated forms of some quantification schemes are shown below:

LDM expression	the corresponding Prolog clause
exists QE	solvable(subst_of(QE'))
exists ! QE	uniquely_solvable(subst_of (QE'))
forall QE holds p	forall(subst_of(QE'),p')

L = list(f(X)   list_of_solutions
    forall QE)   subst_of(QE'),f(X,Z),Z,L)

X = the QE   the_solution(subst_of(QE'),E),
                       unify(E,X)

where QE' is the internal form of QE, p' is the Prolog clause corresponding to p.

6   Conclusions and Further Plans

Though the system described here is only a first version of the complex LDM system to be developed, it seems to be a useful software development tool. Before creating an improved version, of course, we have to use it extensively in order to gain more experience. Beside improving the services of the system, we are planning to extend it with functions to help the multilevel development process. The first step towards this aim has already been made: our system is also able to handle the algorithmic elements of LDM. The next planned extension steps are the verification of the compatibility of LDM levels and providing semiautomatic, user-driven transformations to help transition between levels.

References

Balogh, K., Zs. Farkas, E. Santane-Toth, and P. Szeredi. (1982). "Software Development in LDM." Proc. of "Specification and Design of Software Systems" Conference on Operating Systems, Visegrad (Hungary) (ed. by E. Knuth and E. J. Neuhold). Lecture Notes in Computer Science 152, Springer Verlag, pp. 56–83.

Bendl, J., P. Koves, and P. Szeredi. (1980). The MPROLOG system. Preprints of the Logic Programming Workshop (ed. S-A. Tarnlund), Debrecen, Hungary, pp. 201–209.

Bjorner, D., and C. B. Jones (editors). (1978). The Vienna Development Method: The Meta-Language. Lecture Notes in Computer Science 61, Springer Verlag.

Davis, R. E. (1982). "Runnable Specification as a Design Tool." In Logic Programming (ed. by K. L. Clark and S.-A. Tarnlund), Academic Press, pp. 141–149.

MPROLOG Language Reference Manual & MPROLOG User's Guide. 1983. Institute for Coordination of Computer Techniques, Budapest, Hungary.

Szeredi, P., K. Balogh, E. Santane-Toth, and Zs. Farkas. (1980). LDM—a Logic Based Software Development Method. Preprints of the Logic Programming Workshop (ed. S-A. Tarnlund), Debrecen, Hungary, pp. 160–171.

Additional Sources

The following reports describe (in Hungarian) the development of LDM and its applications:

Software design in LDM—case studies. (1979). Series SOFTTECH, Vol. D37, SZAMKI, Budapest.
The LDM design language and method. (1979–1980). Vol. I-III. Series SOFTTECH, Vol. D47-D49, SZAMKI. Budapest, Hungary.
The LDM system—a design outline. (1979). Series SOFTTECH, Vol. D46, SZAMKI, Budapest, Hungary.
User's manual of the LDM3 system. (1983). SZKI, Budapest, Hungary.

CHAPTER 7

Towards a Derivation Editor[1]

Agneta Eriksson
Anna-Lena Johansson
Sten-Åke Tärnlund

UPMAIL
Uppsala Programming Methodology and Artificial Intelligence Laboratory
Department of Computing Science, Uppsala University
P.O. Box 2059, S - 750 02 Uppsala, Sweden

1   Introduction

We shall take up a programming calculus proposed by Hansson and Tärnlund (1979a,b) based on a natural deduction system. Although some of our results are specific to this system, corresponding results can usually be found, for example, in the systems of Green (1969a, 1969b), Manna and Waldinger (1971), Clark (1977), Hogger (1979), Kowalski (1979), and Clark and Darlington (1980). In our programming calculus a program Ψ can be obtained by constructing a derivation Π from a set of definitions of data structures Δ and computable relations Γ. In this way a program can be viewed as a theorem in the calculus (see Hansson and Tärnlund, 1979a). Alternatively, a program can first be written down as a conjecture and then justified by showing a theorem Θ, for example about correctness (see Clark and Tärnlund, 1977). These two approaches have the advantage of providing us with more exact information about our programs than is usual, but their drawback is that in order to obtain this information we have to carry out quite a few detailed derivation steps, in fact, easily several hundreds for nontrivial programs (see Hansson, 1980). This complexity is regrettable because deriving programs or theorems about programs can be interesting in itself, and moreover, could have important applications whenever we are using a computer. Eventually our problem may be solved by automated deduction methods so we can obtain the desired derivations automatically, but these methods do not seem to be available yet. As we shall see, a derivation editor can be helpful for studying and manipulating derivations.

We shall focus on four classes of derivations that we shall describe schematically.

---

[1] This work is supported by the National Swedish Board for Technical Development (STU).

(i) A program Ψ is deduced by a derivation Π_i from definitions of data structures Δ and definitions about computable relations or functions Γ.

$$\frac{(\Delta) \quad (\Gamma)}{\Pi_i}$$
$$\overline{\quad \Psi \quad}$$

(ii) A program Ψ is verified by a derivation Π_{ii} of a theorem Θ from the definitions Δ and Γ.

$$\frac{(\Delta) \, (\Gamma) \, (\Psi)}{\Pi_{ii}}$$
$$\overline{\quad \Theta \quad}$$

(iii) A program Ψ' is transformed by a derivation Π_{iii} from a program Ψ and the definitions Δ and Γ.

$$\frac{(\Delta) \, (\Gamma) \, (\Psi)}{\Pi_{iii}}$$
$$\overline{\quad \Psi' \quad}$$

We have until now been interested in using the editor to derive or to prove properties about a program. Let us take a further step and also consider running a logic program Ψ i.e. constructing a proof Π_{iv} of a theorem Λ from the program Ψ, that we may have derived formally (case *i*) or obtained by transformation (case *iii*) or written down intuitively and then verified (case *ii*). In contrast to cases *(i)*–*(iii)* where we use full first order logic, we only use Horn clauses for case *(iv)*.

(iv) A logic program Ψ is run by constructing a derivation Π_{iv} of a theorem Λ from Ψ.

$$(\Psi)$$
$$\frac{\Pi_{iv}}{\Lambda}$$

An interesting point about logic programming is that the derivation Π_{iv} can be carried out automatically and so fast in the Prolog systems (see Roussel, 1975 and Warren, 1977) that it can be viewed as a computation. This fact makes logic programming a good idea (see Hayes, 1973; Colmerauer, Kanoui, Pasero, and Roussel, 1973; Kowalski 1974; 1979).

The structures and properties of these four classes of derivations can be different depending on the logical systems, speed of derivation (computation), and the employed derivation methods. For example, in case *(iv)* when a programmer writes his programs he has the derivation Π_{iv} in mind and works implicitly with the control component of logic programs. A characteristic nature of the derivations Π_{iv} is that their length depends on the length of the input. It is not difficult to write a program and give it an input so the derivation grows (automatically) beyond say, 10,000 steps. The fact that such long derivations can be interesting is a new result coming from logic programming, and surprisingly enough it has turned out to be very practical. For the classes (*i*)–(*iii*) derivations of say, 5,000 steps would probably also lead to interesting applications and give formal developments of nontrivial programs, and moreover interesting theorems about programs.

2   Logic System

We are using a natural deduction system for derivations (*i*)–(*iii*) in our programming calculus, but the first logic programming systems are Prolog systems using Robinson's resolution principle (1965) for derivations of type (*iv*). The programming calculus of Hansson and Tärnlund (1979a,b) made this distinction between the two logic systems. There is a slight drawback to using two different logic systems, but the only way of employing one system would have been to use a resolution system for derivations (*i*)–(*iii*) as well, as Clark (1977) and Hogger (1979) do, because at that time it was not known how to obtain a derivation of type Π_{iv} in a natural deduction system.

However, since then methods for programming in natural deduction have been developed (see Hansson and Haridi, 1981; Hansson, Haridi, and Tärnlund, 1982; Haridi, 1981; and Tärnlund, 1981) so we can make use of a natural deduction system as a single logic system for derivations of all the four classes (*i*)–(*iv*).

Deriving programs or proving theorems with a derivation editor is an interactive process between informal reasoning by the user and formal reasoning by the computer, and it is desirable to get this dialogue as smooth as possible. Therefore, it is interesting to take up natural deduction systems since they are results of attempts to characterize informal reasoning. Thus unformalized arguments preserve their structure when they are formalized, e.g. hypothetical reasoning. We shall make use of the normal form theorem (Hauptsatz) for natural deduction systems by Prawitz (1965) and Stålmarck (1983) which corresponds to an analogous theorem for the sequent calculus by Gentzen (1934).

3   Editing techniques

Besides normal properties of advanced text formatters for manipulation of structured text, we want something more of a derivation editor. We shall introduce these properties generally and illustrate them by a few examples.

3.1   Substitutions

Already simple rules for substitution make derivations with identity shorter, and moreover, a staccato style of writing a derivation usually gives concise presentations.

Let us illustrate this by proving McCarthy's (1978) challenge that an append program is associative. This derivation is of type (*ii*) in our classification in the introduction.

The append program, where ϕ denotes the empty list and the dot, ., is an infix list operator, is defined as follows:

Definition 1[2]

$$app(\phi,x) = x$$
$$app(u.x,y) = u.app(x,y)$$

The derivation has the following steps:
Induction base:

$app(app(\phi,y),z)$	$= app(y,z)$	substitution Definition 1
	$= app(\phi,app(y,z))$	substitution Definition 1

Induction step:

$app(app(u.x,y),z)$	$= app(u.app(x,y),z)$	substitution Definition 1
	$= u.app(app(x,y),z)$	substitution Definition 1
	$= u.app(x,app(y,z))$	substitution induction hypothesis
	$= app(u.x,app(y,z))$	substitution Definition 1

We thus get the following result by an induction schema on lists (see Clark and Tärnlund, 1977):

Theorem 1

$$\forall x \forall y \forall z (app(app(x,y),z) = app(x,app(y,z)))$$

We are using substitution as a derived rule of inference that can be justified by the following axioms for identity which Gödel (1930) showed complete.

Axiom 1

$$\forall x(x = x)$$

Axiom 2

$$\forall x \forall y (F(x) \wedge x = y \rightarrow F(y))$$

---

[2] We omit universal quantifiers in front of programs.

However, these axioms would not give us the condensed proofs above, but a derivation of about 20 steps in a natural deduction system.

3.2 Outlines of derivation structures

The editor makes use of the normal form theorem to construct an outline of a derivation. Informally the theorem says that a deduction of a theorem is carried out by breaking down its premises into parts by elimination rules for the connectives and quantifiers and building up the theorem by introduction rules. This idea is illuminated in Figure 7.1, where we derive a program from a specification, that is a derivation of type (*i*) in our classification in the introduction. We employ a specification of an insert relation on ordered binary trees (see Hansson and Tärnlund, 1979a,b).

Definition 2

$$\forall w \forall v \forall w'(insert(w,v,w') \leftrightarrow orderedtree(w) \wedge label(v) \wedge orderedtree(w') \wedge$$
$$\forall v'(v' \in w' \leftrightarrow v' = v \vee v' \in w))$$

We shall also write down the specifications for the relation orderedtree and the relation that an element belongs to a tree ($\in$).

Definition 3

orderedtree(ϕ)
$$\forall x \forall u \forall y(orderedtree(t(x,u,y)) \leftrightarrow label(u) \wedge orderedtree(x) \wedge orderedtree(y) \wedge$$
$$\forall v(v \in x \rightarrow v < u) \wedge \forall v(v \in y \rightarrow v > u))$$

Definition 4

$$\forall v \neg(v \in \phi)$$
$$\forall v \forall x \forall u \forall y(v \in t(x,u,y) \leftrightarrow v = u \vee v \in x \vee v \in y)$$

Provided that we or the editor can fill in the missing steps in the outline indicated by Infer in Figure 7.1, we arrive at the following theorem that also is one of four cases of a logic program for inserting an element into an ordered binary tree. In fact, a complete derivation consists of about 150 steps.

$$insert(t(x,u,y),v,t(x',u,y)) \leftarrow v < u \wedge label(v) \wedge orderedtree(t(x,u,y)) \wedge insert(x,v,x')$$
$$(1)$$

3.3 Corresponding derivations

The editor is guided by the user to find a derivation Π_1 of the theorem (1), from the data structure defined in Definition 3 and the relations defined in Definition 2

$$\begin{array}{ll}
\rlceil v < u \wedge \text{label}(v) \wedge \text{insert}(x, v, x') \wedge \text{orderedtree}(t(x, u, y)) & \text{hypothesis} \\
\quad \text{orderedtree}(t(x, u, y)) & \wedge E \\
\quad \text{insert}(x, v, x') & \wedge E \\
\quad \text{orderedtree}(x) \wedge \text{orderedtree}(x') \wedge \text{label}(v) \wedge & \text{substitution Definition 3} \\
\qquad \forall v'(v' \in x' \leftrightarrow v' = v \vee v' \in x) \\
\quad \text{orderedtree}(x) \wedge \text{orderedtree}(y) \wedge \text{label}(u) \wedge & \forall E \text{ Definition 3} \\
\qquad \forall v(v \in x \to v < u) \wedge \forall v(v \in y \to v > u) \\
\quad \text{orderedtree}(x') & \wedge E \\
\quad \text{orderedtree}(y) & \wedge E \\
\quad \text{label}(u) & \wedge E \\
\quad \rlceil v' \in x' & \text{hypothesis} \\
\qquad \vdots \\
\quad \lfloor v' < u & \text{Infer} \\
\quad v' \in x' \to v' < u & \to I \\
\quad \forall v(v \in x' \to v < u) & \forall I \\
\quad \forall v(v \in y \to v > u) & \wedge E \\
\quad \text{orderedtree}(x') \wedge \text{orderedtree}(y) \wedge \text{label}(u) \wedge & \wedge I \\
\qquad \forall v(v \in x' \to v < u) \wedge \forall v(v \in y \to v > u) \\
\quad \text{orderedtree}(t(x', u, y)) & \text{substitution Definition 3} \\
\quad \text{label}(v) & \wedge E \\
\quad \rlceil v' \in t(x', u, y) & \text{hypothesis} \\
\qquad \vdots \\
\quad \lfloor v' = v \vee v' \in t(x, u, y) & \text{Infer} \\
\quad v' \in t(x', u, y) \to v' = v \vee v' \in t(x, u, y) & \to I \\
\quad \rlceil v' \in t(x, u, y) \vee v' = v & \text{hypothesis} \\
\quad \rlceil v' \in t(x, u, y) & \text{hypothesis} \\
\qquad \vdots \\
\quad \lfloor v' \in t(x', u, y) & \text{Infer} \\
\quad v' \in t(x, u, y) \to v' \in t(x', u, y) & \to I \\
\quad \rlceil v' = v & \text{hypothesis} \\
\qquad \vdots \\
\quad \lfloor v' \in t(x', u, y) & \text{Infer} \\
\quad v' = v \to v' \in t(x', u, y) & \to I \\
\quad v' \in t(x', u, y) & \vee E \\
\quad v' \in t(x, u, y) \vee v' = v \to v' \in t(x', u, y) & \to I \\
\quad (v' \in t(x, u, y) \vee v' = v \to v' \in t(x', u, y)) \wedge & \wedge I \\
\qquad (v' \in t(x', u, y) \to v' = v \vee v' \in t(x, u, y)) \\
\quad v' \in t(x', u, y) \leftrightarrow v' = v \vee v' \in t(x, u, y) & \leftrightarrow I \\
\quad \forall v'(v' \in t(x', u, y) \leftrightarrow v' = v \vee v' \in t(x, u, y)) & \forall I \\
\quad \text{orderedtree}(t(x, u, y)) \wedge \text{orderedtree}(t(x', u, y)) \wedge \text{label}(v) \wedge & \wedge I \\
\qquad \forall v'(v' \in t(x', u, y) \leftrightarrow v' = v \vee v' \in t(x, u, y)) \\
\lfloor \text{insert}(t(x, u, y), v, t(x', u, y)) & \text{substitution Definition 2} \\
v < u \wedge \text{label}(v) \wedge \text{insert}(x, v, x') \wedge \text{orderedtree}(t(x, u, y)) \to & \to I \\
\quad \text{insert}(t(x, u, y), v, t(x', u, y))
\end{array}$$

Figure 7.1. An outline of a derivation.

and 4. Now a study of the derivation Π_1 shows that there is a corresponding derivation Π_2 of a theorem corresponding to (1), where the tree $t(x',u,y)$ corresponds to the tree $t(x,u,y')$, the relation less than, $<$, corresponds to the relation greater than, $>$, and the assumption insert(x,v,x') corresponds to the assumption insert(y,v,y').

If the editor could use these correspondences to show that there exists a derivation Π_2 of the following theorem

$$\text{insert}(t(x,u,y),v,t(x,u,y')) \leftarrow v > u \wedge \text{label}(v) \wedge \text{orderedtree}(t(x,u,y)) \wedge \text{insert}(y,v,y')$$

(2)

it would save us 150 steps. Although the program in (2) is one of the four cases of the insert program, it requires about half of the entire derivations of our insert program, and thus the editor relieves us from a significant amount of work.

3.4   Derivations with auxiliary theorems

For constructing derivation outlines, we mentioned that the editor makes use of the normal form theorem in a natural deduction system (or sequent calculus). Such derivations have the subformula property, i.e. each formula in a derivation is a subformula of the theorem. However, when we are building up a calculus we want to save auxiliary theorems for later use and not prove them anew each time. This is a typical way of working in a Hilbert system, but this approach does not preserve the subformula property. However, it can save substantial efforts so we want an editor also to use this method. Let us illustrate this technique on an example where we use Theorem 1. A programmer may for reasons of efficiency transform a recursive program to an iterative one. It is in general simpler to write and easier to understand a recursive program. So it would be desirable if this process could be simplified by an editor for example, and thereby guaranteed that the obtained iterative program follows from the original recursive one. Here, we are using the name recursive for the idea of increasing a stack when the program is running, and not self-reference.

Definition 5

$$\text{rev}(\phi) = \phi$$

$$\text{rev}(u.x) = \text{app}(\text{rev}(x),u.\phi)$$

To transform this recursive program into an iterative version, we could use the methods of Manna and Waldinger (1971) and introduce a special induction schema for iteration. The drawback of this method, as also pointed out by Manna and Waldinger, is that we end up with too many induction schemata. In contrast we shall solve the problem by a definition that relates the recursive program (that we write rev) and the iterative reverse (Rev), where we use the additional argument, y, for a memory space that is a linearly increasing function of the input, so the program can thus be implemented without popping and pushing a stack when running.

Definition 6

$$\forall x \forall y (Rev(x,y) = app(rev(x),y))$$

Our derivation of the iterative program makes use of the idea of substitution in section 3.1 and the result in Theorem 1 that the append program app is associative. The derivation is of type (iii) in our classification in the introduction.

$$
\begin{array}{ll}
Rev(\phi,y) = app(rev(\phi),y) & \forall E \text{ Definition 6} \\
\qquad\quad = app(\phi,y) & \text{substitution Definition 5} \\
\qquad\quad = y & \text{substitution Definition 1} \\
Rev(u.x,y) = app(rev(u.x),y) & \forall E \text{ Definition 6} \\
\qquad\quad = app(app(rev(x),u.\phi),y) & \text{substitution Definition 5} \\
\qquad\quad = app(rev(x),app(u.\phi,y)) & \text{substitution Theorem 1} \\
\qquad\quad = app(rev(x),u.app(\phi,y)) & \text{substitution Definition 1} \\
\qquad\quad = app(rev(x),u.y) & \text{substitution Definition 1} \\
\qquad\quad = Rev(x,u.y) & \text{substitution Definition 6}
\end{array}
$$

We have thus derived the following iterative program from the recursive program in Definition 5.

Theorem 2

$$Rev(\phi,y) = y$$

$$Rev(u.x,y) = Rev(x,u.y)$$

4   Conclusions and Results

We have given examples, from the three classes (i)–(iii) of derivations in our classification in the introduction, with as short derivations as possible that illustrate editing techniques desirable in an editor. However, reasonings on realistic logic programs, of course, have much longer derivations, but for reasons of space we have to omit them here. In a graduate course on logic programming during the academic year 1981–1982 the students derived and verified logic programs available in published papers (see e.g., Johansson, 1983). The students either developed their own editors or used the derivation editor NATDED (see Eriksson and Johansson, 1981) implemented in Prolog (Pereira, Pereira and Warren, 1978). Although these editors did not have all the derivation techniques implemented that we have proposed here, the students were able to formally derive most of the lemmas and theorems in Clark and Tärnlund (1977). In particular, they gave a formal proof of the correctness theorem[3] for the insert relation.

$$\forall w \forall v \forall w' \text{orderedtree}(w) \wedge \text{label}(v) \wedge \text{insert}(w,v,w') \rightarrow \text{orderedtree}(w') \wedge \forall u(u \in$$
$$w' \leftrightarrow u = v \vee u \in w))$$

This proof has more than 600 steps in a natural deduction system.

A derivation editor in which we can carry out the derivation techniques we have discussed, improves our ability to formally derive, verify or transform logic programs. This fact improves the strength of logic programming as a computational formalism.

We should mention two related systems, although their design principles are different from those of our derivation editor. Weyhrauch's (1975) FOL-system uses a natural deduction system and it can also be used as a derivation editor, in fact Hansson (1980) derived programs in more than one hundred steps. The Edinburgh LCF (see Gordon, Milner and Wadsworth 1977) supports interactive formal proofs and it contains a metalanguage for programming proof strategies and a family of deductive calculi.

References

Clark, K. L. (1977). *Verification and Synthesis of Logic Programs*. Research report, Department of Computing, Imperial College.
Clark, K. L., and J. Darlington. (1980). "Algorithm Classification through Synthesis." *The Computer Journal* 23, no 1.
Clark, K. L., and S-Å. Tärnlund. (1977). "A First Order Theory of Data and Programs." IFIP-77, Toronto, North Holland, pp. 939–944.
Colmerauer, A., H. Kanoui, R. Pasero, and P. Roussel. (1973). *Un Systéme de Communication Homme-machine en Français*. Research report, Groupe Intelligence Artificielle, Université Aix-Marseille II.
Eriksson, A., and A-L. Johansson. (1981). *NATDED, a derivation editor*. UPMAIL, Computing Science Department, Uppsala University.
Gentzen, G. (1935). "Untersuchungen über das logische Schliessen." *Matematische Zeitschrift*, 39.
Gordon, M., R. Milner, and C. Wadsworth. (1977). Edinburgh LCF, *Internal report CSR-11-77*, Department of Computer Science, University of Edinburgh.
Green, C. C. (1969a). "Theorem proving by resolution as a basis for question-answering systems." *Machine Intelligence* 4, Edinburgh University Press, pp. 183–205.

---

[3] Boyer, R. and Moore, J. (see 'A Fully Automatic Proof of the Correctness of an Ordered Tree Insertion Function', Institute for Computing Science, The University of Texas at Austin, ICSCA-CMP-36, May 1983) have in a functional formalization automatically derived two theorems that correspond to the correctness theorem in our relational formalization. Unfortunately, there seems to be a slip in their formulation that allows them to prove that an incorrect program is, in fact, correct.

Green, C. C. (1969b). *The Application of Theorem Proving Question-Answering Systems*. Ph.D. Thesis, Stanford University, Stanford, California.

Gödel, K. (1930). "Die Vollständigkeit der Axiome des logischen Funktionenkalküls." *Monatshefte für Mathematik und Physik,* vol. 37, pp. 349–360.

Hansson, Å. (1980). *A Formal Development of Programs*. Ph.D. Thesis, Department of Information Processing and Computer Science, The Royal Institute of Technology and The University of Stockholm.

Hansson, Å., and S. Haridi. (1981). "Programming in a Natural Deduction Framework." *Proc. Functional Languages and their Implications for Computer Architecture.* Göteborg, Sweden.

Hansson, Å., S. Haridi, and S-Å. Tärnlund. (1982). "Properties of a Logic Programming Language." *Logic Programming.* (Eds) Clark and Tärnlund, Academic Press, London.

Hansson, Å., and S-Å. Tärnlund. (1979a). *A Natural Programming Calculus*. Proc. IJCAI-6, Tokyo Japan.

Hansson, Å., and S-Å. Tärnlund. (1979b). *Derivations of Programs in a Natural Programming Calculus.* Electrotechnical Laboratory, Tokyo.

Haridi, S. (1981). *Logic Programming Based on a Natural Deduction System.* Department of Computer Science, The Royal Institute of Technology, Stockholm, Sweden.

Hayes, P. J. (1973). "Computation and Deduction." *Proc. 2nd MFCS Symposium.* Czekoslovakian Academy of Sciences.

Hogger, C. (1979). *Derivation of Logic Programs.* Ph.D. Thesis. Department of computing and control, Imperial College, London.

Johansson, A-L. (1983). *Results of Program Derivations in a Derivation Editor.* NATDED, UP-MAIL, Computing Science Department, Uppsala University.

Kowalski, R. A. (1974). "Predicate Logic as Programming Language," *Information Processing* 74, 569–574.

Kowalski, R. A. (1979). *Logic for Problem Solving.* Artificial Intelligence series, (Ed.) Nilsson, N. J., North Holland.

Manna, Z., and R. Waldinger. (1971). "Toward Automatic Program Synthesis." *CACM* 14(4), 151–165.

McCarthy, J. (1978). *ACM SIGPLAN History of Programming Languages,* Conference, ACM, pp. 215–223.

Pereira, F., L. Pereira, and D. Warren. (1978). *User's Guide to DECsystem-10 PROLOG.* Department of Artificial Intelligence, University of Edinburgh.

Prawitz, D. (1965). *Natural Deduction. A Proof-Theoretical Study.* Ph.D. Thesis, Almqvist and Wiksell, Stockholm.

Robinson, J. A. (1965). "A Machine-Oriented Logic Based on the Resolution Principle." *Journal of the Association for Computing Machinery* 12, pp. 23–41.

Roussel, P. (1975). *PROLOG, Manuel de Reference et d'Utilisation.* Groupe Intelligence Artificielle, Université Aix-Marseille II.

Stålmarck, G. (1983). *Strong normalization for complete 1st order classical natural deduction.* Stockholm.

Tärnlund, S-Å. (1981). *A Programming Language Based on a Natural Deduction System.* UPMAIL Report, Computing Science Department, Uppsala University.

Warren, D. (1977). *Implementing PROLOG—Compiling Logic Programs, 1 and 2.* D.A.I. Research Report No 39, 40, University of Edinburgh.

Weyhrauch, R. (1977). *FOL: A Proof Checker for First-Order Logic.* Stanford AI. Lab. Memo AIM-235.1.

PART IV
APPLICATIONS

CHAPTER 8

Teaching Logic as a Computer Language in Schools

Richard Ennals

Department of Computing
Imperial College of Science & Technology, London SW7 2BZ
England

1   Background

Logic has long been a subject of academic interest in schools. The classical Western intellectual tradition places great emphasis on reasoning, and since the ancient Greeks formal logic has been used to describe patterns of argument. Logic can be said to provide a backbone for the various disciplines: in the past it was indirectly taught through the medium of Latin or Euclidean geometry. Neither of these is now popular, and it can be argued that logic should be taught in its own right, as providing an insight into the workings of the various disciplines through the representation and manipulation of knowledge.

Academic research in the fields of metamathematics and computer science has produced logic programming. Kowalski (1974, 1979) was able to suggest the procedural interpretation of declarative sentences of logic for problem-solving, and Colmerauer implemented Prolog in Marseille in 1972, opening a new area for academic exploration and exploitation. Early work with the language Prolog (PROgramming in LOGic) had a technical orientation that reflected its mathematical and theoretical origins in mechanical theorem-proving. Logic is also of use as a computer language in less abstract areas.

Recent approaches to mathematics teaching have emphasized the logical operations involved in problem-solving, and have focused on areas such as set theory in a way that traditional teaching failed to do. Kowalski (1982) tried introducing logic programming in some experimental lessons at the school attended by his children, and this experience led to the project "Logic as a Computer Language for Children" based at Imperial College and with lessons at Park House Middle School in London.

This project has had the support of the U.K. Science and Engineering Research Council since September 1980, and of the Nuffield Foundation since October 1981. Its aims were to develop teaching materials to teach logic as a computer language to children aged ten to thirteen and to develop a child-oriented microcomputer implementation of Prolog. In the first instance a pilot class aged 10–11 was to be taught for a year, with the course being repeated in two subsequent years, and the pilot class was to receive further lessons to assess the long term effects of the course.

2   The initial pilot class

Classroom teaching of logic commenced in the first week of the project. McCabe (1981) developed micro-Prolog (Clark, Ennals and McCabe, 1982) and this was available in the classroom from the third month of the project. The pilot class was taught for seventy minutes on each of two afternoons per week, with one microcomputer and a large television monitor for the use of the class of thirty children. The lessons were given in time normally allocated to mathematics and to "Activities," and the class was the better of two mathematics sets.

The first introduction consisted of the writing of simple descriptive sentences of the form:

> Individual   relationship   Individual

such as:

> John   likes   Mary

The binary infix notation was used, provided by the micro-Prolog program SIMPLE, as it produced a more friendly syntax. It was emphasized that this language, though similar in appearance to English, was not to be confused with it, by using sentences that were logically correct though nonsense in English, such as:

> Jubjub   burbles   Bandersnatch

The form of the sentence was emphasized, and the children adopted the conventions of underlining names of relationships.

The next step, having constructed a simple database of descriptive sentences, was querying the database. The simplest queries, using the command "is," make a YES/NO query out of a sentence, such as:

> is (John likes Mary)
> YES
> is (Jubjub burbles Jabberwock)
> NO

Two points immediately arise. The name of a relationship must be the same in the query as in the program, often breaking with conventions of correct English (after all, this is not English). Answers to queries depend solely on the contents of the program or database. If the information named in the "is" query cannot be found and proved to be true, the answer "NO" will be given, indicating "Not proved." This rests on the closed world assumption: this has to be made explicit to a class or audience from the beginning to avoid misunderstanding.

More complex, or "molecular" questions followed, such as:

> is (John likes Mary and
> Mary likes John)

which will receive the answer "YES" only if each of the individual atoms of the question does so.

More information is required from a database than merely "YES" or "NO". A second form of query was introduced, using the command "which", such as:

> which (x: x burbles Bandersnatch)

This query has two arguments: the first, in this case "x," is the output template. The second, in this case "x burbles Bandersnatch" is the condition to be satisfied. Substitutions for "x" in sentences of the form "x burbles Bandersnatch" are required. The answer has the form:

> Jubjub
> No (more) answers

The letters x, y and z, in upper or lower case, and followed by numbers if desired, are used as variables. Upper and lower case characters otherwise can be used to name relations or (unvarying) individuals at the discretion of the user.

A number of exercises followed involving querying of databases made up of atomic sentences as above. The children would both formulate the appropriate queries and give the answers they would expect from the computer. Such exercises use, but do not depend on, the computer, as the logic used is human logic that is simply regarded by the computer as a computer language.

The children were by this time writing their own programs (Ennals, 1981) describing a vast range of subjects of their own choice: the solar system, the weather, cars, European capitals, winners of the World Cup, their own families, likes and dislikes. They either typed in their own programs, having practised on dummy keyboards; or when time ran out, handed in their books for the programs to be typed in by the teacher or part-time secretary.

Using the analogy of reading passages for comprehension in learning a foreign language, more complex programs were used in class, describing subject matter of interest to the class: a fictitious holiday on the "Costa Della Rocca," the family tree of a group of Nigerian cats, the Romans in Britain. These involved the use of molecular sentences, which they had not previously used themselves.

Molecular sentences were described as having the form:

Conclusion   if   Conditions

such as:

John friends-with-Mary -if John likes Mary
and Mary likes John

Fred parent-of Sid if Fred father-of Sid

The children had to get used to the Horn clause constraint of only being allowed one conclusion per sentence. At first no variables were used, but then exercises were introduced translating between English and Prolog.

English: Fred likes anything which is covered in custard.
Prolog: Fred likes x if x is-covered-in custard

(It has to be pointed out that this Prolog sentence could also mean "Fred likes anyone who is covered in custard.")

English: Everyone likes anyone who is a pupil at Park House.
Prolog: x likes y if y is-a-pupil-at Park-House

The teaching of the definition of relations was facilitated by the introduction of semantic networks as an alternative representation. The convention of solid lines for conditions and dotted lines for conclusions was adopted. For example, to produce a definition of "grandparent" the children first drew a network based on their own family, such as:

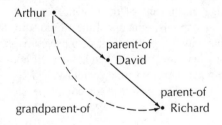

They then translated the network into a Prolog program:

Arthur grandparent-of Richard if Arthur parent-of David and
David parent-of Richard

They then drew a network of the pattern involved:

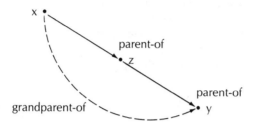

and translated that into a Prolog program:

x grandparent-of y if x parent-of z and
z parent-of y

This graphic representation also helped in the introduction of the "ancestor" relation, where the recursion had a clear visual analogue. A long family tree of the Tudor royal family could be covered by the two-line definition of "ancestor". As one child said "it just goes on and on" and another group attempted to use the program to trace ancestry back to Adam and Eve.

Arithmetic was introduced initially as another example of querying a data base. Micro-Prolog has built-in relations LESS, SUM and TIMES, which notionally involve querying built-in databases for the arithmetical operations. The arithmetic was integers only, and queries took the form:

is (7 LESS 8)
YES
is (SUM (4 5 9))
YES

which (x: SUM (9 8 x))
17
No (more) answers
is (TIMES (5 4 25))
NO

which (x: TIMES (6 9 x))
54
No (more) answers

Use of these operations was reinforced by problem exercises of the kind that is common in their mathematics lessons. It should be noted that SUM handles both addition and subtraction, and TIMES both multiplication and division, emphasizing the reversability of operations.

By this stage a number of the programs written by the children were becoming extremely lengthy. The tendency was to produce a mass of atomic sentences, with considerable caution over the use of molecular sentences. Some economy could be achieved by the introduction of list structures.

This new level of complexity was introduced gradually. Lists were first introduced as individuals, to be treated as such without accessing their internal structure. For instance, we could have the program:

(Philip Elizabeth) parents-of Charles

which we could query:

which (x: x parents-of Charles)
(Philip Elizabeth)
No (more) answers

List processing concepts such as list membership, list length and appending of lists were all shown in action for a considerable time before explanation of their recursive programs was attempted.

3   Experimental teaching of mathematics and history

The class teacher, Mr. Della-Rocca, is the teacher whose approach first inspired the project at Park House. There is a remarkable consistency between his approach to mathematics and the approach offered using Prolog. This has been tested by using Prolog with a mathematics class of 12-year-olds. They have done little written work, but after a grounding in database querying, we have often introduced Prolog into mathematics lessons. Simple equations, digital roots, finding of averages, problems involving volume: all have involved the class breaking down a problem into subproblems and describing relations, enabling the computer to produce solutions to their problems. This descriptive approach has enabled the class to use complex logical programs such as list length, recursive adding of lists of numbers, and constructing sets of all solutions.

The headmaster of the school, Mr. King, teaches history, and was interested in using the computer to help in his interrogation of census information. Many British history teachers have been concerned with historical evidence, and have wished to introduce their pupils to the practical work of the historian. He had a copy of the census returns for the area around the school for the year 1871, and the class worked in groups to transcribe it from the original. The census is recorded in a regular form, and it was straightforward to record each entry as a Prolog sentence using lists, preserving the original text in its entirety and adding only brackets. For example, one sentence reads:

(Belvedere House) person ((Henry Holland) Head M 47 Male
(Linen Manufacturer and Merchant) (Dorking Surrey))

Individual items from the list could be identified using pattern-matching sentences, defining relations such as "job," "sex," "birthplace," "age." For instance, to find out Henry Holland's occupation, you would ask

which (x: (Henry Holland) job x)

To find out who was born in Dorking, Surrey, you would ask

which (x: x birthplace (Dorking Surrey))

To find out the names and occupations of women over 40 you would ask

which (x y: x sex F and
x age z and
40 LESS z and
x job y)

The class and teacher had no prior experience of the computer, but had grasped that they needed to describe things clearly, to state criteria for their conclusions. At the beginning of the lesson a definition of wealth was put forward. A Head of Household has a wealth determined by the number of servants employed in the household. Our program makes a list of such servants, and counts the number of members of the list.

x wealth y if x relation Head and
z is-all (X: X relation Servant and
X live-at Y and
x live-at Y) and
z length y

They were then able to ask about people's wealth and occupation, and investigate any anomalies. They offered definitions of social class in terms of occupation, and obtained lists of professional and manual workers. The use of Prolog had enabled them to augment their own deduction: they were better able to frame a query than to perform the search themselves, and they could check the appropriateness of the answers that they received. They left with a series of further historical questions to which their census sample could not provide an answer, and having experienced positive rewards for clear thinking.

4   Logic across the curriculum

If our original claim about logic providing a backbone for the various disciplines is to be made credible, we must produce working programs that are of practical use. I have above described practical work done in mathematics and history: an attempt is now being made to identify core concepts and processes to be represented in Prolog. In history work is being done in representing historical knowledge in Prolog to extend the scope of classroom teaching. This can be in the form of computer-aided simulation, information retrieval from any source where the representation is consistent, and in representing models of historical explanation (Ennals, 1982).

In science a lead was provided by one of the pilot class, Jolyon Ralph. Having written programs about the solar system, rock formations, and minerals, he embarked upon a program based on the periodic table of the elements. The basis of the program is a description of each of the elements in terms of its name, weight, symbol and number. He then proceeded to list the formulae of certain compounds, using a simple notation, e.g.

Water Compound (H 2 O)

From this one could ask:

which (x: x in Water)
Hydrogen
Oxygen
No (more) answers

He used this program for "in":

x in y if y Compound z and
X belongs-to z and
X stands-for x

This uses the "belongs-to" program for list membership, and a program describing symbols and the chemical elements for which they stand.

Next he evolved a more complex representation for the formulae, e.g.

Water Comp ((H 2) (O))

This involved a more complex program to break down the formulae, called "is-in". From this one could ask:

> which (x: x is-in Water)
> (2 Hydrogen)
> (1 Oxygen)
> No (more) answers

Using information about chemical reactions in certain experiments he is able to define physical and chemical properties, and he is able to generate correct chemical nomenclature from knowledge of the ratio of numbers of atoms of different elements.

In French another one of the pilot class, Alex Ashworth, made the start. He represented his French vocabulary homework as a Prolog program. This aroused the interest of the head of French, who was curious as to whether French grammatical rules of the kind he taught in class could be handled. He produced rules for the possessive adjective, partitive article and forms of the perfect tense for representation in Prolog. Let us develop an example using the rules for the partitive article. Our initial vocabulary is

> (I cut)   means (Je coupe)
> (bread) means (pain)

We have a simple rule for the partitive article, which says that two words or phrases take the partitive article "du" if the second of them is a masculine singular noun

> (x y) parts-to (du) if y is (masculine noun) and
> y is (singular)

We have not so far stipulated that the first element of the pair should be a verbphrase.

We can add information about our example

> (pain) is (masculine noun)
> (pain) is (singular)

We can now add a simple definition of "trans-to"

> (x y) trans-to (z X Y) if x means z and
> y means Y and
> (z Y) parts-to X

This will give us translation of the individual components and will also apply our grammatical rule. We can test that

> which (x: ((I cut) (bread)) trans-to x)
> ((Je coupe) (du) (pain))
> No (more) answers

The trouble here is that there are too many brackets breaking up the natural language. We would prefer to see the complete sentence as a whole rather than a list of words or phrases. If we add the program for "appends-to", which takes two lists and puts them together to make one combined list,

> (() x) appends-to x
> ((x|y) z) appends-to (x|X) if (y z) appends-to X

then we can quickly remove such brackets, by using "appends-to" a number of times, as follows

> x translates-to (y z X) if
> (Y Z) trans-to (y z X) and (Y Z) appends-to x
>
> x translates y if x translates-to (z X Y) and
>   (z x) appends-to Z and
>   (Z Y) appends-to y

These last few sentences need not be explained to the children: it is their result that is important. If we now use the "one" command, which gives us answers one at a time, we can ask:

> one (x: (I cut bread) translates x)
> (Je coupe du pain).

or

> one (x: x translates (Je coupe du pain))
> (I cut bread).

The same program serves for translation of English to French or French to English as it purely consists of descriptions of relations, with no control information or restriction. It can also be used to generate pairs of translated sentences, using the form:

> which (x y: x translates y)

5   The classroom experience: a comparison of the first two pilot classes

Both of the two pilot classes, taught in successive years, were of children aged 10–11, approximately twenty-six in each class, and were taught in collaboration with their regular mathematics teacher, Mr. Kenneth Della-Rocca, for two hours and twenty minutes each week on a regular timetabled basis throughout the school year. Each was the better of two mathematics sets in their year-group, and contained a considerable range of ability. The first class had the use of one computer and a large television screen from November, the second had the computer from the start of the course in September. In each case children would also use the computer on a voluntary basis at lunchtimes and after school, working on their own individual and group programs. The first class had assistance at the keyboard from the project secretary while the second class made use of the experience of the first, both at the keyboard and in writing programs. The second class had occasional access to further microcomputers in the classroom, and a growing number were also acquiring "computer literacy" on personal computers at home. The second class also benefited from the greater availability of example programs, and from the fact that ten of their subject teachers attended courses in the use of the materials. Above all, of course, the second class benefited from the experience and mistakes made by the researchers and the first class, and worked on a refined version of the same materials.

In both cases, the sequence of topics introduced was as follows:

Writing simple sentences
Asking simple questions to databases
Asking complex questions to databases
Writing simple programs
Using complex sentences
Writing complex sentences
Defining relations (using networks)
Using lists as individuals
Using list processing
Recursive programs

6   Areas of difficulty

Briggs (1982) found in a series of interviews and tests that although the level of interest and enjoyment was high in both classes, the degree of understanding was on the whole much higher in the second class, despite their shorter experience. He identified areas of difficulty experienced by the first class:

Forms of queries
The use of variables
Translation from natural language into logical notation
The use of rules
Lists as individuals
List processing

In this light the teaching method was modified for the second class in a number of ways.

1. The importance of motivating examples was clear: An advance in formal representation can be motivated by the content of current examples. The introduction of a list notation, for instance, was motivated by a class activity writing a narrative account of events in the Falkland Islands, and the need to describe and distinguish (British troops) from (Argentinian troops) and (President Reagan) from (President Galtieri). One pupil was happily writing programs with lists on his first day as he wished to describe German fighter planes from the Second World War, and an experienced friend showed him how he had tackled a similar subject.
2. More use was made of graphic representation in classroom explanation. In particular, the use of semantic networks in introducing the defining of new relations was extremely valuable, and recursive programs could be given a visual analogue: for instance in tracing the ancestry of the Tudor royal family back to Adam and Eve.
3. Less new topics were handled by the second group and more examples used on each, increasingly derived from the children's own programs.
4. Lessons were less teacher-centered, and contained a higher proportion of discussion initiated by the class. New levels of difficulty were introduced in response to demand rather than with rigid planning. Complex issues could be raised in discussion that provided an appropriate framework for later written work: the retrieval of information from programs using lists was motivated by probing questions from the class. For instance, shown how to find the first or second member of a list, they insisted on knowing how to find the last member and could follow the declarative reading of the appropriate recursive program.

Weir (1982) made a detailed analysis of children's difficulties in learning "Simple Prolog," discussed possible changes in the syntax, and argued for a more profound change in the learning environment. He identified common mistakes in the framing of queries, the use of parentheses, and in translation from English into Horn clause logical form. Using new language features implemented with Sergot (1983), he proposed that children learn to ask questions by answering them. The "Query-the-User" facility enables the user to be treated as an extension of the computer's database, to be questioned when information is needed to help in the solution of a problem. We can learn a language like micro-Prolog through using it, as we learn our native tongue, as well as by having it explained in a formal way. A child can learn the structure of simple queries through both asking and answering questions, with the format of questions being asked by the computer mirroring questions asked by the user. Children can respond correctly to questions before they have mastered the structure well enough to ask questions themselves. In working at answering the questions the child is developing some understanding of their structure, just as we can learn a natural language from hearing it spoken and taking part in two-way conversations.

Weir outlines the potential benefits of the new interactive facilities which are now in classroom use:

1. They overcome the problems of framing queries.
2. They aid the declarative reading of programs.
3. They provide a natural way for developing and representing knowledge in simple classroom "expert systems."
4. They make the computer more conversational.
5. They provide insight into the use of rules.

7   Teaching Logic as opposed to teaching Prolog

It must be emphasized that the project is concerned with the teaching of logic, realized as a computer language, and not with the teaching of computer programming in a particular language such as Prolog. The classroom approach is wholly declarative, with no concern for computational efficiency. Issues of ordering of atoms in clauses, of loops, of left recursion and of negation by failure are dealt with pragmatically in terms of observed behavior of example programs, and not in terms of some complex underlying model of the machine, which largely drops out of consideration. Work has been done primarily using a simple front-end program to micro-Prolog, but the same materials have been used with a front-end program on the DEC-10 Prolog, and the PDP-11 Prolog running in Unix. From the child's point of view it should not matter what machine or particular language implementation is being used: our concern is with the power of logic as a tool. We are certainly not committed to a particular machine architecture or means of evaluating queries: no explicit technical account is given of backtracking, use of imperative features or extralogical control. A clear description of a subject can be regarded as a specification and run as a program.

8   A comparison with the Logo project

A common motivation can be seen for much of our work and that of the Logo project both in the United Kingdom and North America (Papert et al., 1979; Papert, 1980; Howe, O'Shea, and Plane, 1979). Papert's enthusiasm for the computer as a powerful tool for children is supported by the ease with which children and teachers use micro-Prolog to describe and explore subjects of their own choice.

It may be helpful to point out some contrasting aspects of the two research approaches:

1. Work with Logo has been based on intensive individual use of the computer, while with Prolog the computer to date has been regarded as a resource for the whole class.
2. Much Logo work has been with small classes of four pupils, whereas we have been working with full classes of twenty-six to thirty pupils.
3. Logo research has typically involved intensive involvement of teachers and university staff, whereas our work has been done with the normal class teacher with support from an individual researcher. Increasingly, work with Prolog is being initiated and carried out by the classroom teachers independently of the researchers.
4. Some Logo research has been based on 4 hours per pupil per week: we have used 2 hours and 20 minutes per week with the pilot classes.
5. Logo programs have been typically restricted to the domain of Turtle geometry: Prolog programs are used across the curriculum and can incorporate Turtle geometry among graphics features (Julian, 1982; Ball, 1982).
6. The Logo project to date has placed more emphasis on individual cognitive styles, compared with our class teaching approach with individual programs and projects.
7. There has to date been more emphasis on formal evaluation of Logo, with a greater range of sources of experimental data.
8. Until recently Logo has run on a limited number of nonstandard microcomputers. However, soon both Logo and Prolog should be readily accessible for school use on a wide range of existing microcomputers.
9. We appear to have placed a greater emphasis on teacher involvement and courses for teachers, leading to a network of experimental activities.

9   Application areas

Apart from the pilot work with children, the project materials are being used for:

1. An Information Technology course as a descriptive tool for introducing data processing, word processing and programming.

2. Related work with trainees at Information Technology centers.
3. Development of Computer Assisted Learning materials in History.
4. Developing simple expert systems.
5. Introducing Computer Science both to teachers and students.
6. Computer Assisted Learning materials in Mathematics, Science, French and Sociology.
7. Courses for primary and secondary school teachers.

10   Issues of evaluation

The "superclass" phenomenon has been noted: extravagant claims can be made for the initial experimental classes using a new language, whether it be Small-talk, Logo or Prolog, and yet the project can sink without traces left on general educational practice. There is clearly a case for the Stanford practice (Suppes and Morningstar, 1972) of not carrying out full formal evaluations on initial groups, with all the inevitable distortions and overoptimism by committed innovators.

I have reported above on some informal evaluation carried out by participating B.Sc and M.Sc students. Further reports have been published and circulated following a wide range of visits by interested individuals and organizations. Formal evaluation will require agreement on a framework, criteria, personnel, institutions, timescale, report format and intended use of such an evaluation.

The planning of such evaluation has begun. In the meantime, work continues exploring such areas as the use of graphics, development of CAL packages to the specification of subject teachers, and the provision of software tools for use by teachers.

References

Ball, D. (1982). *PROLOGO: Turtle graphics in micro-PROLOG on the Research Machines 380Z.* University of Leicester (unpublished).

Briggs, J. (1982). *Teaching Mathematics with PROLOG.* Bachelor of Science Thesis, Dept. of Computing, Imperial College, London.

Clark, K. L., J. R. Ennals, and F. G. McCabe. (1982). *A micro-PROLOG Primer* (revised edition). Logic Programming Associates, London.

Clark, K. L., and F. G. McCabe (1984). *Micro-PROLOG: Programming in logic.* Englewood Cliffs, NJ: Prentice-Hall.

Clark, K. L., F. G. McCabe and P. Hammond. (1982). "PROLOG: A Language for Implementing Expert Systems. In *Machine Intelligence* 10, E. Hayes, D. Michie, Y-H. Pao (eds.).

Ennals, J. R. (1981). *Logic as a Computer Language for Children.* DOC 81/6, Dept. of Computing, Imperial College, London.

Ennals, J. R. (1982). *Beginning micro-PROLOG.* Ellis Horwood and Heinemann Computers in Education. (2d edition 1984, New York: Harper & Row)

Ennals, J. R. (1983). "Artificial Intelligence." In *State of the Art Report on Computer Based Learning.* N. J. Rushby, Ed. Pergamon Infotech 1983.

Ennals, J. R. (1985). *Artificial intelligence: Applications to logical reasoning and historical research*. London: Ellis Horwood.

Howe, J. A. M., T. O'Shea and F. Plane. (1979). "Teaching Mathematics through LOGO programming: An Evaluation Study." In *Proceedings of IFIP Working Conference on CAL*, London.

Julian, S. (1982). *Graphics in micro-PROLOG*. M.Sc Thesis, Dept. of Computing, Imperial College, London.

Kanoui, H. and M. van Caneghem. (1980). *Implementing a very high level language on a very low cost computer*. Groupe d'Intelligence Artificielle, Universite d'Aix-Marseille, Luminy.

Kowalski, R. A. (1974). "Predicate Logic as Programming Language." *Proceedings IFIP Congress*.

Kowalski, R. A. (1979). *Logic for Problem Solving*. North-Holland Publishing Company.

Kowalski, R. A. (1982). "Logic as a Computer Language for Children." In *Proceedings of European Conference on Artificial Intelligence*, Orsay, 1982, and in *New Horizons in Educational Computing*, M. Yazdani (ed.), Ellis Horwood, 1983.

McCabe, F. G. (1981). *micro-PROLOG Programmers Reference Manual*. Logic Programming Associates, London.

Kriwaczek, F. R. (1982). *Some applications of PROLOG to decision support systems*. Master of Science Thesis, Dept. of Computing, Imperial College, London.

Papert, S. (1980). *Mindstorms: children, computers and powerful ideas*. Harvester Press.

Papert, S., D. Watt, A. di Sessa, and S. Weir. (1979). *Final Report of the Brookline LOGO project*. AI Lab Memo 545, Massachusetts Institute of Technology.

Ridd, S. (1982). *An Investigation of PROLOG as an aid to French Teaching and Language Translation*. Bachelor of Science Thesis, Dept. of Computing, Imperial College, London.

Robinson, J. A. (1983). "Logical Reasoning in Machines," In *Intelligent Systems*. Hayes J. E., Michie, D. (eds.), Ellis Horwood.

Sergot, M. (1983). "A Query-the-User Facility for Logic Programming," In *Integrated Interactive Computing Systems*. P. Degano and E. Sandewall (eds.), North-Holland Publishing Company.

Suppes, P., and M. Morningstar. (1972). *Computer-Assisted Instruction at Stanford*. Academic Press.

Weir, D. J. (1982). *Teaching Logic Programming: An Interactive Approach*. M.Sc Thesis, Dept. of Computing, Imperial College, London.

CHAPTER 9

A Prolog Simulation of Migration Decision-Making in a Less Developed Country

John W. Roach

Department of Computer Science

Theodore D. Fuller

Department of Sociology
Virginia Polytechnic Institute and State University
Blacksburg, Virginia 24061

1   Introduction

In this paper we present the initial results of a collaboration between sociological theory and artificial intelligence practice. Artificial intelligence provides a means of creating new kinds of models in the social sciences. Prolog provides an opportunity for social scientists to build programs that simulate the cognitive, emotional, and interactional behavior of human beings, using easily modifiable, modular rules. If the social rules that constrain human behavior can be expressed in Prolog rules, the result will be a "working model," that is, a model that can replicate the behavior of human beings rather than merely explain it.

Very few examples of this approach are extant in the sociological literature. Portions of Homans' (1961) exchange theory of social behavior, well-known within sociological circles, have been represented in a working model by Gullahorn and Gullahorn (1963). Faught, Colby, and Parkison (1974), in their work on PARRY, and Abelson's (1973) belief system work are both similar to our approach. Explicitly rule-based theories of communication and interpersonal behavior are found in Cronen *et al* (1982) and Cushman *et al* (1982). Certain other literature, such as Reiss' (1960) theory of the stages of a love relationship and Goffman's (1974) theory of interpersonal behavior, while not at all relying on the same approach, appear to be amenable to representation as working models.

The specific application is to represent the migration decision-making process of villagers in Thailand. The resulting simulation is a very different approach from normal sociological research, and is an approach we believe to be extremely promising.

Models are normally used to illuminate or explain behavior. The working or operational model idea, however, is somewhat different as articulated by Reynolds (1971):

> there is another type of activity that is different from constructing theories. This other activity is to develop a process that will reproduce the same patterns of empirical data that are found in specific concrete situations.

The working model demands significantly greater development in consistency, detail, and precision than any other notion of a model: it must be executable by a computer. It is true that this approach could be developed in another language such as Fortran (or Turing machine language for that matter), but the ease of development and modifiability would be prohibitive.

The working model approach offers unique advantages and unique challenges. The greatest challenge is finding the correct means of specifying social processes in terms of computable rules. Turning theories into programs is difficult in any field, but the social sciences have typically not emphasized process models. Basically, this means that new kinds of theories must be developed to account for social processes: The methodology feeds back to influence the way theories are made. Thus, learning to think in terms of Prolog influences the kinds of theories originated.

The working model approach has powerful advantages to offer. For example, its testability does not depend on statistical analysis. Furthermore, working models can be repeatedly tested. That is, the same experiments can be run repeatedly, with variations, in order to determine the validity of some hypothesis. A simulation of a social situation could even include a role for an experimenter to "participate" in the simulation. Different levels of sophistication are possible, with the most advanced, intelligent simulations not yet implementable.

2   Advantages of Prolog for Sociologists

One of the advantages of using Prolog as a language to model social and cognitive processes is that the basics of the language can be learned fairly easily by individuals who have relatively little experience with computer languages. The second author, a sociologist, did most of the programming for this illustrative exercise using Virginia Tech Prolog running on a VAX 11/780 under VMS (Roach and Fowler (1983)). Relatively little instruction in the language (approximately six lecture hours) was required. This suggests that other social scientists—or others unfamiliar with Prolog—can easily learn enough about the language to utilize it in their own research problems.

1. The language is highly modular. Each axiom might be thought of as a subprogram with local variables. Since there are no global variables, the programmer need not attend to the problem of having the flow of control mixed with the flow of information as in conventional languages.
2. Programs can easily be extended to include new axioms. In languages such as Fortran or GPSS, serious complications can arise when the programmer attempts to modify a working program. The new code must be spliced into the execution flow of the program. With Prolog, such problems are minimized. Although the ordering of axioms can be used as a tool to control the execution of the program, in many cases totally new axioms can be added without regard to their position relative to other axioms.
3. The relational nature of the language lends itself to easing the representation problem. Cognition as inference and computation as inference fit together remarkably well. Using the rule-based production system of Prolog, it becomes relatively straightforward to represent the contingencies under which actors in social settings engage in particular actions or make particular inferences. Furthermore, it is easy to specify different sets of contingencies that produce particular consequences. Although social scientists recognize that there are many contingencies that impinge on social behavior, these contingencies are difficult to represent in the linear models and cross-tabular analyses that are common in sociology and other social sciences.

3   The Migration Decision-Making Simulation

The simulation discussed here is a program of about seven pages written in Virginia Tech Prolog (Roach and Fowler (1983)) and is rather simple compared with what could be ultimately achieved. It simulates the cognitive decision facility of Thai villagers considering migration to some city. Included in the simulation are rules defining social norms such as deference to parents, social desirability such as the quality of the schools, etc. Several types of knowledge and information are represented by rules in the program:

1. Descriptions of the villagers themselves, including their social roles and personal inclinations.
2. Evaluations the villagers made of the villages, and
3. Conditions prevailing in several cities that are possible destinations.

The model contains several stages, reviewed below. More detail is given in Roach and Fuller (1982).

1. It must be determined whether the villager is satisfied with the village. Satisfaction with the village is determined by averaging the evaluations of

several aspects of village life (e.g., quality of life, riskiness of life, working conditions, child-rearing conditions), weighted by the importance of each aspect to specific individuals.

2. If the person is looking for a place to move, he reviews the places that he knows about, in order to select the best destination.

3. Reviewing the places that he is familiar with, the villager selects as the best destination the one that seems to offer the most promising conditions, keyed to the age, sex, and skill level of the villager.

4. If the best available destination appears to be better than the village, the person decides to move. This decision is based on a comparison of the evaluation score of the best destination versus the evaluation score of the village.

5. The villager may not actually move even if he has decided to move. This is true because certain obstacles may prevent him from doing so. One obstacle would be the disapproval of the villager's father. This obstacle could exist if the villager is a child (i.e., son, daughter, son-in-law in the current household). However, the model asserts that father will not object to any move to a town in the same region as the village. Another obstacle would exist if the villager has substantial household responsibilities that he cannot easily transfer to another family member. If the evaluation scores of the best destination and the village diverge greatly, in favor of the best destination, then the villager perceives relatively great benefits to moving. In this case, and in the absence of great household responsibilities, the villager will move whether or not the father approves. Some villagers ("young turks") will disregard social rules and move if they want to, regardless of responsibilities or father's agreements.

These rules are implemented as follows:

```
((move *person *location *score) if
     (decidemove *person *location *score)
     (noblockmove *person *location *score))
((noblockmove *person *stayinvillage *score))
((noblockmove *person *location *score) if
     (or (fatheragree *person *location)
         (benefitshigh *person *location *score))
     (responsibility *person low))
((noblockmove *person *location *score) if
     (description *person *listing)
     (member youngturk *listing))
((responsibility *person low) if
     (description *person *listing)
```

(child *person)
(northeast *location))

Additional rules defining the child relation conform to notions of kinship in Thai culture. Logic programming, then, turns out to be a natural vehicle for coding the social and individual cognitive processes needed to simulate migration decision behavior.

A simulation involving three fictitious villagers was run to illustrate the functioning of the migration model. Uthai is dissatisfied and decides to move to Khon Kaen with his father's approval; Samboon is satisfied with the village and decides to stay; Pranee is dissatisfied with the village but because she lacks urban skills concludes she would be no better off by moving.

4   Discussion of the Model and its Validity

The second author has lived and worked among the rural Thais whose migratory decisions are being modeled. The production rules comprising the working model are based on his observations and systematic research (Fuller *et al* (1983). The "behavior" of several prototypical villagers has been traced through the model. Where specific numeric values are required, these were assigned to these composite prototypes on the basis of knowledge about actual villagers.

Validation is a key issue in developing this kind of model. Quantitative approaches to sociological research rely on statistical theory and either random assignment of cases to treatment categories or scientific sample design. This approach to validation seems less relevant to the testing of working models. One approach to validation of such models is what would be termed a "Turing test" in computer science or "face validity" in social science. Essentially the question would be: Does the model produce realistic results? Does the model produce intelligent behavior—that is, behavior which is appropriate to the circumstances? If this can be achieved through a rule-based production system implemented in a Prolog program, then there is a sense in which a stronger theory has been imbedded in the Prolog program than is imbedded in statistically-oriented theories of social behavior. Applying this criterion to the working model presented in this paper, we would argue that the model in fact behaves in a reasonable fashion.

5   Future Directions

Additional elaboration of the cognitive processing could be considered at most stages in the model. The model reported here is sufficient as an illustration of the working model concept for sociology. The description below identifies some possible elaborations. For example, an older dissatisfied villager might seek means to improve his crop yield through use of pesticides and fertilizers in order to make more money. The model needs more explicit goal representations together with operators for achieving those goals. Such an extension can be achieved in Prolog, as shown in Warren (1974).

A more elaborate model could take account of the extent and accuracy of the information that the villager possesses about the destination. For example, if the villager lived and worked in the town for a period in the past, his confidence in information about the town will be more complete and accurate than if he is making judgments based on information from friends who have gone there.

Social rules for negotiation between children and parents over permission to move could be added to the model. Rather than simply identify the best destination, the villager might rank order his preferences among those destinations which he perceives as being better than the village. If the father vetoes the first, the villager might attempt to secure approval for his second choice, and so forth.

The model in this simulation might be lifted to a more general cognitive model. That is, with a restructuring of the knowledge base, the model might simulate migration from the farm to the city in the United States, or exiting from any unsatisfactory social situation.

6   Conclusion

Past work in sociology has concentrated on statistical models that aim to explain social phenomena. In this paper we have presented a method of creating new models for social science using logic programming languages such as Prolog. The initial version of a migration decision-making simulation was discussed and related to the concept of a working, or operational model. The interplay of individual, personal decision and social rules was explored with a program written in Prolog. Although this simulation program uses a simplistic design, it can be readily extended under a more comprehensive theory, one of the major advantages of using a rule-based programming language. The major thrust of this work has not been to create sophisticated logic programming code, rather it has been to demonstrate the feasibility of creating a program to model social interactions based on a production rule representation.

Thai government planners are concerned that Bangkok is growing too rapidly, and consequently they are seeking means to encourage the growth of other urban centers. This enterprise is likely to be successful only if we understand the decision-making structure used by villagers (i.e., potential migrants). Prolog has proven to be a most useful tool in this initial investigation into representing and applying the social rules shaping migration patterns in Thailand.

References

Abelson, R. P. (1973). "The structure of belief systems." In *Computer models of thought and language*. R. C. Schank and K. M. Colby, eds., San Francisco, CA.: W. H. Freeman.

Bannister, D. and F. Fransella. (1971). *Inquiring man, the theory of personal constructs*. London: Penguin.

Berlo, D. K. (1977). "Modeling the communication process," In *Readings in human communication*. T. M. Steinfatt, ed., Indianapolis: Bobbs-Merrill.

Cronen, V. E., W. B. Pearce, and L. M. Harris. (1982). "The coordinated management of meaning: A theory of communication." In F. E. X. Dance (ed.) *Human communication theory*. New York: Harper and Row.

Cushman, D. P., B. Valentinsen, and D. Dietrich. (1982). "A rules theory of interpersonal relationships." In F. E. X. Dance (ed.) *Human communication theory*. New York: Harper and Row.

Faught, B., K. M. Colby, and R. C. Parkinson. (1974). *The interaction of inferences, affects, and intentions in a model of paranoia*. Stanford Technical Report, AIM-253.

Fuller, T. D., P. Kamnuansilpa, P. Lightfoot, and S. Rathanomongkolmas. (1983). *Migration and development in modern Thailand*. Bangkok, Thailand: Social Science Association of Thailand.

Goffman, E. (1974). *Frame analysis*. New York: Harper and Row.

Gullahorn, J. T. and J. E. Gullahorn. (1963). "A computer model of elementary social behavior." pp. 375–385 In E. A. Feigenbaum and J. Feldman (eds.) *Computers and Thought*. New York: McGraw-Hill.

Homans, George. (1961). *Social behavior: Its elementary forms*. New York: Harcourt, Brace, and World.

Meehan, J. R. (1980). *The metanovel: writing stories by computer*. New York: Garland Publishing Co.

Reiss, I. (1960). "Toward a Sociology of the Heterosexual Love Relationship" *Marriage and Family Living* 22(May) pp. 139–145.

Reynolds, P. D. (1971). *A primer in theory construction*. Indianapolis: Bobbs-Merrill.

Roach, J. W. and G. S. Fowler. (1983). "The HC Manual: Virginia Tech PROLOG." Department of Computer Science, Virginia Polytechnic Institute and State University, Blacksburg, Virginia.

Roach, J. W. and T. D. Fuller. (1982). "A Prolog Simulation of Migration Decision Making in a Less Developed Country." in *Proceedings of the First International Logic Programming Conference*.

Warren, D. H. D. (1974). *Warplan: a system for generating plans*. University of Edinburgh School of Artificial Intelligence, Memo no. 76.

CHAPTER 10

A Prolog Implementation of a Large System on a Small Machine

Luís Moniz Pereira
António Porto

Departamento de Informática
Universidade Nova de Lisboa
2825 Monte da Caparica
Portugal

1   Introduction

The system we describe here is a natural language (Portuguese) question-answering system for aiding in the planning of research investment in Portugal. It knows about interactions between scientific disciplines and development goals, interactions among sciences themselves and interactions among goals. The data was gathered in several nationwide meetings, following a procedure recommended by UNESCO (Caraça and Pinheiro, 1981: UNESCO, 1977).

This system was implemented using a slightly modified version of RT-11 Prolog (see appendix in Clocksin and Mellish (1981)) on two small LSI-11 based machines with 64K/128K bytes of central memory and dual single/double density floppy disks. The hardware restrictions strongly influenced the design considerations.

The system is made up of two main modules : the *natural language interpreter* and the *query evaluator*.

The natural language interpreter divides itself into two sub-modules : a *lexical parser* and a joint *syntactic/semantic parser*. The lexical parser accepts input from a terminal and produces a list of morphological tokens, which are used by the syntactic/semantic sub-module to produce a Prolog goal expression which corresponds to the semantics of the natural language query.

The query evaluator includes the procedures needed to execute the Prolog goal expression produced by the natural language processor. A large part of it is an external database of Prolog clauses stored in disk files. A goal involving disk access is executed in two steps : first there is a planning stage whereby a new subgoal is produced, and then this new subgoal is executed — it will only access the relevant files, and timing of its operations has been optimized.

2   The domain

The system deals with *sciences* and *development goals*.

Sciences are divided into main branches (e.g., pure sciences), each one of these into groups (e.g., physics) and each group into individual disciplines (e.g., optics).

Development goals are divided into groups (e.g., agriculture), which in turn are divided into individual goals (e.g., cereals).

There are 110 scientific disciplines and 78 individual development goals.

The system is supposed to know about several types of correlations between sciences and goals, between sciences and other sciences, and between goals and other goals.

3   The natural language interpreter

The system's linguistic competence is obtained by means of a lexical and syntactic/semantic analysis, transforming a natural language query into a Prolog goal expression.

The modules which perform this task were adapted from a general grammar for the Portuguese language initially developed for another application. We shall not go into details here ; for that the reader is referred to Pereira et al (1982).

3.1   Lexical analysis

Our lexical analysis replaces words in the input sentence by their corresponding lexical categories (noun, verb, . . .) with syntactic and semantic readings. This is done by making each word access a *dictionary*.

Since RT-11 Prolog only gives us indexing on the predicate names, the dictionary consists of a set of single clauses for unary predicates whose names are the actual words that we want to access the dictionary.

In general there is a lexical entity corresponding to each word, but sometimes several words are grouped to form a single noun, e.g., pure sciences. For possibly handling several words, the dictionary clauses would have to use a difference-list pair for processing the input string instead of accepting a single input word, thus making the dictionary too large (the *whole* dictionary must be available in memory). Therefore we preferred to use single-word abbreviations of all multi-word nouns. For this to be practical a menu-type consulting service was introduced for querying about abbreviations.

3.2   Syntactic/semantic analysis

The syntactic/semantic analysis is realized by means of a grammar defined in terms of context-sensitive rules with syntactic and semantic controls. These rules handle the fundamental structures of the Portuguese language, including features such as extraposition and intersentential ellipsis.

The syntactic and semantic analysis are not carried out separately but in a mixed way, no parse tree being built. This allows a compact grammar, important in view of the memory restrictions, and is efficient by reducing search upon early semantic check failures.

4   The database

The system database has two different parts. One is small and contains information on the hierarchical division of sciences and development goals. The other one is large and contains data on correlations.

4.1   Hierarchical description

Each hierarchical definition is a unit clause whose predicate name is the internal code for some group of sciences or development goals, and whose two arguments are the number of elements in that group and a list containing their names.

Internal codes are used as predicate names both for efficiency (RT-11 indexing) and space-saving (one less argument).

The internal code was designed for easy manipulation of information : the 1st group in the 2nd branch of sciences has the code s21.

A hierarchical description clause can be used to generate the codes for the elements of a group (and thus to build goals for accessing their own hierarchical description clauses), or to get their names from their codes.

4.2   Correlations

Handling of information about correlations was critical in terms of system feasibility and performance, involving both space and time considerations.

The basic information available consisted of three arrays with the self and cross-correlations of individual scientific disciplines and development goals. Given the size of those arrays (110×78, 110×110 and 78×78) where each element was to be represented as a clause, there was no space in central memory to hold all that information simultaneously. It was therefore necessary to split the arrays into sub-arrays that could be individually consulted. The natural choice was to split them along the boundaries between the groups of elements. Fortunately this division was regular enough that no file remained oversized. For a decision of when and how to ``page out'' consulted files to consult a new one, the system should know about available core. Since no RT-11 Prolog system predicate does this, and even though we could implement such a predicate not much core was available anyway, we opted for the simple strategy of always retracting the clauses of a consulted file before consulting a new one.

In order to consult each correlatation file when needed, its name should be related to the names of the two groups therein represented. In fact, we chose to use the name obtained by just appending the codes of the two groups, eg. **s21d1.**

Inside the file, elements of the two groups are just represented by small integers (from 1 to the number of elements in the group).

Correlations are defined by a predicate with the same name as the file, using only clauses for the **non-zero** correlation values, like

$$s21d1(4,7,2) :- !.$$

followed by a single clause for the value *zero* :

$$s21d1(\_,\_,0) :- !.$$

(where the cut is not necessary but provides a uniform pattern for retracting s21d1 clauses). This allows a considerable saving of disk space, since the most common correlation value is zero.

The use of a default clause screened by cuts in previous clauses is standard practice in Prolog programming. Its major drawback is that such clauses can only be used to test cases for the values of arguments, not to generate the domain of values. If needed, generation must be carried out by a previous call to some generator predicate.

Our system does need to scan domains, in order to compute mean values for correlations. This is done by generating integers, for whose bounds the file contains a clause defining the dimensions of the sub-array :

$$dim(s21d1,7,9).$$

There is also a clause relating a general correlation predicate **cor** to the file-specific correlation predicate :

$$cor(s21d1,X,Y,N/4) :- s21d1(X,Y,N).$$

This clause represents a general technique for turning an n-ary relation into m (n−1)-ary relations, m being the number of atomic values of some argument of the n-ary relation. The gain in time is provided by the extra level of indexing. The gain in space derives from the reduction of one argument. These gains grow with the number of tuples in the n-ary relation and decrease with larger m. They must make up for the overhead (time and space) of the extra translation code. This code may be of two kinds - a single call for runtime construction of a call to one of the (n−-1)-ary relations (as in the dictionary call in the lexical parser), or m specific calls to those relations (as above).

The use of file-specific correlation predicates was designed before the decision was made to allow no more than one correlation file in memory, for it was then necessary to use the file name in the correlation call to access only the relevant information. Now it is possible to use just a single correlation predicate in all files, as they are in memory only one at a time.

An important time-related problem had to be tackled, involving the way correlations are computed.

The correlation between two basic elements (eg. optics and cereals) is found by a simple lookup of a clause after consulting the appropriate file.

To find the correlation between a basic element and a group (eg. optics and agriculture) one must consult the corresponding file, get the correlations between the basic element and each element of the group, and compute their mean value.

Now, to find the correlation between two groups (e.g., physics and agriculture), having consulted the relevant file one would get the correlations for all pairs of elements of the two groups and then average them. This may already take some time, but worse is to find the correlation between a basic element and a super-group (eg. cereals and pure sciences) that calls for consulting a different file for each group within the super-group. Still worse cases are easily imagined.

The way out is to do some *preprocessing* of correlations once and for all, and keep the results in files similar to the ones containing the basic information.

Having every single correlation precomputed was absolutely out of the question, so one had to decide which ones to precompute. Fortunately the regular hierarchical nature of the domain lends itself to a neat and efficient solution.

Let us say that an element's *level* is 0 if it is a basic element, 1 if a group of basic elements, etc. Then the solution is to have a file for every two groups whose level difference is *even*. This guarantees that for any single correlation computation only *one file* will be consulted, and no more than *one row or column* of the corresponding array will be searched, thus limiting the evaluation time for a single correlation (of course some queries may involve several single correlations).

The initial files are for pairs of groups of level 1. From these we construct all other needed files, using a preprocessor written in Prolog that uses the hierarchical definitions.

All needed files fit into a single-sided double-density floppy disk.

5   Query evaluation

The goal expression which comes out of the natural language processor eventually contains calls to evaluate correlations. All such calls are of the form

correlation(X,Y,V)

where X and Y define what are the elements whose correlation is wanted in V. This may represent a single correlation or several of them, if X or Y are of the form

$$each(G)$$

in which case V will hold the value of the correlation for just one element of the group G, the set of solutions being explored by backtracking.

As already said, the evaluation of **correlation** proceeds first through a *planning* stage before actually consulting files and computing correlations. This is done by having an intermediate predicate evaluate everything that is deterministic, and build a new goal expression to be launched afterwards:

$$correlation(X,Y,V) :- eval\_plan(X,Y,V,Goal), Goal.$$

Execution of **eval_plan** follows these steps:

1. Analysis of **each** quantification in the X and Y arguments;
2. Assessment of level difference;
3a. Construction of the names of the files to be consulted;
3b. Construction of goals to generate elements of groups;
4. Assembly of the postponed goal expression;

The postponed goal expression may include goals waiting for clauses to be consulted from a file, arithmetic calls waiting for arguments to become instantiated, and nondeterministic goals. The optimal order among them must be produced to avoid unnecessary backtracking. Knowledge is used of which goals become deterministic when some other goals are executed.

So, far from using a general query planner, we just wrote clauses for **correlation** that perform the planning in a highly optimized way for the tasks at hand.

6   System performance

The first implementation of this system was made on a machine with an LSI-11/03 processor and 64K bytes of main memory.

To get the system to run with such a small amount of main memory available, one had to resort to the technique of chaining various modules (separate programs), using a disk file to pass information from module to module. This was achieved by making RT-11's procedure for chaining programs available inside Prolog.

Three modules had to be chained: the lexical parser (because of the size of the dictionary); the syntactic/semantic parser; and the query evaluator, that chained again to the lexical parser for the next query.

The main consequence was that a great part of the time required for answering a query was lost in the process of loading the next module from disk.

The answer to a typical query took about 16 seconds to be computed, thus distributed:

Lexical analysis	3
Chaining	4
Syntactic/semantic analysis	2
Chaining	4
Query evaluation (1 file consulted)	4

The system is now installed on a PDP-11/23, where extended memory (128K bytes), faster processor and better disk access have much improved the system's performance.

Instead of chaining three modules, we now have two permanent Prolog jobs in memory, communicating through a message queue handler provided by RT-11 (working in main memory), using standard Prolog I/O (with extended device name recognition).

One of the jobs does the syntactic/semantic analysis, while the other one reads the user query and performs the lexical analysis and query evaluation.

A typical query is now answered in just about 5 seconds:

Lexical analysis	1.5
Syntactic/semantic analysis	1
Query evaluation (1 file consulted)	2.5

7   Summary of techniques

We will try to summarize the space- and time-saving techniques that were incorporated in the system.

7.1   Using arguments as predicate names

This is done to achieve one more level of indexing than what the system provides. Besides speed-up, it may save space.

We have used it for the dictionary access, for searching through hierarchical definitions, and to evaluate correlations for different groups.

7.2   Splitting an external database into small files

This is done to access a database that will not fit into the main memory. It is practical only if accesses can be foreseen to be generally circumscribed to fixed small groups of data. This is usually true for hierarchically organized data with a regular distribution.

This was used to handle data on correlations.

7.3   Preprocessing of some values

This is required for interactive question-answering systems where the user should not wait for lengthy computations. The aim should be to put a limit on the length of the expected computations. This is dependent on the spreading of operations over the basic data. Operations on sets (e.g., mean value, maximum) of data with regular hierarchical organization are usually good candidates for preprocessing.

We preprocessed correlations for all pairs of elements with even level difference, to limit the range of the expected correlation computation to at most one row or column in one file.

7.4   Representation for sparse arrays

If there is one more common value for the elements of an array one can gain space and time by making the clauses for the other values deterministic, by using a cut, and using a last single clause with the common value for unspecified arguments.

This was the representation used for the correlation arrays.

7.5   Special-purpose planning

Complex computations involving deterministic parts inside nondeterministic ones can be made more efficient by programming a planning phase that executes everything deterministic and produces a new goal expression to be executed in the end, where the order of goals was planned to take advantage of foreseen runtime determinism.

The general correlation predicate was defined that way.

7.6   Communicating programs

If the total code for a system is too large to be run as a single program it may be split into several programs that either call one another or are run concurrently, passing messages in memory or through a disk file.

Our two implementations both used communicating programs.

Acknowledgments

This work was done under contract with Portugal's *Junta Nacional de Investigacão Científica e Tecnológica* (JNICT).

References

Caraça, J.M.G. and J.D.R.S. Pinheiro. (1981). *Prioridades em ciência e tecnologia — identificação de áreas prioritárias em I&D*. Junta Nacional de Investigação Científica e Tecnológica.

Clocksin, W.F. and C.S. Mellish. (1981). *Programming in Prolog*. Springer-Verlag.

Pereira, L.M., E. Oliveira, and P. Sabatier. (1982). "An expert system for environmental resource evaluation through natural language." In *Proceedings of the First International Logic Programming Conference*, ed. ADDP, Marseille.

UNESCO. (1977). *Méthode de détermination de priorités dans le domaine de la science et de la technologie*. Etudes et documents de politique scientifique n.40, UNESCO.

CHAPTER 11

MYCIN: The Expert System and Its Implementation in LogLisp

Sanjai Narain

The Rand Corporation
1700 Main Street
Santa Monica, California 90406

1 Introduction

MYCIN is a "rule-based" expert system. Expert knowledge has been organized on a set of mutually independent IF-THEN decision rules. A consultation is the result of inference using these rules. The advantages of a rule-based organization are well-known (Shortliffe, 1976). First, human experts find it a convenient formalism around which to express their knowledge. This facilitates transfer of expertise from the human to the computer. Second, it is conceptually easy to devise an explanation system for such an organization. Third, if rules are mutually independent, new rules representing new packets of knowledge may easily be added to the knowledge base of the expert system. This also simplifies the search for inconsistencies and contradictions in the knowledge base. Last, the simple structure of rules simplifies the design of a natural language front-end to the expert system.

Since 1974 we have witnessed the emergence of the field of logic programming first proposed by Kowalski and Colmerauer (Kowalski, 1974; Colmerauer, 1975). Logic programs consist of a set of axioms in Horn Clausal form (see next section). Each axiom may be interpreted as a logical statement in IF-THEN format. It may also be interpreted as a procedure to be executed by an interpreter (Kowalski, 1974). Computation is the result of a top-down inference using a proof procedure that is known to be sound and complete for Horn Clauses. The proof procedure may also be viewed as an interpreter that calls procedures represented by the clauses of the logic program. Logic programming systems have an inbuilt and fully general pattern-matching facility based upon the unification principle (Robinson, 1965). They are also equipped with an automatic backtracking facility for the exploration of alternative paths to a solution. Several implementations of logic programming are now available mostly as various versions of the programming language Prolog. The most well known among these is the Edinburg Prolog (Warren et al., 1977) in which programs may be compiled to execute as efficiently as compiled Lisp programs for similar tasks. A recent implementation, LogLisp (Robinson and Sibert, 1980) extends Lisp to provide primitives for programming in logic.

In view of these features—well understood framework for deductive, rule-based problem solving, inbuilt pattern matching, automatic backtracking and efficient implementations—logic programming systems are an attractive medium for symbolic computation and the writing of intelligent computer programs, in particular, expert systems. Logic programming has already been applied to areas such as natural language processing, databases, expert systems, symbolic algebraic manipulation, program transformation and verification, object-oriented programming, planning and inductive inference.

As a further example of the application of logic programming, it is the intention of this paper to outline the structure of MYCIN's rule-based inference, to show its reformulation in LogLisp, and finally to outline the advantages of a LogLisp approach for expert system development.

2   Overview of LogLisp

LogLisp is an extension of the Lisp programming language to provide primitives for programming in logic. These primitives in themselves embody a complete programming language called Logic.

A logic program in LogLisp consists of a conjunction of facts or assertions called Horn clauses, each of the form:

$$[A \langle— B1 \& B2 \& \ldots \& Bk]   k\rangle=0$$

to be read as "A holds if all of the conditions Bi hold". A and each Bi are predications of the form:

$$(R\ tl\ t2\ \ldots\ tn)   n\rangle=0$$

where R is the name of a relation and each ti is a term, either an identifier or a function application of the form:

$$(F\ x1\ x2\ \ldots\ xm)   m\rangle=0$$

where F is a function symbol and each xi is itself a term.

All identifiers beginning with a lower case letter are treated as variables. The back arrow and the ampersand are syntactic sugar and are understood if omitted.

All variables in an assertion are universally quantified.

If A is of the form (R tl . . . tn), the assertion:

$$[A <- B1 \& B2 \& \ldots \& Bk]$$

asserts that the relation R between tl through tn holds if each of the conditions, B1 through Bk holds. The set of all such assertions is called 'procedure' R. Procedure R is then a complete definition of the relation R. Thus, procedure INSERT for inserting an element into a list consists of the following three assertions:

$$[(INSERT\ u\ NIL\ (:\ u\ NIL))\ <-\ ]$$
$$[(INSERT\ u\ (:\ x\ y)\ (:\ u\ (:\ x\ y))\ <-\ ]$$
$$[(INSERT\ u\ (:\ x\ y)\ (:\ x\ z))\ <-\ (INSERT\ u\ y\ z)]$$

where ':' is an arbitrary function symbol in the role of the Lisp 'CONS' and NIL is the empty list.

Let S be a set of assertions. A 'query' on S is a conjunction Q of conditions:

B1 & B2 & . . . &Bk, where each Bi is a predication and k>0

All variables in a query are existentially quantified.

Let x1 x2 . . . xn be the variables occurring inside Q. To 'run' this query is to show:

S implies that there exist x1 x2 . . . xn such that
B1 & B2 & . . . Bk.

This is the top-level 'goal'. This goal may be achieved by achieving each of a set of subgoals, that is by proving each of B1 through Bk. The proof of the top level goal is one of existence. If the proof terminates successfully, it would effectively bind x1 x2 . . . xn to terms such that:

B1 & B2 & . . . Bk.

Values of x 1 . . . xn can thus be 'computed'. In general, if Bi is to be proved and Bi is of the form (R tl t2 . . . tk), Bi is unified or matched against the head of each assertion under procedure R. When a successful match occurs a substitution environment is generated, and the body of the matching assertion is instantiated with this environment. Each predication in the instantiated body becomes a subgoal to be proved once again via exactly this same procedure. This proof procedure is called LUSH resolution, a top-down procedure which is both sound and complete for Horn clauses (Hill, 1974).

So for example, if the query:

$$(INSERT\ 1\ (:\ 2\ (:\ 3\ NIL)\ z)$$

is run in the presence of procedure INSERT, z will be bound to:

(: 1 (: 2 (: 3 NIL))) or
(: 2 (: 1 (: 3 NIL))) or
(: 2 (: 3 (: 1 NIL))).

One, a fixed number, or all solutions can be found by using the LogLisp primitives THE, ANY or ALL respectively. Thus typing:

(THE z (INSERT 1 (: 2 (: 3 NIL) z))

will return one of the above three lists.

It is noteworthy that no analogs of the selector functions CAR and CDR are needed here for dealing with lists. Rather it is possible to deal directly with patterns, or generalized representations of data structures (a list is just NIL or (: u v) where u is the head and v is the tail). This is made possible by the unification pattern-matching inherent in the proof procedure.

Such programming in logic has long been the basis of all versions of the Prolog language. However in LogLisp it is also possible for Lisp and Logic to interact intimately to provide a rich programming environment (Robinson & Sibert, 1980). For example it is possible for predications in the IF portion of a rule to be Lisp functions that are interpreted as true if they return a non-NIL value. Such functions can be used to simulate procedural behavior, causing side-effects or "actions". Sequential behavior can be simulated by specifying the order in which predications are proved, either inside a query or inside the premise of an assertion or by arranging to use clauses in a definite order.

3   MYCIN

This section outlines four major aspects of MYCIN's rule-based expertise, namely, data structures used, the structure of decision rules, the inference mechanism, and the explanation system.

3.1   Data Structures

MYCIN uses the term "context" to represent objects occurring inside a consultation. Examples of objects are the patient, cultures isolated from his body, organisms present in those cultures or drugs administered against those organisms. All contexts in a particular consultation are arranged hierarchically inside a tree structure called a "context tree." An example of a possible context tree is:

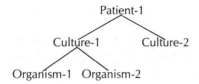

The context tree gives structure to the clinical problem and helps to infer relationships between contexts during a consultation.

Each context has a set of attributes called clinical parameters. Parameter values are stored inside four-tuples each of the form:

⟨parameter context val cfac⟩

where "cfac," in MYCIN's model of inexact reasoning, represents the degree of belief, in the hypothesis that the value of "parameter" of "context" is "val." All data on the patient are represented in the form of such four-tuples.

A consultation consists of growing the context tree and inferring values of certain relevant parameters for certain relevant contexts.

3.2   Structure of Decision Rules

MYCIN's knowledge base consists of about 200 decision rules each of the form:

IF ⟨PREMISE⟩ THEN {cfac} ⟨ACTION⟩

⟨PREMISE⟩ is a usually a conjunct of a set of conditions each of the form

(SAME C P VAL)

SAME is a Lisp function that returns a value representing the certainty factor associated with the hypothesis that the value of parameter "P" of context "C" is "VAL." If, however, this certainty factor is less than 0.2, SAME returns NIL instead, signifying that the condition (SAME C P VAL) failed to be met.

⟨ACTION⟩ is usually a conclusion about the value of a certain parameter for a certain context.

{cfac} is a measure of belief of the domain expert in the validity of the rule.

If all the conditions in the ⟨PREMISE⟩ succeed, i. e. none of them return NIL, the certainty factor associated with the conclusion of the rule is calculated usually as the product of {cfac} and the minimum of certainty factors returned by conditions in ⟨PREMISE⟩.

As an example, the English and InterLisp versions of a typical MYCIN rule, RULE147 are:

IF: 1) The site of the culture is CSF, AND
           2) There is significant disease associated with
              the occurrence of this organism, AND
           3) The culture was obtained via an L.P. or a
              cisternal tap

THEN: There is strongly suggestive evidence (0.9)
           that Meningitis is an infectious disease
           diagnosis for the patient.

PREMISE: ($AND (SAME CNTXT SITE CSF)
                (SAME CNTXT SIGNIFICANCE YES)
                (SAME CNTXT LP_OR_CIS YES))
ACTION: (CONCLUDE CNTXT INFECT MENINGITIS TALLY 0.9)

3.3   Inference Mechanism

MYCIN's inference is performed in a goal-oriented fashion. Each parameter has a property called UPDATED-BY which is a list of rules that could help in the inference of the value of this parameter for a certain context. For example, to determine the disease that the patient is suffering from (value of parameter INFECT for the context patient), MYCIN tries each rule in the UPDATED-BY list of INFECT, and, in particular, RULE147 above. To try this rule it must evaluate each of the conditions in the PREMISE of this rule. To evaluate the second condition in the PREMISE, MYCIN must know the value of parameter SIGNIFICANCE. MYCIN then retrieves the list of rules on the UPDATED-BY property of SIGNIFICANCE and tries each rule in that list in turn. It continues to reason backwards in this manner and if at any stage it finds that it does not have enough information in its database to evaluate the condition at hand, it queries the user.

3.4   Explanation System

MYCIN's explanation system monitors the consultation and, at any time, is able to provide answers to several types of user questions about the state of the consultation. Two major types are HOW and WHY questions.

A HOW question is used to ask MYCIN how it arrived at a given conclusion. To answer such a question, MYCIN looks at the set of successfully evaluated rules, picks out those rules that had the given conclusion in their ACTION portion, and simply displays those rules or their rule numbers.

A WHY question is used to ask MYCIN why it is prompting the user for a certain piece of information. To answer a WHY question MYCIN displays its current chain of reasoning, which is essentially the chain of rule calls extant at that point.

The explanation system helps the user not only to understand the course of the consultation but also to debug and validate the expert system.

4   MYCIN in LogLisp

This section describes the implementation of the MYCIN system in LogLisp, and is organized exactly as the preceding section. We show how the specification of the preceding section was translated into a LogLisp program.

4.1   Data Structures in LogLisp

Any context tree may be described by listing all its edges. An edge may be represented by an unconditional clause denoting the parent-offspring relationship.

For example, the context tree:

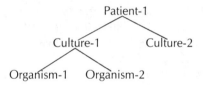

may be described completely by the following set of unconditional clauses:

[(CULTURE (PATIENT 1) (CULTURE 1))]
[(CULTURE (PATIENT 1) (CULTURE 2))]
[(ORGANISM (CULTURE 1) (ORGANISM 1))]
[(ORGANISM (CULTURE 1) (ORGANISM 2))]

where CULTURE and ORGANISM are relation names. With such a representation it is very simple to infer relationships between contexts at runtime. For example to relate an organism to a patient one may write the rule:

[(ORGANISM_OF pat org) <− (CULTURE pat cult)&
                          (ORGANISM cult org)]

to be read as:

"org" is an organism of patient "pat" if there exists a culture "cult" which is drawn from "pat," and "org" was observed inside "cult."

Patient data are stored inside unconditional assertions of procedure CONCLUSION, each of the form:

[(CONCLUSION source parameter context value cfac)].

where "source" represents the source (a rule number or the user) from which the four-tuple ⟨parameter context value cfac⟩ was acquired.

Each such assertion has exactly the same interpretation as that of MYCIN's four-tuples except that the source information is also present.

The uncertainty "cfac" is easily represented in the form of an extra argument to CONCLUSION.

4.2   MYCIN Rules in LogLisp

MYCIN's RULE147 in section 3.2 above has been translated into LogLisp as:

```
((INFECT patient MENINGITIS cfac)
    <- (RULE 147)
    & (CULTURE patient (CULTURE k))
    & (ORGANISM (CULTURE k) organism)
    & (SAME (CULTURE k) SITE CSF cf1)
    & (SAME organism SIGNIFICANCE YES cf2)
    & (SAME (CULTURE k) LP_OR_CIS YES cf3)
    & (TALLY (cf1 cf2 cf3) tally)
    & (CONCLUDE INFECT patient MENINGITIS cfac tally 0.9))
```

This is one of 7 rules under procedure INFECT and is also in IF-THEN format. All rules of inference have been translated in similar fashion. In general, for each parameter P, a LogLisp procedure P has been defined. Procedure P contains translated versions of all rules that, in MYCIN, were listed on the UPDATED-BY property of parameter P.

To infer the value of INFECT for "patient" by this rule, each of the conditions in the PREMISE of this rule is executed. The first condition represents the rule number and always succeeds. It also serves as a record keeping device for use in the explanation system as described in section 4.4. Given a "patient," successful execution of the second condition results in binding "k" to a number such that (CULTURE k) is a culture drawn from the patient. Similarly, successful execution of the third condition results in binding "organism" to an actual organism observed inside (CULTURE k). A call to procedure SAME performs exactly the same computation as a call to the function SAME in MY-CIN would. If this call is successful, it binds its last argument to the certainty factor value that a call to MYCIN's SAME would have returned. In particular, procedure SAME first obtains a set of hypotheses regarding a parameter using the scheme outlined in the next section. Procedure TALLY computes the minimum of the certainty factors returned by the different calls to SAME and binds the result to "tally." Finally, procedure CONCLUDE binds "cfac" to the product of "tally" and 0.9, the rule certainty factor, and adds to the database the assertion:

[(CONCLUSION (RULE 147) patient INFECT MENINGITIS cfac)]

It may be seen that given the same initial data, this method of representation and execution of rules leads to conclusion of exactly the same data as would be in MYCIN.

4.3   Hypothesis Inference in LogLisp

The query invocation:

(ALL (infect cf) (INFECT (PATIENT 1) infect cf))

will, given the above representation of rules, return a list of pairs (infect cf), such that each value of "infect" will represent an infection that (PATIENT 1) is suffering from and each associated "cf" will represent the corresponding certainty factor. The query is processed in a goal-oriented fashion because of the procedure used by the LogLisp interpreter. The procedure call:

(INFECT (PATIENT 1) infect cf)

will match the head of each assertion under procedure INFECT. So each rule under that procedure will be tried, exactly as was the case in MYCIN.

If hypotheses are to be collected only from the currently available patient data, the following query invocation is used:

(ALL (infect cf) (CONCLUSION source INFECT (PATIENT 1) infect cf))

Hypotheses for all other parameters are also inferred in this way. Thus the inference mechanism of MYCIN is exactly simulated.

4.4   The Explanation System

In the design of the explanation system, explicit use was made of LogLisp's facility for calling Lisp from inside Logic assertions.

Every clause under procedure CONCLUSION contains information about the source from which the hypothesis contained in that clause was inferred. This makes it very simple to answer HOW questions. For example if the user wishes to know how the system inferred that the identity of Organism-1 was E_COLI, LOGLISP would collect the list of rules used to infer this hypothesis by evaluating:

(ALL rule (CONCLUSION rule IDENT Organism-1 E_COLI cf))

and then display each rule in that list.

A WHY question is essentially a request to display the current reasoning chain. The reasoning chain at any time is the chain of rule calls extant at that time. The housekeeping necessary to determine this chain is accomplished as a side-effect of evaluating the first condition in a LogLisp rule. For example, if the LogLisp rule is numbered X, the first condition in that rule is:

(RULE X).

The evaluation of this condition results in pushing X onto a global stack (that grows downwards) called CURRENT_RULES. Thus the top of the stack always represents the rule being currently considered. If during the consideration of Rule X, Rule Y is referenced, we first push a separator symbol ' ‖ ' before pushing Y on CURRENT_RULES. At any time, to determine the rule that called Y, we "climb" the stack until we find the ' ‖ ' symbol. The rule number immediately above it represents the rule that called Y. In a similar way the rule that called X may be determined, and the chain of rule calls may be determined.

Details of how the stack is maintained may be found in Narain (1981).

5   Other Aspects of MYCIN Translated

MYCIN was translated more completely than might have been implied by the above account, and details may be found in Narain (1981). Besides the function SAME, all other functions occurring in premises of MYCIN rules (about 15 in number) were also translated. A mechanism for the growth of the context tree at runtime was implemented to simulate that of MYCIN. MYCIN's method of preventing reasoning loops at runtime was also implemented. All diagnostic rules, about 103 in number, (including rules with disjuncts in the PREMISE) were translated into assertions of LogLisp. MYCIN's model of inexact reasoning was completely reexpressed in LogLisp. The translated version does runtime type checking of user responses in exactly the style of MYCIN. A simple browser for the knowledge base was also built.

6   Aspects of MYCIN Not Translated

Because of the unavailability of MYCIN's algorithms used for implementing its natural language front-end, and because designing such a front-end is a nontrivial problem in itself, there is no facility in the translated version for English-like discourse with the system in the style of MYCIN.

Therapy recommendation in MYCIN was done using algorithmic means, and not using rule-based reasoning. For this reason, and also because of the unavailability of the relevant algorithms, the therapy recommendation capability of MYCIN was also not translated.

7 Space and Time Requirements

MYCIN was implemented in InterLisp on a DECsystem-10 running the TENEX operating system. The total space requirement for InterLisp, the compiled MYCIN program, the knowledge base, knowledge tables and working area was about 245K words of memory. The total interaction time elapsed during the consultation at the beginning of (Shortliffe, 1976) was about 20 minutes.

LogLisp is written in Rutgers-UCI Lisp on a DECsystem-10 running the TOPS-10 operating system. The total space requirement for Lisp, LogLisp, the translated knowledge base, Lisp functions, and working area was about 150K words. The total CPU time for the diagnosis portion (including explanations) of the consultation in (Shortliffe, 1976) was about 2.5 minutes.

8 Comparison with Other Prolog Approaches for Expert System Building

Most other Prolog-based expert systems (Clark & McCabe, 1980; Hammond, 1980; Pereira et al., 1982) use essentially the same approach as outlined in this paper. Data structures are handled using pattern-matching, IF-THEN rules are represented using Horn Clauses under procedural or declarative interpretation, and the inference engine is built on top of the resident Prolog theorem-prover. Since the Prolog theorem-prover is already quite powerful, inference engines built on top of it are very compact.

An elegant implementation of an explanation system in Prolog is given by Clark and McCabe. The implementation is essentially declarative yet practical and efficient.

The expert system in Pereira et al. (1982) has a powerful natural language capability, and demonstrates clearly the utility of Prolog for expert systems. It is shown how Prolog forms a common medium for integrating knowledge base, inference, explanation and natural language interface.

Of course, at present, Prolog implementations like Edinburgh Prolog or C-Prolog are much more efficient than most Lisp-based implementations, so Prolog-based expert systems are likely to deliver much more efficient performance.

Also, Prolog implementations are available on small machines (Pereira et al., 1982) and so there exists the possibility of building expert systems even in installations not having large expensive machines running Lisp.

9   Advantages of the LogLisp Approach

Since LogLisp is inherently a rule-based programming system, all the advantages of MYCIN's rule-based organization are carried over to the translated system. These advantages include (a) ease of representation of expert knowledge (b) modularity of knowledge base and consequent dynamic reasoning chain and (c) simple design of user interfaces like explanation systems or natural language front-ends. The presence of Lisp made it very convenient to do arithmetic, build the explanation system and design the input-output user interface.

In addition, there are several other advantages to programming inside a logic programming framework and these are now outlined.

First, to capture any kind of reasoning in a computer program one will have to define some kind of logic. Since logic programming systems have their basis in formal logic, they are an obvious choice for the writing of such computer programs. For one is then able to draw upon well understood and powerful ideas of formal logic in thinking about new ideas, for example inductive inference (Shapiro, 1982), planning (Warren, 1974), database design (Kowalski, 1981), natural language understanding (McCord, 1982), meta-level inference (Bundy & Welham, 1981) or concurrent processing (Shapiro & Takeuchi, 1983). The important role that logic plays in the representation of knowledge and common-sense reasoning is argued in depth in Moore (1982) and Kowalski (1979).

Second, since the inference procedure used in logic programming has been shown to be sound and complete (Hill, 1974), if bad conclusions are reached, one changes the axioms and not the inference procedure. This shifts the burden of writing intelligent computer programs from redesigning the inference procedure to better ways of structuring knowledge. Moreover, one can now explore, independently of applications, techniques of implementing the inference procedure in progressively better ways. The results of such an investigation are the very efficient Prolog implementations currently available.

Since this abstract machinery is also a "very high level" one, it is possible to write both exceptionally clear as well as efficient programs. One is not forced to make tradeoffs between clarity and efficiency, as is too often the case with Lisp. Logic programming systems are, for this reason, truly higher-level than Lisp.

Third, the heuristic of separating the logic component of an algorithm from its control component is an extremely important one for managing the complexity inherent in large-scale artificial intelligence software development. Logic programming systems allow one to use this heuristic directly. This is made possible by the dual interpretation of logic programs (logical and procedural) and good examples of such programming are the natural language programs implemented in Prolog, e.g. in McCord (1982), which may be read as expressions of a certain grammar, but which may also be executed to parse natural language queries.

Fourth, because a logic programming system is also a complete programming language, representation of uncertainty offers no conceptual problems. Any model of uncertainty may be implemented in such a language, just as it would be in any other programming language.

Last, unification pattern-matching is a powerful tool for dealing with arbitrarily complex data structures. This lends tremendous expressive power to logic programs which may therefore be used to represent knowledge in a wide range of domains. This is in contrast to many other so-called domain-independent AI languages. For example, in one such language, EMYCIN (van Melle, 1980), one is still constrained to use a context tree and ⟨attribute object value⟩ triples to organize knowledge. Such a method of organizing knowledge may of course not be natural or even possible in many domains.

Moreover pattern recognition is one activity humans do very well. Hence it seems that a language based upon pattern recognition may have an excellent chance of providing tools for modeling intelligent human performance.

Acknowledgments

I am immensely grateful to Professor J. A. Robinson for his guidance, and for suggesting the idea of translating MYCIN. I am also very grateful to Professor E. E. Sibert for his help and assistance during the development of this translation.

References

Bundy, A. and W. Welham. (1981). "Using meta-level inference for selective application of multiple rewrite rule sets in algebraic manipulation." *Artificial Intelligence*, Vol. 16, No. 2, May.

Clark, K. L. and F. McCabe. (1980). *PROLOG: A language for implementing expert systems.* Department of Computing and Control, Imperial College of Science and Technology, University of London, England.

Clark, K. L. and S. A. Tarnlund. (1977). "A first order theory of data and programs." *Proceedings of IFIP Congress 77,* Toronto, Ontario. August 8–12.

Colmerauer, A. (1975). "Metamorphosis Grammars." *Natural Language Communication with Computers,* ed. L. Bolc. Lecture Notes in Computer Science 63, Springer Verlag, New York 1978.

Hammond, P. (1980). *Logic Programming for Expert Systems.* Master of Science Thesis, Imperial College, London.

Hill, R. (1974). *LUSH resolution and its completeness.* DCL Memo 78, Department of Artificial Intelligence, University of Edinburgh, 1974.

Kowalski, R. A. (1974). "Predicate Logic as Programming Language." *Proceedings IFIP Congress.*

Kowalski, R. A. (1979). *Logic for problem solving.* Elsevier: North Holland.

Kowalski, R. A. (1981, July). *Logic as a Database Language.* Department of Computing, Imperial College, London, England.

McCord, M. (1982). "Using slots and modifiers in logic grammars for natural language." *Artificial Intelligence.* 18(3).

McDermott, D. (1980). *The PROLOG phenomena.* SIGART Newsletters, (July).

Moore, R. (1982). "The role of logic in knowledge representation and commonsense reasoning." *Proceedings of the National Conference on Artificial Intelligence*, Pittsburgh, PA., August 18–20.

Narain, S. (1981). *MYCIN: The expert system and its implementation in LOGLISP*. Tech. Report, School of Computer and Information Science, Syracuse University, Syracuse, NY (August).

Pereira, L. M., P. Sabatier and E. Oliveira. (1982). "Orbi: An expert system for environmental resources evaluation through natural language." *Proceedings of the First International Logic Programming Conference*, Faculte des Sciences de Luminy, Marseilles, France, (September 14–17).

Pereira, F. and D. H. D. Warren. (1980). "Definite Clause Grammars for Natural Language Analysis—A Survey of the Formalism and a comparison with Augmented Transition Networks." *Artificial Intelligence*, 13(3).

Robinson, J. A. (1965). "A machine-oriented logic based on the resolution principle." *Journal of the Association for Computing Machinery* 12, pp. 23–41.

Robinson, J. A. and E. E. Sibert. (1980). *Logic programming in LISP*. Tech Report, School of Computer & Information Science, Syracuse University, (November).

Shapiro, E. and A. Takeuchi. (1983). "Object-Oriented Programming in Concurrent Prolog." *New Generation Computing*, 1(1). Springer Verlag.

Shapiro, E. (1982). *Algorithmic Program Debugging*. ACM Distinguished Dissertation Series, MIT Press, Cambridge, MA. 1982.

Shortliffe, E. H. (1976). *Computer based medical consultations: MYCIN*. Elsevier Computer Science Library.

van Emden, M. H. (1977). "Programming in resolution logic." *Machine Intelligence* 8, pp. 266–299.

van Melle, W. (1980). *EMYCIN: A domain independent production rule system for consultation programs*. Ph.D. Thesis, Computer Science Department, Stanford University.

Warren, D. H. D. (1974). *WARPLAN: A system for generating plans*. Memo No. 76, Department of Computational Logic, University of Edinburgh, Edinburgh EH8 9NW, (June).

Warren, D. H. D., L. M., Pereira, and F. Pereira, (1977). "PROLOG - the language and its implementation compared with LISP." *Proceedings of a symposium on AI and Programming Languages*, SIGPLAN Notices, 12(8), and SIGART Newsletters 64, (August) pp. 109–115.

CHAPTER 12

Can Drawing Be Liberated from the von Neumann Style?[1]

Fernando C.N. Pereira

Artificial Intelligence Center
SRI International
Menlo Park, California 94025

1   What's in a Drawing?

The problems discussed in this paper and the solutions proposed arose from trying to simplify the writing of computer-aided design applications by defining design databases in logical rather than physical terms. From this new point of view, a design database is just a collection of logical statements about the objects being designed.

Apart from the basic relationships between parts of the design, a design database must contain statements that specify the *views* relevant to different aspects of the design activity. Drawings are an essential element of the design activity. Therefore, a design database must include statements that specify a visual representation for the objects described by the database. Furthermore, it is generally the case that the most convenient form of user access to a design database is through drawings of its contents.

A graphical interface to a database must provide means for **viewing** the contents of the database and for **building** objects through graphical operations. These two classes of operations correspond directly to the usual database operations of query and update. It seems to be the case that, with current implementation techniques for graphical interfaces, the computation of the graphical view of the database is related only in an "ad hoc" way to the translation of graphical input into changes to the database.

The main objective of this paper is to show how to give nonprocedural,

[1] The work described in here was carried out at EdCAAD in the Department of Architecture of Edinburgh University, under grants SERC grants GR/B 79493 and GR/A 88774. The preparation of this paper was partly supported by SRI International. This is an enlarged and revised version of the article of the same name that appeared in the Proceedings of the Annual Meeting, Databases for Business and Office Applications, Database Week, San Jose, May 23–26 1983, edited by Eric D. Carlson, copyright 1983, Association for Computing Machinery, Inc.

logical descriptions of the **structural mapping** between objects and their graphical representations that can be used both for graphical output and for graphical input. In other words, the same description is used to view graphically the contents of the database and to **identify** what objects are meant in user commands given in graphical terms. We will see that the logical statements describing the structural mapping are runnable programs in the logic programming language Prolog (Clocksin and Mellish, 1981; Warren, Pereira, and Pereira, 1977; Roussel, 1975).

For a single representation to be used both for viewing the contents of a database and for identifying which objects in the database correspond to features of the drawing, the representation must be **invertible.** With an invertible representation, we can both go from objects to their images and from images to those parts of of the database that correspond to the images. Invertibility imposes heavy constraints on the representation method. For example, a representation method based on a general-purpose programming language with graphics primitives (**procedural representation**) will not be invertible, because it is manifestly impossible to derive from features of a drawing the parts of the program that produced those features. In contrast, a **structural representation** with a a one-to-one correspondence between graphics primitives in the drawing and data structures in the database is clearly invertible.

CMU's Glide language for 3-D geometric modeling (Eastman and Henrion, 1978) and the Sticks & Stones functional notation for VLSI design (Cardelli, 1981; Cardelli and Plotkin, 1981) are extreme examples of procedural representation languages. Geometric modeling systems based on instantiation of prototypes (Braid, 1973), and graphics systems based on the same idea (ten Hagen et al., 1980) stand at a halfway position. A graphics system with a simple display file is a straightforward example of a pure structural representation.

The nature of the two representation methods just described has critical practical consequences. As I noted before, some form of invertibility, the ability to go from a drawing to its representation, is essential for interactive editing. Structural representations are invertible, and therefore allow interactive editing, but do not support general operations for putting pictures together from other pictures, deriving pictures from prototypes, or specifying classes of objects to be edited. In contrast, procedural representations support general languages for specifying complex pictures, but do not support facilities for recovering the constituents of a picture from the finished picture.

The examples in the two sections that follow show that logic programming can indeed help us to combine the advantages of structural and procedural representation methods. This is due to the fact that suitably constructed Prolog programs are **multipurpose** (Warren, Pereira, and Pereira, 1977), that is, the procedures in the program can be used both to compute some results from some inputs and to compute which inputs would generate given results. In other words, suitably constructed logic programs are invertible.

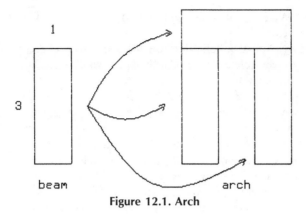

Figure 12.1. Arch

2 A Logic of Pictures

The discussion in this section builds on two empirical observations about physical assemblies (and pictures):

1. Complex objects are made of simpler objects.
2. New objects (or pictures) are often made by replicating, with some transformation, some existing object (picture).

I will give now a logical description of the "arch" of Figure 12.1[2] The structure of the arch can be represented by the following clauses:

> part(leftcolumn,arch).
> part(rightcolumn,arch).
> part(crossbeam,arch).
>
> instance(leftcolumn,beam,id).
> instance(rightcolumn,beam,translate($2^\circ 0$)).   (1)
> instance(crossbeam,beam,rotate(-90,$0^\circ 0$) ○ translate($0^\circ 4$)).
>
> primitive(beam)
>
> graphics(beam,line($0^\circ 0,1^\circ 0$)).
> graphics(beam,line($1^\circ 0,1^\circ 3$)).
> graphics(beam,line($1^\circ 3,0^\circ 3$)).
> graphics(beam,line($0^\circ 3,0^\circ 0$)).

---

[2] All the examples are two-dimensional for simplicity.

For example, clause (1) states that rightcolumn is an instance of beam translated by the vector (2,0).

When run by Prolog, a definition like the above can be used to check that objects satisfy given relationships or to compute which objects are in a given relationship with others.

The example program I have just given might seem no different from a program in some object definition language, such as Glide (Eastman and Henrion, 1978). However, in such a language, names such as line or translate have a fixed interpretation. In contrast, in definite clauses a name, be it a predicate name, a functor name or an atom name, has no predefined meaning. Thus, the clauses that were proposed to describe Figure 12.1 would have the same effect if part were replaced everywhere by detail. The names used in the example, however, are there for some reason: they were chosen to indicate the **intended** meaning of the clauses. That is, part is meant to represent the part-whole relationship, instance to represent the "transformed instance of" relationship, translate to represent a translation operator, ○ to represent composition of spatial transformations, and so on. But this intended meaning can only be made concrete if we add two ingredients:

- The viewing mapping between objects without parts (atomic objects) and graphic representations.
- The structural rules that determine the representation of complex objects from those of their components.

I will now discuss how to give structural rules, which are most important from the point of view of this paper. The question of the mechanisms for viewing the atomic objects will not be discussed further.

Structural rules are themselves definite clauses, but more complex than those shown above. The ones below are sufficient to complete the example.[3]

$$in(Part, Obj) \Leftarrow basic\_part(Part, Obj).$$
$$in(Part \cdot Trans, Obj) \Leftarrow$$
$$\qquad instance(Obj, Proto, Trans),$$
$$\qquad in(Part, Proto).$$

$$basic\_part(Obj, Obj) \Leftarrow primitive(Obj).$$
$$basic\_part(SubPart, Obj) \Leftarrow \qquad\qquad\qquad\qquad (2)$$
$$\qquad part(Part, Obj),$$
$$\qquad basic\_part(SubPart, Part).$$

For example, clause (2) above can be read as "SubPart is a basic part of Obj if Part is a part of Obj and SubPart is a basic part of Part." The relation

---

[3] I follow the Edinburgh Prolog convention of capitalizing variable names.

in(Part,Obj) is intended to hold between an object Obj and any **virtual primitive** Part that is indivisible and contributes to the structure of Obj. A virtual primitive is either a **primitive**, satisfying the predicate primitive, or an object derived through the application of geometric transformations to a primitive.

To derive actual graphical representations, besides the structural rules we need rules that relate the graphics of an object to the graphics of its parts. The relationship visible, defined by the rules below, holds between an object and a **graphic sign** if the sign belongs to the graphics of one of the parts of the object.

$$\text{visible(Obj,Sign)} \Leftarrow \hspace{4cm} (3)$$
$$\text{in(Part,Obj)},$$
$$\text{visible(Part,Sign)}.$$
$$\text{visible(Obj} \cdot \text{Trans,Sign)} \Leftarrow \hspace{3cm} (4)$$
$$\text{visible(Obj,Sign0)},$$
$$\text{apply(Trans,Sign0,Sign)}.$$
$$\text{visible(Obj,Sign)} \Leftarrow \text{graphics(Obj,Sign)}. \hspace{2cm} (5)$$

The rules for the visible relationship can be understood as follows. Rule (3) states that *Obj* has Sign in its graphic representation if Part is in Obj and Part has Sign in its representation. Rule (4) states that an object Obj transformed by Trans (written as Obj · Trans) has Sign in its representation if Obj has Sign0 in its representation and Trans applied to Sign0 gives Sign. The predicate apply just applies geometric transformations, and therefore we do not need to examine it further. However, for what follows it is important that apply be invertible in the limited sense of being able to compute one of its arguments given the other two. This is not problematic, because a reasonable set of geometrical transformations will satisfy that property, being mathematically a group.

With the above definitions, the graphic representation of a set of objects specified by some predicate object can computed and displayed by

$$\text{show} \Leftarrow$$
$$\text{setof(Sign,Obj^(object(Obj),visible(Obj,Sign)),Signs)},$$
$$\text{present(Signs)}.$$

where the setof metalogical operator defines Signs as the set of signs Sign such that there is an object Obj such that Obj is one of the specified objects and Sign is part of the graphic representation of Obj. The predicate present takes a set of graphic signs and presents them. If the (graphic) side-effects implicit in the predicate present strike the reader as improper in the context of logic programming, one may think instead of the presentation operation as being embedded in the top level of a Prolog interpreter that treats specially terms denoting graphic signs and displays them rather than printing them as terms in the usual way[4].

---

[4] I am indebted to Maarten van Emden for this suggestion.

3   Pointing at Things

Pointing at a drawing with some pointing device[5] is the natural means of referring to the objects depicted which we want to operate on. In general, pointing
operations are *ambiguous,* that is, several different objects could be meant by the
operation. Whereas the identification of which objects are meant is in general a
very difficult question, we will see later that in the present framework it is
possible to derive reasonable guesses.

The usual situation in a complex drawing will be that a pointing operation will
unambiguously identify a **hit set** of atomic graphical entities, and the identification task will be to go from those atomic objects to a set of objects in the database
whose graphics include those graphical entities.

For power and generality, a pointing operation may be a combination of
actual physical pointing with a specification of constraints (the **hit class**) to help
identify the objects being referred to.

In conventional picture editors, identification is conceptually simple because
of the limited repertoire of objects that may be built and referred to. Objects are
either primitives (lines, text strings, etc) or complex objects made of simpler
objects, but in which the simpler objects have lost their individuality (ISO
Working Group, 1982; Bijl and Nash, 1981). Therefore, from the point of view
of identification we have a single level of atomic objects without any internal
structure. In the same way, primitive text editors have commands to identify a
particular character or a particular line in the text, but cannot identify lines with a
given internal structure. In picture or text editors of this kind, the pointing
expressions of the user language are all of the form

⟨pointed positions, hit codes⟩

where the hit codes are used to select from all the (atomic) objects whose views
contain some graphics in the hit set, those in some particular predefined subclass
(for example, line segment, symbol).

Another kind of pointing, **specialization**, is available in some drawing systems (Applied Research of Cambridge, 1980). The target set identified by a
specialization is the set of all occurrences of a given subobject, where those
occurrences have been created through instantiation of a common prototype. I
will have more to say about prototypes and instances in Section 5. For now, it is
enough to note that this kind of pointing operation may be seen as drawing an
arbitrary distinction between objects that are the same from the user's point of

---

[5] In GKS terms, a pick or locator device (ISO Working Group, 1982), which is used to point at
graphics or locations on the screen. I will leave aside the computer graphics issues of how the bottom-
level graphics machinery derives from this input a hit set of atomic graphic objects (segments in GKS
parlance).

view, but that do not come from the same prototype. For example, of two apparently identical arches X and Y, X could be an instance of an arch prototype, and Y an assembly of three instances of the beam prototype. X could be identified as a specialization of "arch," whereas Y could not. This shows particularly well how the internal organization of the drawing system imposes "ad hoc" constraints on the user language. At the machine level, instances of prototypes are stored in the database as descending from the prototype. It is therefore easy to go from the prototypes to the instances. The pointing operation does not identify "all X's," where X is a *description* of the prototype, but only "all descendants of X." The way in which the picture has been put together has here an incurable influence on the class of identifiable objects.

We have seen so far two kinds of seemingly arbitrary limitations in the user language for pointing:

- Loss of the substructure of objects
- Identification of pointed objects governed by features of the database that are inaccessible to the user.

By using the methods of the last section, we are going to see now how these problems can be solved.

4   Structural Rules and the Identification Problem

We can now give a quite general description of the identification problem in terms of structural rules. Essentially, we can use the fact that the predicate visible as defined in Section 2 can be inverted provided that the predicates instance, part, graphics and apply are also invertible. The first three are defined exclusively by atomic facts and therefore are trivially invertible. The predicate apply can also be made invertible as discussed in Section 2.

I assume the user input provides a hit set of atomic graphic objects as those generated by the visible predicate. The hit classes also derived from the user input are seen as names for conditions that an object must specify to be the target of the pointing operation. Then, the identification problem for a pair

$$\langle \text{graphic object, hit class} \rangle$$

can be simply described by the rule:

$$
\begin{aligned}
&\text{target(GraphicObject,HitClass,Object)} \Leftarrow \quad\quad\quad (6)\\
&\quad\text{visible(Object,GraphicObject),}\\
&\quad\text{satisfies(Object,HitClass).}
\end{aligned}
$$

where satisfies defines whether an object satisfies the conditions named by a hit class.

The hit classes allowed by the user language could range from the names of primitives to complex conditions expressed in the same language as the structural rules. For example, the following clauses partially define an arch hit class:

$$\text{satisfies(Object,arch)} \Leftarrow \text{arch(Object)}.$$

$$\text{arch(Object)} \Leftarrow \text{instance(Object,arch,\_)}.$$
$$\text{arch(Object)} \Leftarrow \tag{7}$$
$$\text{setof(Part,basic\_part(Part,Object),Set)},$$
$$\text{arch\_shape(Set)}.$$

Arches occur by this definition in two ways: as instances of an arch prototype, and as "ad hoc" arches made of independent parts partially defined by clause (7). The meaning of clause (7) is that an object whose (basic) parts form an arch shape is an arch. In this way we restrict arch objects to those that are instances of the arch prototype or assemblies defined by part clauses that satisfy the arch_shape predicate. Yet another possibility would be to accept as an arch any set of unrelated objects satisfying arch_shape. Such (as one might say) "epiarches" would not have atomic names as other objects, but would instead be named by terms representing the sets of their basic parts. The computational cost of searching for "epiarches" is clearly much heavier than that of looking for the two other kinds of arches defined by the clauses above. The definition of arch_shape, which just checks that the basic parts are beams with coordinates satisfying the appropriate constraints, is bulky but straightforward, and is therefore omitted.

In a more realistic setting, rule (6) would be replaced by a rule that takes into account the context-dependent **focus** of the interaction. We can formalize focus as a predicate which takes a context and an object, and checks that the object is "in focus" in that context. The revised rule is as follows:

$$\text{target(GraphicObject,HitClass,Object,Context)} \Leftarrow$$
$$\text{visible(Object,GraphicObject)},$$
$$\text{satisfies(Object,HitClass)},$$
$$\text{focus(Context,Object)}.$$

In our arch example, we could have the following definition for focus:

$$\text{focus(arches,Arch)} \Leftarrow \text{arch(Arch)}.$$
$$\text{focus(beams,Beam)} \Leftarrow \text{beam(Beam)}.$$

where the arch and beam predicates identify arches and beams respectively. In a building application, pointing at a line segment might identify a wall if we are working at the floor plan level, but might identify a house if we are working at the site plan level.

This notion of focus will also be useful in viewing the database to avoid the presentation of irrelevant detail.

The distinction between context and hit class is that the hit class is supplied directly by the user's pointing action, whereas the context is given by the overall placement of the pointing action in the course of the interaction. An analogy with the use of pronouns in English may help clarify this point. In the contrasting sentences

> Mary has a house, but John hates *it*.
> Mary has a house, but John hates *her*.

the clause "Mary has a house" sets the context whereas the pronoun, "*it*" or "*her*," identifies an entity by its interaction with the context. In our domain, hit classes play a similar role to pronouns in that they usually come from a small predefined set, but in combination with an interaction context are capable of identifying a large variety of objects.

5   New From Old

In the examples of the last section, we have encountered a very simple mechanism for defining objects from others through transformations. The term "prototype" was used above to refer to objects that are transformed in this way. However, whereas the prototypes of the last section were fully defined, in general a prototype will only describe an aspect of an object, leaving undefined (**uninstantiated**) other aspects. Prolog programming gives us an effective means for dealing with partly defined or **parameterized** objects. For example, the following clauses define two parameterized prototypes beam(Length) and arch(Width,Height) leaving unspecified the length of beams of width 1 and the width and height of arches.

```
prototype(arch(Width,Height)).

part(leftcolumn(Height),arch(Width,Height)).
part(rightcolumn(Width,Height),arch(Width,Height)).
part(crossbeam(Width,Height),arch(Width,Height)).

instance(leftcolumn(Length),beam(Length),id).
instance(rightcolumn(Width,Height),
         beam(Height),
         translate((Width-1)^0)).
```

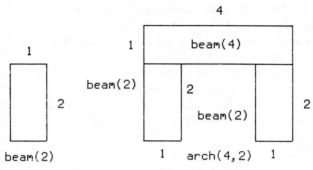

Figure 12.2 Parametrized Arches

instance(crossbeam(Width,Height),
    beam(Width),
    rotate(-90,0ˆ0) ○ translate(0ˆ(Height+1)))).

prototype(beam(Length)).

graphics(beam(Length),line(0ˆ0,0ˆLength)).
graphics(beam(Length),line(0ˆ0,1ˆ0)).
graphics(beam(Length),line(1ˆ0,1ˆLength)).
graphics(beam(Length),line(0ˆLength,1ˆLength)).

These clauses correspond directly to their counterparts in Section 2, except that now object names are not atomic, but instead have arguments for the unspecified dimensions. Figure 12.2 shows some instances of the prototypes.

Besides prototyping, other combination operations between objects are easily defined. For instance, a union relationship to make a new object containing all the parts of two other objects can be interpreted by the following additional clauses for in:

in(Part,Obj) ⇐
    union(Obj1,Obj2,Obj),
    in(Part,Obj1).
in(Part,Obj) ⇐
    union(Obj1,Obj2,Obj),
    in(Part,Obj2).

The specific union objects will be defined by clauses for union[6]. The two clauses for in state that a part is in a union object if it is in one of the two objects in the union.

---

[6] Union is a predicate, rather than a functor that combines two object names into a new object name, to guarantee that spurious union objects are not generated when the definition of in is used for identification of objects rather than for viewing.

Work is being done on even more powerful methods of object definition in definite-clause logic for graphics databases. Of particular interest are definition operators analogous to those provided in regular expressions and context-free grammars (Cardelli, 1981; Hopcroft and Ullman, 1979) that can be used to define generic objects containing arbitrary numbers of parts where the location and dimensions of each part are defined relatively to those of the other parts and the overall assemblage is defined by further constraints. Such operators can be applied, for example, to fill a region with instances of a given prototype.

6   Updating the Database

The method of representation described in the preceding sections is very closely related to that provided by relational databases. All the basic object definition predicates (part, instance, primitive, graphics and prototype) can be identified with relations in a relational database. The predicate instance is the only one that has an implicit fuctional dependency, from its first argument to each of its other arguments. The techniques for updating Prolog databases described by Parsaye (1983) may therefore be applied here.

Because, in our databases, objects are described in a piecemeal fashion, it is perfectly acceptable to modify only part of the description of an object, or to modify all objects that use a prototype by modifying the prototype. The easiest way to visualize what happens to the objects described by the database when the database is updated is to see an update as a mapping of an extensional version of the predicate in (the set of tuples in in) to another such set of tuples. The correspondence between updates of the base relations and changes in the extension of the in relation is defined by the structural rules.

Because objects containing instances of prototypes may change if the prototypes are changed, we need to be able to copy an object, by creating a new object containing the parts of another, directly, without relying on the prototype instances contained in the old object. The old and new objects will be exactly the same from the point of view of the in predicate but their internal structure will be different, with the new object being a one-level assembly of atomic parts. The copy operation can be defined as a global database update operation along the lines

$$copy(Old, New) \Leftarrow$$
$$for\_all(Part, in(Part, Old), add(part(Part, New))).$$

where for_all and add are extralogical operators[7] that iterate over the tuples of a relation and add new tuples to the database, respectively.

---

[7] The theory of giving nonprocedural meaning to such operators is discussed by Kowalski (1980).

In a related paper (Swinson et al., 1983) a method for updating and maintaining the integrity of Prolog design databases is discussed.

7 Implementation

SeeLog, a graphics front-end for Prolog databases based on an early version of the methods described here has been implemented by combining a Prolog interpreter with the GiGo window graphics manager (Rosenthal, 1983) on a VAX 11/750 under 4.1 Berkeley Unix[8].

SeeLog allows the user to give a declarative description not only of drawings but also of the screen layout and scaling properties of windows. SeeLog manages the relationship between primitive objects and their graphical representations so that the display is automatically updated when the Prolog database changes and graphics input is efficiently related to primitive objects in the database. SeeLog is being reimplemented and extended to add a more flexible screen model and to improve the speed of redisplaying and input interpretation. SeeLog is being used to demonstrate Prolog programming techniques for computer-aided architectural design (Giraud, 1982; Swinson, 1982).

Although the definitions of in and visible fully describe the graphical content of a database, in a large database it is not practical to rely solely on those definitions to interpret user input. Some form of "backwards indexing" from parts to the objects that contain them is clearly desirable. It is possible to provide such information in the form of additional redundant clauses in the database. Of course, a specification of the functional dependency of the indexing clauses on the base clauses will be required to ensure correct updating.

8 Conclusion

A method for relating objects in a design database to their graphical representations has been presented. The foundation of the method is the use of definite-clause logic both as a description language and, in the form of Prolog, as a programming language for representing objects and the relations between objects and between objects and their graphical representations. From the point of view of graphical operations, the main advantage of the method is that the same logical statements can be used to compute the images of objects and to interpret graphical input in terms of the objects in the database. The method also makes the definition of parameterized objects as easy as that of constant objects. There is potential for extending this work to encompass more powerful object combination operations such as indefinite iteration and space-filling.

---

[8] Unix is a trademark of Bell Laboratories.

References

Applied Research of Cambridge. (1980). *General Drafting System, System Overview*, ref. no. GDS|S2. Cambridge, England.

Bijl, A. and J. Nash. (1981). "Progress on Drawing Systems." *Computer-Aided Design*, Vol. 13, No. 6, pp. 351–357 (November).

Braid, I.C. (1973). *Designing with Volumes* (Cantab Press, Cambridge, England).

Cardelli, L. (1981). "Sticks & Stones: an Applicative VLSI Design Language." Internal Report CSR-85-81, Dept. of Computer Science, University of Edinburgh, Scotland (July).

Cardelli, L. and G. Plotkin. (1981). "An Algebraic Approach to VLSI Design." *VLSI 81 International Conference*, Academic Press.

Clocksin, W.F. and C.S. Mellish. (1981). *Programming in Prolog*. Springer-Verlag, Berlin, West Germany.

Eastman, C.M. and M. Henrion. (1975). *GLIDE: A System for Implementing Design Databases*. Research Report 76, Institute of Physical Planning, Carnegie-Mellon University (December).

Giraud, C. (1982). *The Presque-Half Plane: Towards a General Representation Technique*. In preparation. Describes a new geometric modeling technique based on the combination of point set and edge representations.

Hopcroft, J.E. and J.D. Ullman. (1979). *Introduction to Automata Theory, Languages, and Computation* (Addison Wesley, Reading, Massachussets).

ISO Working Group TC97/SC5/WG2. (1982). "Graphical Kernel System (GKS) - Functional Description." ISO TC97/SC5/WG2 Document N117, International Standards Organisation (January).

Kowalski, R. A. (1980). *Logic for Problem Solving*. New York: North Holland.

Parsaye, K. (1983). "Database Management, Knowledge Base Management and Expert System Development in Prolog," *Proc. of 1983 ACM Database Week*, ACM.

Rosenthal, D.S.H. (1983). "Managing Graphical Resources," *Computer Graphics*, 17(1) pp. 38–45 (January).

Roussel, P. (1975). *Prolog: Manuel de Référence et Utilisation*. Technical Report, Groupe d'Intelligence Artificielle, Université d'Aix-Marseille II, Marseille, France.

Swinson, P.S.G. (1982). "Logic Programming - a Computing Tool for the Architect of the Future," *Computer-Aided Design*, Vol. 14, No. 2 (March).

Swinson, P.S.G., F.C.N. Pereira and A. Bijl. (1983). "A Fact Dependency System for the Logic Programmer." *Computer-Aided Design*, 15 (4), 235–243.

ten Hagen, P.J.W., T. Hagen, P. Klint, H. Noot, H.J. Sint and A.V. Veen. (1980). *Mathematical Centre Tracts*. Volume 130: *Intermediate Language for Pictures*, Amsterdam: Matematisch Centrum.

Warren, D.H.D., L.M. Pereira and F.C.N. Pereira. (1977). "Prolog—The Language and its Implementation Compared with Lisp," *SIGPLAN/SIGART Newsletter*, ACM Symposium on A.I. and Programming Languages (August).

CHAPTER 13

Experience with Specification and Verification of a Complex Computer Using Concurrent Prolog

Norihisa Suzuki

The University of Tokyo
Japan

1   Introduction

We will be putting very complex computer systems into chips that are only available in very large-scale mainframe computer systems today. In such VLSI (very large-scale integration) chips, sophisticated control structures like pipelines and concurrency that are useful in obtaining high performance will be used extensively. Even in conventional computers where debugging is easier, taking out all the bugs is a major problem. It was reported that a very complex memory system contained 50 bugs when the first breadboard model was created (Clark et al., 1981). Therefore, a very important issue in VLSI chip design is to take out all the bugs before the mask is produced so that we do not have to repeat the expensive process of mask design. An important step in creating a correct design is to generate functional specifications in a very high-level language and to debug these specifications against many test data. We developed a VLSI specification language called Sakura based on a highly-typed, algorithmic language Mesa (Mitchell et al., 1979). A detailed description of Sakura was reported previously (Suzuki and Burstall, 1981). In this paper we will take a very different approach to functional specification and verification; we use a more high-level, functional language, Concurrent Prolog. We specify a complex memory system of a high-performance personal computer, the Dorado (Lampson and Pier, 1981). We will describe techniques to specify hardware in Concurrent Prolog and discuss the comparison of these two experiences.

I had an opportunity to write microcode for an undebugged Dorado, which is a complex, pipelined computer (Lampson et al., 1981). When we encountered the most difficult bug, it took two of us three days to create a test case so that the bug was isolated and regenerated repetitively. The bug only appeared under the following circumstances: the instruction pipeline was first full, then it was emptied by a jump, and at the same time an interrupt occurred. We first noticed this bug only after running the most complex software system written for the computer; all the other programs including a compiler, an editor, and a loader could run successfully. This experience told us that it is extremely important to have a very large library of software to test new computers in order to make them reliable if we are to use conventional design and debug methodologies. Transistor-level logic simulation is much too slow for complete debugging of VLSI circuit design. Therefore, the only practical approach to create complex, reliable VLSI chips is to create a breadboard model using TTL circuits and to run the software on it. When we are convinced that the breadboard model works reliably, we can create a chip by directly converting TTL (transistor-transistor logic) circuits to corresponding MOS (metal-oxide-semiconductor) circuits.

This approach has been working so far but it limits the scope of VLSI chips in four ways:

1. It is a slow and expensive process, since we have to build a TTL prototype.
2. We cannot exploit all the potentialities of MOS circuits; path transistors will not be used. Therefore, the resulting chips can be large and inefficient.
3. Since prototypes are much larger than the chips and cannot be easily replicated, this approach does not work for multiprocessors.
4. If we are to build computers with new architecture, this approach may not usually be very effective, since we do not have a large library of programs.

The alternative approach we are taking is to use functional simulators. We specify the functionality of the computer in a high-level language; then, test programs are run on this functional specification. Since functional specifications are written at an abstract level they usually run much faster than the transistor-level logic simulators. Thus, we may be able to create VLSI chips without building breadboard prototypes.

Once the top-level protocols are rigorously defined, there are a number of ways to create masks that satisfy these protocols reliably. We are confident that design automation (DA) tools are becoming quite adequate for such tasks. Electric and timing characteristics of building blocks such as adders, shifters, and registers can be precisely obtained by advanced circuit simulation programs on supercomputers. The logical behavior of the entire chip can be rapidly obtained by the logic simulators.

Therefore, a major issue in creating complex VLSI chips is to give the top-level protocol specifications in a very high-level language and verify that the protocol specifications actually satisfy what we want.

We designed a VLSI modeling language called Sakura and specified a complex VLSI multi-microprocessor system (Suzuki and Burstall, 1981). Sakura is a derivative of a strongly-typed algorithmic language, Mesa (Mitchell et al. 1979).

We added several features that, we felt, are useful for hardware specifications. There have been few real attempts to use a strongly-typed language for hardware specification. Many errors, such as misconnections and underspecifications, were found at compile-time; we were very satisfied with the use of a strongly-typed language.

After the entire specification was written and was successfully compiled, we ran it with several test programs. We discovered a number of bugs in the specification, but most of them were introduced when the formal specification was created from the natural language prose specification.

Another lesson we learned from this exercise was that randomly created test data are not very useful. It is much more effective if we know the implementation, and select test data carefully so that critical logic can be tested often.

It is also very important to be able to observe internal states, since the input and output sequences do not often reveal errors. For example, a cache is considered incorrect if it contains two copies of the same main memory block. However, from the outside it is merely a somewhat inefficient cache.

On the other hand, as long as we rely on simulation, the hardware is just as good as the test data. This is the severe limitation of this methodology. Most of the widely used computers have hardware bugs; they occur sufficiently rarely that people are no longer bothered by the bugs. However, if we want to become perfect, the only technique theoretically known to take out all the bugs is verification. People think that this might be a good idea, and many efforts are spent to make verification practical; so far very few systems really work.

We will explore a methodology in between the functional simulation and the formal verification. We specify hardware just as in the formal verification. We give input and output assertions in predicate calculus. Then instead of showing that output assertions will be satisfied by hardware for all the inputs that satisfy input assertions, we only show that this relation holds for some selected inputs. We actually run the triple—input assertion, hardware specification, and output assertion—against test data. The advantage of this method over the functional simulation is that the output data is automatically checked for correctness. The advantage over the formal verification is that they can be executed so that we do not have to worry about inefficiencies of theorem-provers.

We chose Prolog as the language to write input and output assertions as well as hardware specifications. Prolog is the natural choice for writing executable assertions, since it is based on logic and much research has been done to create efficient and convenient Prolog programming systems. We actually used Concurrent Prolog (Shapiro, 1983), a derivative of Prolog developed by Ehud Shapiro; this language has multiprocessing primitives so that it is suited for description of hardware. Hardware specification is also written in Concurrent Prolog so that input and output assertions can be executed together with the hardware specification. Even though Prolog is used in much automatic programming research, we believe that our way of using Prolog is new. What we were doing is to execute requirement specifications, which are input and output assertions, together with implementation specifications, which are hardware specifications, on test data to check consistency. Because of the characteristics of Prolog, assertions can be executed directly. We chose the Dorado memory system as the target of specification (Clark et al., 1981). We selected it because the details of the implementation are published, it has a very complex memory system, and is implemented and widely used.

2   Brief Introduction to Concurrent Prolog

Concurrent Prolog is a superset of Prolog with multiprocessing features. These new features are:

2.1   Parallel And

Written as

$$P :- A \: // \: B.$$

A and B are executed concurrently; if both succeed, then P succeeds.

2.2   Communication

Communication among processes is accomplished by parameters. If two processes want to communicate, they have the same variables as the parameters. The direction of the information flow is one-way. The receiver of the information has read-only variables; they are distinguished by putting ? as a suffix, as in

$$A(X) \: // \: B(X?).$$

In this case the data is only passed from A to B. More than two processes can be the writers and readers. Writers have to write the same data; otherwise, the computation fails. The information is broadcast to all the receivers. Actual data are passed by queries. When B tries to know the information passed from A, it unifies some patterns against the input parameter X; if the unification is successful, B knows that the matched data is what was actually sent. If nothing is sent, B ought to be suspended. Therefore, processes are suspended when unification occurs with bound variables and unbound read-only variables. It is also possible to say

$$wait(X)$$

on a read-only variable X. The process will be suspended until X becomes bound.

2.3 Commit operator

The backtracking and parallel computation may cause quite undeterminable behaviors. During the computation of a predicate, several backtracks may take place; therefore, the values of parameters may change several times before they settle for the final values. Since the communication is done through parameters, other processes may obtain intermediate values, which may be quite different from the final values of the parameters. If this is allowed, the relative speed of the processes determine the result of computation: an undesirable characteristic for a concurrent language. In Concurrent Prolog, the control of backtracking is done by commit operators. The body of the predicate is separated into two parts by a commit operator "|" and any effects that happened before the commit operator will not appear to the outside through parameters. However, backtracking is free to occur before the commit operator without causing any effects to other processes. Once the commit operator is executed, the execution is deterministic; backtracking is not allowed.

3 Specification Methodology

Methods used to describe highly concurrent circuits are described. In this description we take the stand that the hardware is described hierarchically. At each level, the building components are called circuits, which are connected together by wires.

3.1 Circuits

Each circuit is represented by a predicate. Circuits communicate among themselves through wires. The wires are represented by the parameters of the predicates. Circuits have to receive an infinite chain of signals and produce an infinite chain of result signals. These infinite chains are represented by sequences.

Consider a circuit for generating error correcting codes. It is described by the following predicate ECGen:

```
ECGen([In | InTail], [Out | OutTail]) :-
    generate(In, Out), ECGen(InTail?, OutTail).
ECGen([], []).
```

ECGen receives a sequence of signals, the head of which is In, and produces a sequence of signals, the head of which is Out. Out is produced from In by the predicate generate, and the following signals are accepted by recursively calling ECGen. The fact that InTail is a read-only variable to this second call means that the call is held until some input comes in.

3.2   Representing semantics of hardware by timed-event history

We now have circuits and wires to represent the physical structure of hardware. If we provide a sequence of data at the input, we would obtain a sequence of data at the output.

This is not enough for hardware simulation. We need to represent timings. We need to capture the facts that data are coming at certain clock times and there are delays at each circuit, and some synchronization may take place because of these timings.

We first introduce a clock so that all the components operate at the same time. We describe how to implement a clock later. Then we can write a predicate describing a circuit's behavior at a certain time. We also attach a time to each datum in the input stream denoting the arrival of the datum. We also attach time to the data in the output stream.

In this way we can describe the behavior of a circuit by a timed input stream and a timed output stream. These are, however, not sufficient in most cases, because what is important is the internal behavior of circuits for a given input. That is the dataflow view of the circuits. Here is the input sequence. Each datum in the sequence may go through different subcomponents, or different events. We keep track of what events each datum went through at what time.

Instead of looking at the circuit as producing results, we look at a timed input sequence and an output sequence, each datum of which has a history of subcomponents it went through.

Then the description of ECGen may become as follows:

```
ECGen([],[],X).
ECGen(I,O,[Clock | NextClock]) :-
    wait(Clock),
    ECGenTail(I,O,[Clock|NextClock]).
ECGenTail([[In,InTime,InHistory]|InTail],
    [[Out,OutTime,OutHistory]|OutTail],[Clock|NextClock]) :-
    InTime>=Clock |
        generate(In,Out),
        OutTime is InTime+2,
        append(InHistory,[[ecGen,InTime,OutTime]],OutHistory),
        ECGen(InTail?,OutTail,NextClock).
ECGenTail(I,O,[Clock|NextClock]) :-
    ECGen(I?,O,NextClock).
```

The first statement of ECGen is the terminal condition. The second statement asks the clock to advance to the next tick, and waits until Clock holds the real time. Then it computes the error correcting code in ECGenTail when the right time comes. The first statement of ECGenTail shows that it takes a sequence of triples and produces a sequence of triples. The first element of the triple is the datum, the second is the arrival time of the datum, and the third is the history of events of this datum. In the body, first it checks whether the system time has come to the input time. If not, nothing is done because the checking is done before the commit operator. If the time has come, it computes the output data, the output time, and creates the output history and proceeds to accept the next datum by recursively calling ECGen. If the time has not come, it merely fails, and the second statement of ECGenTail is executed. It advances to the next time.

3.3   Parallel circuits

Circuits essentially operate in parallel; in order to represent these parallelisms we use the concurrency of Concurrent Prolog. Signals can be transmitted to concurrently running processes quite easily by supplying a sequence to all the processes that are connected. The output must, however, be merged to form a single output sequence. Consider for example a memory system consisting of two parts, one of which stores the lower half of the address space while the other stores the upper half. When one wants to access data, the fetch command with an address is sent to both modules and the data comes out from the one which holds it. This can be specified as follows:

```
System :-
    Processor(X) //
    Memory(0, 999, X?, Out1) //
    Memory(1000, 1999, X?, Out2) //
    Merge(Out1?, Out2?, Out).
```

The Memory is specified as:

```
Memory(Low, High, [Address | InTail], [[hit, Data]|OutTail]) :-
    Low<=Address, Address<=High |
      getResult(Address, Data),
      Memory(Low, High, InTail?, OutTail).
Memory(Low, High, [Address | InTail], [[miss, 0] | OutTail) :-
    Memory(Low, High, Intail?, OutTail).
Merge([[hit, Data1]|In1], [[miss, Data2]|In2], [Data1|Out]).
Merge([[miss, Data1]|In1], [[hit, Data2]|In2], [Data2|Out]).
```

3.4   Clock

Since the hardware system reports all the events by the time when they occur it is essential to have a clock. Once the clock is working and all the circuits can obtain the time, there would not be any scheduling problem, since each circuit looks at the time and is invoked at the right time.

The requirement for the clock is that it produces times continuously. In our system we would like a clock to be producing an infinite sequence of numbers: [0, 1, 2, . . .]. This may be a problem, since if the clock has too high a priority, it is taking up all the time producing a continuous sequence of numbers, so that other processes cannot proceed.

The solution to this problem shows a very clever use of Concurrent Prolog. Even though, the communication is one-way because of the read-only variables, one can actually transmit values back and forth. This is done by sending a skeleton from the sender to the receiver: then the receiver puts a value inside the skeleton. Using this technique, we make the clock to be the receiver of the skeleton. Other circuits need to look at the clock in order to tell the time. Whenever this happens, they send skeletons to the clock. The clock is suspended waiting for some request, and as soon as it receives a request it sends back the time. This is explained by the following example:

```
System :-
  Clock(X?) //
  Processor( . . . , X) //
  Memory( . . . , X) //
  IO( . . . , X).
```

Now the clock is defined as:

```
Clock(Time) :-
  ClockNext(0, Time).
ClockNext(S, [S | Tail) :-
  U is S+1,
  ClockNext(U, Tail?).
```

Each circuit has the following form:

```
Memory( . . . , [Time | T]) :- . . . .
```

Then the suspended ClockNext is invoked and fills in the time at the head of the list.

These are all the methodologies we used to describe the Dorado memory system.

4   Description of the Dorado Memory System

The Dorado is a high-performance personal computer designed and built at the Xerox Palo Alto Research Center (Lampson et al., 1981). Even though the Dorado is a personal computer, it uses the most sophisticated hardware technologies and mechanisms available only in today's large mainframe computers, such as ECL (emitter-coupled logic) logic and cache memory. Unlike most other cache memory systems, the Dorado cache retains written data as long as the cache block is not flushed out. Cache keys are virtual addresses so that the virtual address to real address translation takes place only when there is a cache miss.

The memory system is made up of pipeline stages and resources. Pipeline stages provide control and are organized into two pipelines: the cache pipeline and the storage pipeline. The cache pipeline consists of ADDRESS and HITDATA stages and the storage pipeline consists of MAP, WRITETR, STORAGE, READTR1, and READTR2 stages. The organization of these stages is shown in Figure 13.1.

Resources provide the data paths and memories. The major resources mentioned in this section are CacheA, CacheD, StoreReg, FetchReg, MapRAM, WriteReg, StorageRAM, and ReadReg.

4.1   Cache Pipeline

4.1.1 ADDRESS stage. Every memory reference is first handled by the ADDRESS stage. This stage checks whether the virtual address is in the cache; if it is, and the reference is a Fetch or Store, ADDRESS starts HITDATA. ADDRESS starts MAP, if a reference misses or is an I/O reference.

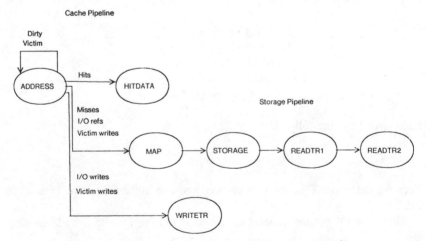

Figure 13.1. Organization of Cache and Storage Pipelines

4.1.2 HITDATA stage. The cache address is passed from ADDRESS; the HITDATA stage fetches a word from CacheD storage into FetchReg register if the reference is a Fetch and stores a word into CacheD from StoreReg register if the reference is a Store.

4.2   Storage Pipeline

4.2.1 MAP stage. The MAP stage translates a virtual address into a real address by looking it up in a hardware table called the MapRAM, and then starts the STORAGE stage. MAP takes 8 cycles to complete, but starts the STORAGE stage at the fifth cycle.

4.2.2 StORAGE stage. The STORAGE stage is started by MAP: it controls the StorageRAM. STORAGE receives 16 words from WRITETR through WriteReg and sends 16 words to READTR1/2 through ReadReg.

4.2.3 WRITETR stage. The WRITETR stage transports a block into WriteReg, either from CacheD or from an input device; it shares WriteReg with STORAGE. It is started by ADDRESS on every write, and synchronizes with STORAGE. The WRITETR takes at least 11 cycles; the next to last cycle waits until the third cycle of STORAGE is started.

4.2.4 READTR1 and READTR2 stages The read operation takes more than 8 cycles because it does error correction and data transport from ReadReg to cache. Therefore, it is split into two stages. On a read, READTR1 shifts words out of ReadReg and through the error corrector. READTR2 reports faults and completes cache read operations either by delivering the requested word into FetchReg (for a Fetch), or by storing the contents of StoreReg into the newly-loaded block in the cache (for a Store).

4.3   Concurrency Control

Since the memory system is pipelined, it is possible that more than one control stage is active. Special mechanisms are implemented to prevent multiple accesses to a single resource.

There are three mechanisms to prevent conflicts:

1.   The memory system rejects requests by asserting Hold, if the memory system cannot accept a new request.
2.   A reference waits in ADDRESS until its immediate resource requirements are met.
3.   All the remaining conflicts are dealt with in a single state of MAP.

The third stage of MAP, denoted as MAP.3 is the only stage to implement
interlocks. The conditions that MAP.3 waits are:

> WRITETR activated by the same reference to pass the fifth stage.
> If the previous reference is a clean miss and this reference is a clean miss,
> MAP.3 waits two cycles.
> When loading and unloading of CacheD occur, conflicts must be avoided.
> MAP.3 waits until WRITETR for dirty victim write reference is started.

5   Specification of the Dorado Memory System

We specified the Dorado Memory system described in Section 4 in Concurrent
Prolog using the techniques in Section 3. The whole specification is given in the
appendix. In this listing, we only treated Fetches and Stores; other types of
references can be accommodated very easily. We made some simplifications: the
cache memory is fully associative and the size of a block of cache is one word.
We have not treated the faults; in order to treat faults completely, the intermediate results in the pipeline have to be written in the register called history. Since
the description of the management of the history register is completely missing
from the report (Clark et al., 1981), we decided not to treat these cases.

The top-level predicate corresponding to the entire memory system is called
Memory. The description closely parallels the organization of the Dorado memory system control structure shown in Figure 13.1.

```
memory(InStream, OutStream) :−
    clock(S?) //
    addressHead(InStream, X1, S) //
    hitDataHead(X1?, O1, S) //
    mapHead(X1?, X2, 0, S) //
    writeTrHead(X1?, X2?, X5, S) //
    storageHead(X2?, X5?, X3, S) //
    readTr1Head(X3?, X4, S) //
    readTr2Head(X4?, O2, S) //
    merge2(O1?, O2?, OutStream).
```

The predicate clock is the same clock described in 3.4, and produces an infinite
sequence of numbers, [0, 1, 2, . . .]. The predicate merge2 merges the two
sequences O1 and O2 to produce the behavior of the system against the input
sequence: O1 is the cache hit sequence and O2 is the cache miss sequence. The
other seven predicates correspond to the pipeline stages.

The behavior of the Dorado memory system is described in the paper by
giving several examples, showing how data goes through pipeline stages. We
checked each case by giving an input sequence and an environment so that the

desired effects would occur. The output sequence was checked against the diagrams given in the report.

An interesting case is a dirtymiss because it is quite complicated. A dirtymiss occurs when a fetch or store misses a cache, and the cache is full. Then an empty space has to be made in a cache before a block can be brought in from the main memory. Therefore, a victim, the block to be emptied, is found; the victim has been written by the processor since it was brought in from the main memory, so the contents of the cache block is different from the corresponding location in the main memory. Therefore, the block is called dirty, and it has to be written back to the main memory. So a memory reference actually creates two data streams. From the description of the dirtymiss, it seems that the data stream of writing back the dirty victim should proceed before the data stream of reading in the target block. However, that sequence of steps has an unfortunate consequence that the data to be transferred to the processor comes out late. So in the actual implementation, the data stream to bring in the block from the main memory proceeds first.

We tested this case by supplying the input sequence

[[fetch, 15, _, 0]].

The environment has been set up so that this will cause a cache miss, and the victim is dirty. Then the output is

[[address, 0, 0],
[map, 1, 8],
[storage, 6, 13],
[readtr1, 13, 20],
[readtr2, 20, 27]],
[[address, 1, 8],
[map, 9, 16],
[writetr, 2, 17],
[storage, 14, 21],
[readtr1, 21, 28],
[readtr2, 28, 35]].

This has the same behavior as the one described in the Dorado report; thus, we verify the specification for this particular case.

6 Conclusion

A functional description of a complex memory system of a high-performance personal computer was written in Concurrent Prolog. The input and the output assertions were also written in Concurrent Prolog so that the consistency between implementation specifications, functional specifications, requirement specifications, and input and output assertions are checked by running the program with some data.

Since we showed that we can write functional specifications using a general purpose language, it is not necessary to create a special purpose functional simulation language. It is very important and useful to write requirement specifications, when we are to create rigorous, reliable functional specifications. One can find out logical flaws in writing requirement specifications. What is more important is that we can easily check the consistency between two specifications by executing them so that bugs are discovered at the early stages of design.

Using Concurrent Prolog for functional specifications is new. We found several advantages of Concurrent Prolog for such purposes. First of all, it is very easy to write and debug Concurrent Prolog programs. It is like writing Lisp, but one can use pattern-matching and backtracking. We wrote the Dorado specification in a week; it took us about a month to describe a memory system of similar complexity in Sakura. The majority of time was spent in debugging when we used Sakura, because we had to rely on the Mesa debugger, which does not have a good debugging facility for concurrent programs. In the future, a crucial factor in the cost of VLSI chip development will be the amount of time taken for design. The use of Concurrent Prolog may well be very important in such circumstances.

There are a couple of drawbacks in using the current Concurrent Prolog system. One drawback is that the language does not have the flexibility of Lisp, so that the user cannot manipulate processes in his programs. Therefore, he cannot write schedulers himself. This prevented us from writing a more sophisticated simulation system. Right now, all the circuits are watching the clock tick by tick, and perform the operation on data when the time comes that is written on the data. This might be quite inefficient if the number of ticks that each circuit has to wait is very large. One can avoid this in a truly time event driven simulator in which each circuit tells the scheduler when it wants to perform an operation. The scheduler has an access to such information for all the circuits, and it essentially gives a control to the circuit which wants to perform the earliest. When the control comes back, it gives the control to the next earliest process. Sakura was implemented this way. In order to achieve this in Concurrent Prolog, we need to write a scheduler, which knows how many processes are running, and which processes should be run next. This, I believe, can be done in Concurrent Prolog, but not without writing a lot of programs.

The second drawback is that the current implementation of Concurrent Prolog is very slow and space-consuming. Research in creating an optimizing compiler following D. Warren (1977) is crucial.

The other drawback is that an efficient random access storage mechanism does not exist. We need such a feature to simulate the storage system of the computer systems. We represented a random access storage by a predicate and used asserta and remove predicates to cause side-effects. This, however, causes sequential search, and can potentially be very inefficient.

Acknowledgment

The author is grateful to Mr. Takeuchi of ICOT for introducing me to and letting me use Concurrent Prolog.

References

Clark, D. W. et al. (1981). *Memory System of a High-Performance Personal Computer*. Technical Report CSL-81-11, Xerox Palo Alto Research Center (January).

Lampson, B. W. and Pier, K. A. (1981). *A Processor for a High-Performance Personal Computer*. Technical Report CSL-81-1, Xerox Palo Alto Research Center (January).

Lampson, B. W. et al. (1981). *Instruction Fetch Unit for a High-Performance Personal Computer*. Technical Report CSL-81-1, Xerox Palo Alto Research Center, (January).

Mitchell, J. G. et al. (1979). *Mesa Language Manual*. Technical Report CSL-79-3, Xerox Palo Alto Research Center (April).

Shapiro, E. Y. (1983). *A Subset of Concurrent Prolog and Its Interpreter*. ICOT Technical Report TR003 (February).

Suzuki, N. and Burstall, R. (1981). "Sakura: a VLSI Modelling Language." *Proc. Conf. on Advanced Research in VLSI*, Dedham, MA: Artech House.

Warren, D. H. D. (1977). *Implementing Prolog—Compiling Predicate Logic Programs*. DAI Research Report 39–40, University of Edinburgh (May).

Appendix: Program Listing

```
memory(InStream, OutStream) :-
   clock(S?) //
   addressHead(InStream, X1, S) //
   hitDataHead(X1?, O1, S) //
   mapHead(X1?, X2, O, S) //
   writeTrHead(X1?, X2?, X5, S) //
   storageHead(X2?, X5?, X3, S) //
   readTr1Head(X3?, X4, S) //
   readTr2Head(X4?, O2, S) //
   merge2(O1?, O2?, OutStream).

addressHead([], [], [Time|Tail]).
addressHead(Itail, Otail, [Time|AS]) :-
   wait(Time),
   address(Itail, Otail, [Time|AS]).
```

```
address([[Command,Va,Idata,Itime]|Itail],Otail,[Time|AStail]) :-
  Time)=Itime|
    stAddrTime(Itime,StartTime),
    finAddrTime(StartTime,Otime),
    call(cacheSearch(Va,Result,Addr)),
    print('***address time='), print(Time), print(' '), print(Result),
    print(' CacheAddrIs='), print(Addr), nl,
    nextAddress([Command,Va,Idata],Result,Addr,Itime,Otime,Itail,
      Otail,AStail).
address(I,O,[Time|S]) :- addressHead(I?,O,S).

nextAddress(Instr,hit,Addr,Itime,Otime,Itail,[[Instr,hit,Addr,Otime,
    [[address,Itime,Otime]]]|Otail],AStail) :-
  print([[address,Itime,Otime]]),nl,
  addressHead(Itail?,Otail,AStail).
nextAddress(Instr,cleanmiss,Addr,Itime,Otime,Itail,[[Instr,cleanmiss,
    Addr,Otime,[[address,Itime,Otime]]]|Otail],AStail) :-
  print([[address,Itime,Otime]]),nl,
  addressHead(Itail?,Otail,AStail).
nextAddress(Instr,dirtymiss,Addr,Itime,Otime,Itail,
    [[Instr,cleanmiss,Addr,Otime,[[address,Itime,Otime]]],
    [Instr,dirtymiss,Addr,VicItime,
      [[address,VicItime,VicOtime]]]|Otail],AStail) :-
  VicItime is Otime+1,
  addressHead(Itail?,Otail,Astail).

hitDataHead([],[],[Time|HS]).
hitDataHead(I,O,[Time|HS]) :-
  wait(Time),
  hitData(I?,O,[Time|HS]).

hitData([[[fetch,Va,Idata],hit,Addr,Itime,History]|Itail],
    [[[fetch,Va,Idata],Odata,OHis]|Otail],[Time|HStail]) :-
  Time)=Itime|
    Otime is Itime+1,
    cacheVec(Addr,_,Odata,_),
    print('*** hitData time='), print(Time), nl,
    append(History,[[hitData,Itime,Otime]],OHis),
    print(OHis), nl,
    hitDataHead(Itail?,Otail,HStail).

hitData([[[store,Va,Idata],hit,Addr,Itime,History]|Itail],
    [[[store,Va,Idata],[],OHis]|Otail],
    [Time|HStail]) :-
  Time)=Itime |
    Otime is Itime+1,
```

```
            call(setCacheVec(Addr,Va,Idata,false)),
            print('*** hitData time='), print(Time), n1,
            append(History,[[hitData,Itime,Otime]],OHis),
            print(OHis), n1,
            hitDataHead(Itail?,Otail,HStail).
hitData([_|Itail],[[misses]|Otail],[Time|HStail]) :-
    hitDataHead(Itail?,Otail,HStail).
hitData(I,O,[Time|S]) :-
    hitDataHead(I?,O,S).


mapHead([],[],MapLastBusy,[Time|HS]).
mapHead(I,O,MapLastBusy,[Time|T]) :-
    wait(Time),
    map(I,O,MapLastBusy,[Time|T]).

map([[Instr,hit,Addr,Itime,History]|Itail],
        [[Instr,hit,_,_,_,_,[hit]]|Otail],MapLastBusy,
        [_|MStail]) :-
    mapHead(Itail?,Otail,MapLastBusy,MStail).
map([[[Command,Va,Idata],Miss,Addr,Itime,History]|Itail],
        [[[Command,Va,Idata],Miss,Ra,Addr,Fault,Otime,OHis]|Otail],
        MapLastBusy,[Time|MStail]) :-
    Time)=Itime |
        mapTime(Itime,MapLastBusy,MapItime,Otime).
        call(mapSearch(Va,Fault,Ra)),
        print('*** map time='), print(Time), print(' RA='), print(Ra), n1,
        makeMapHis(History,Miss,MapItime,Otime,OHis),
        mapHead(Itail?,Otail,Otime,MStail).
map(I,O,MapLastBusy,[Time|S]) :- mapHead(I?,O,MapLastBusy,S).

makeMapHis(His,cleanmiss,I,O,OHis) :-
    append(His,[[map,I,O]],OHis).
makeMapHis([[address,AI,AO]],dirtymiss,I,O,[[address,AI,AO],[map,I,O]])
    :- AO is I-1.

mapTime(Itime,MapLastBusy,MapItime,Otime) :-
    max(Itime,MapLastBusy,MapSt),
    MapItime is MapSt+1,
    storageLastBusy(Map3Wait),
    OutMapStTime is MapSt+8,
    OutMap3Wait is Map3Wait+5,
    max(OutMapStTime,OutMap3Wait,Otime).

mapSearch(Va,false,Va).

storageHead([],[],[],[Time|HS]).
```

```
storageHead(M,W,O,[Time|T]) :-
  wait(Time), storage(M,W,O,[Time|T]).

storage([[Instr,hit,Ra,Addr,Fault,MapTime,MapHistory]|MapTail],
    [_|WriteTrTail],
    [[Instr,hit,Ra,Addr,Fault,ReadReg,_|[[ignore]]]|Otail],
    [_|SStail]) :-
  storageHead(MapTail?,WriteTrTail?,Otail,SStail).
storage([[Instr,dirtymiss,Ra,Addr,Fault,MapTime,MapHistory]|MapTail],
    [[Instr,WriteReg,_,WriteTrHistory]|WriteTrTail],
    [[Instr,dirtymiss,Ra,Addr,Fault,Readreg,Otime,OHis]|Otail],
    [Time|SRtail]) :-
  Itime is MapTime-2, Time)=Itime |
  setMemory(Ra,WriteReg),
  Otime is MapTime+5,
  append(WriteTrHistory,[[storage,Itime,Otime]],OHis),
  print('*** storage write time='), print(Time), nl,
  print(OHis), nl,
  storageHead(MapTail?,WriteTrTail?,Otail,SRtail).
storage([[Instr,cleanmiss,Ra,Addr,Fault,MapTime,MapHistory]|MapTail],
    [_|WriteTrTail],
    [[Instr,cleanmiss,Ra,Addr,Fault,ReadReg,Otime,OHis]|Otail],
    [Time|SRtail]) :-
  Itime is MapTime-2, Time)=Itime |
  getMemory(Ra,ReadReg),
  Otime is MapTime+5,
  append(MapHistory,[[storage,Itime,Otime]],OHis),
  print('*** storage read time='), print(Time), a1,
  print(OHis), nl,
  storageHead(MapTail?,WriteTrTail?,Otail,SRtail).
storage(M,W,O,[Time|S]) :- storageHead(M?,W?,O,S).

getMemory(Addr,Val) :- Val=Addr.

setMemory(Addr,Val).

readTr1Head([],[],[Time|Tail]).
readTr1Head(I,O,[time|T]) :-
  wait(Time), readTr1(I,O,[Time|T]).

readTr1([[Instr,Result,Ra,Addr,Fault,ReadReg,Itime,History]|Itail],
    [[Instr,Result,Ra,Addr,Fault,ReadReg,Otime,OHistory]|Otail],
    [Time|R1Stail]) :-
  Time)=Itime |
  Otime is Itime+7,
```

```
        append(History,[[readtr1,Itime,Otime]],OHistory),
        print('*** readtr1 time='), print(Time), nl,
        print(OHistory), nl,
        readTr1Head(Itail?,Otail,R1Stail).
readTr1(I,O,[Time|S]) :— readTr1Head(I?,O,S).

readTr2Head([],[],[Time|[]]).
readTr2Head(I,O,[Time|T]) :—
   wait(Time), readTr2(I,O,[Time|T]).

readTr2([[[fetch,Va,Idata],Result,Ra,Addr,Fault,ReadReg,Itime,History]
        |Itail],
        [[[fetch,Va,Idata],Result,Ra,Addr,Fault,ReadReg,Otime,OHis]|Otail],
        [time|R2Stail]) :—

   Time)=Itime |
      Otime is Itime+7,
      call(setCacheVec(Addr,Va,ReadReg,false)),
      append(History,[[readtr2,Itime,Otime]],OHis),
      print('*** readtr2 fetch time='), print(time), nl,
      print(OHis), nl,
      readTr2Head(Itail?,Otail,R2Stail).
readTr2([[store,Va,Idata],Result,Ra,Addr,Fault,ReadReg,Itime,History]
        |Itail],
        [[[store,Va,Idata],Result,Ra,Addr,Fault,ReadReg,Otime,OHis]|Otail],
        [Time|R2Stail]) :—
   Time)=Itime |
      Otime is Itime+7,
      call(setCacheVec(Addr,Va,Idata,true)),
      append(History,[[readtr2,Itime,Otime]],OHis),
      print('*** readtr2 store time='), print(Time), nl,
      print(OHis), nl,
      readTr2Head(Itail?,Otail,R2Stail).
readTr2(I,O,[Time|S]) :— readTr2Head(I?,O,S).

setCacheVec(Addr,Va,Data,Dirty) :—
   retract(cacheVec(Addr,_,_,_)),
   asserta(cacheVec(Addr,Va,Data,Dirty)).
setCacheVec(Addr,Va,Data,Dirty) :—
   asserta(cacheVec(Addr,Va,Data,Dirty)).

writeTrHead([],[],[],[Time|HS]).
writeTrHead(I,M,O,[Time|T]) :—
   wait(Time), writeTr(IM,MO,[Time|T]).

writeTr([[Instr,dirtymiss,Addr,Itime,History]|I],
```

```
      [[Instr,dirtymiss,Ra,Addr,Fault,MapTime,MapHis]|M],
      [[Instr,WriteReg,Otime,OHis]|O],
      [Time|T]) :-
    WrItime is Itime+1,Time)=WrItime |
      cacheVec(Addr,_,WriteReg,_),
      Otime is MapTime+1,
      print('*** writetr time='), print(Time), nl,
      append(MapHis,[[writetr,WrItime,Otime]],OHis),
      print(OHis), nl,
      writeTrHead(I?,M?,O,T).
writeTr([[_, hit | _] | I], [_| M], [_| O], [_| T]) :-
    writeTrHead(I?, M?, O, T).
writeTr([[_, cleanmiss | _] | I], [_| M], [_| O], [_| T]) :-
    writeTrHead(I?, M?, O, T).
writeTr(A, M, O [Time | S]) :-
    writeTrHead(A?, M?, O, S).

merge2([[misses] | A], [B | C], [B | O]) :-
    merge2(A?, C?, O).
merge2([D | A], [B | C], [D | O]) :-
    merge2(A?, C?, O).
merge2([], [B | C], [B | O]) :-
    merge2([], C?, O).

clock(Cardinals) :-
  clockNext(O, Cardinals).
clockNext(S, [S | Tail]) :-
  U is S+1,
  print(' >> Time is '), print(S), nl,
  clockNext(U, Tail?).
clockNext(S, []).

stAddrTime(Itime, StartTime) :-
  addrTime(LastAddrTime),
  LastAddrTime1 is LastAddrTime+1,
  max(Itime, LastAddrTime1, StartTime).

finAddrTime(St, Fin) :-
  Fin is St,
  retract(addrTime(_)),
  asserta(addrTime(Fin)).

init :-
  asserta(cacheSize(O)),
  asserta(storageLastBusy(O)),
```

```
        asserta(victimAddr(O)),
        asserta(addrTime(O)).

   max(A, B, A) :− A >= B | true.
   max(A, B, B) :− B> A.

   cacheSearch(Va, hit, Addr) :−
      cacheVec(Addr, Va, Data, Dirty).
   cacheSearch(Va, Result, Addr) :−
      nextVicitm(Addr),
      call(victimState(Addr, Dirty)),
      call(cleanOrDirty(Dirty, Result)).

   victimState(VictimAddr, Dirty) :−
      cacheVec(VictimAddr, _, _, Dirty).
   victimState(_, false).

   cleanOrDirty(true, dirtymiss).
   cleanOrDirty(false, cleanmiss).

   nextVictim(Addr) :−
      retract(victimAddr(X)),
      X1 is X+1,
      cacheSize(CacheSize),
      Addr is X1 mod CacheSize,
      asserta(victimAddr(Addr)).

   dorado(In, Out) :− init, memory(In, Out).

   test :−
      dorado([[fetch,15,_,O], [fetch,16_,5], [store,17,_,15]], X),
      write(X).
```

CHAPTER 14

Application of Meta-Level Programming to Fault Finding in Logic Circuits

Kave Eshghi

Logic Programming Group
Department of Computing
Imperial College of Science and Technology
London, England

1   Introduction

FAULTFINDER is a program that diagnoses faults in combinatorial digital circuits. It relies on the input-output behavior of the circuit to achieve this, without requiring access to the circuit elements directly.

In FAULTFINDER, fault diagnosis is viewed as a special case of induction. The goal is to derive the theory of the faulty circuit. The point of departure is the theory of the normal circuit, which is known beforehand. FAULTFINDER devises a set of experiments on the faulty circuit which enable it to derive the theory of this circuit from the theory of the normal circuit. Throughout this process, it uses some assumptions about the nature of 'possible faults' to limit its search.

2   The setup of the faultfinding process

2.1   The objective

There exists a digital circuit whose internal organization (circuit diagram) is known. This circuit develops a fault which causes it to misbehave.

It is required to locate the fault by devising a set of experiments and conducting them on the circuit. The program should devise the experiments, and draw the necessary conclusions from the results of the experiments to find the fault.

2.2   The circuit

The circuit is a combinatorial logic circuit, with a number of input terminals, and a number of output terminals. Only these terminals are accessible to the experimenter. By combinatorial we mean that the circuit does not include any memory elements, so that the state of the output is uniquely determined by the input.

2.3   Faults

Faults are assumed to arise from faulty gates only. It is further assumed that there is only one faulty gate in the circuit.

We assume that a faulty gate has its output 'stuck'; in other words, the output is always the same, independent of the inputs to the gate.

2.4   Experiments

An experiment consists of setting up the input terminals of the circuit to a certain combination, and observing the state of the output terminals.

3   Logic programs as theories of circuit modules

In order to reason about the behavior of circuit modules, they must be represented by a data structure that reflects their internal structure and modes of behavior.

In FAULTFINDER, circuit modules are represented by object level programs. These programs are called the theories of the corresponding circuits.

A theory, T, of a circuit, C, consists of three subtheories:

a.   Description of the circuit (D)
b.   Truth tables of the gates (TB)
c.   General laws of logic circuits (G)

3.1   The Description of a Circuit Module (D)

D is a set of assertions that describes the internal structure of the circuit model, its inputs and its outputs.

The gates of the module are named by a set of names. The input and output terminals of the gates, as well, are labled by a set of names. These labled terminals are called the nodes of the circuit, as shown in Figure 14.1.

Example: In C1

A,B,C,K,E,F,O are nodes,
G1 and G2 are AND gates,
G3 is an OR gate,
A,B are the input nodes of G1,

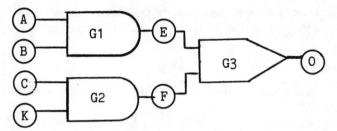

Figure 14.1. The schematic diagram of C1, showing the nodes

E is the output node of G1,
A,B,C,K are the input nodes of C1
O is the output node of C1

D is the description of a circuit iff:
For every gate in the circuit it includes an assertion such as

> GATE(gate-name, gate-type, input-nodes, output-node)

where:

> *gate-name* is the name of the gate,
> *gate-type* is the type of the gate (AND, OR etc.)
> *input-nodes* is a list of the input nodes of the gate,
> *output-node* is the output node of the gate.

It includes an assertion such as

> INPUT-NODES(i),

where i is a list of the input nodes of the circuit;
It includes an assertion such as

> OUTPUT-NODES(o),

where o is a list of the output nodes of the circuit. e.g., this is a description of C1

```
GATE(G1, AND, A.B.NIL, E);
GATE(G2, AND, C.K.NIL, F);
GATE(G3, OR, E.F.NIL, O);
INPUTNODES(A.B.C.K.NIL);
OUTPUTNODES(O.NIL);
```

3.2   The Truth Tables (TB)

TB is a subtheory that specifies the truth tables of the gates in the circuit.
The four place relation

TABLE(gate-name, gate-type, input-list, output)

is used for representing the truth table of a gate. In the above relation,

gate-name is the name of the gate;
gate-type is the type of the gate (AND, OR etc.);
input-list is the list of the states of the input nodes of the gate;
output is the state of the output.

TB has the following property: [|- is the provability relation]
For every gate g in the circuit,

TB |- TABLE(g, gate-type, input-list, output) iff

when the input specified by *input-list* is applied to the gate named by g, the
output that results is the same as *output*. For example, for a normal AND gate
named G,

TB |-TABLE(G,AND,H.H.NIL,H)

etc.
Notice that we must be able to represent faulty gates as well as normal gates.
Thus TB has a set of assertions which specify which gates are normal and which
faulty. These points are discussed in more detail in section 6.

3.3   The General Laws of Logic Circuits (G)

Every node in the circuit can be in one of two states: High or Low. G defines the
relationship between the states of the nodes in terms of their interconnection
through the gates. In particular, the state of the output nodes in terms of the states
of the input nodes are derivable from G.
The main predicate of G is

PREDICT(input-nodes, input-states, output-nodes, output-states)

where:

input-nodes is the list of the input nodes of the circuit,
input-states is the list of the states of these nodes;

output-nodes is the list of the output nodes of the circuit, and *output-states* is the list of the states of these nodes.

Here is a listing of G; it is the same for all circuits.

```
PREDICT(input-nodes, input-states, NIL, NIL);
PREDICT(input-nodes, input-states, node.restnodes, state.reststates)⟨−
        SINGLE-NODE-PREDICT(input-nodes, input-states, node, state),
        PREDICT(input-nodes, input-states, restnodes, reststates);

SINGLE-NODE-PREDICT(input-nodes, input-states, node, state)⟨−
        MEMBER-OF(input-nodes, node),
        STATE-OF(input-nodes, input-states, node, state);
SINGLE-NODE-PREDICT(input-nodes, input-states, node, state)⟨−
        GATE(gate-name, gate-type, gate-input-nodes, node),
        PREDICT(input-nodes, input-states, gate-input-nodes, gate-input-states),
        TABLE(gate-name, gate-type, gate-input-states, state);

MEMBER-OF(x.rest,x);
MEMBER-OF(x.rest,y)⟨-MEMBER-OF(rest,y);

STATE-OF(node.restnodes, state.reststates, node, state);
STATE-OF(x.restnodes, y.reststates, node, state) ⟨−
        STATE-OF(restnodes, reststates, node, state);
```

4   Some Terminology

4.1   Input Term

The input term is the term I(input-nodes, input-states) where *input-nodes* is the list of the input nodes and *input-states* is the list of the states of these nodes.

4.2   Output Term

The output term is a term such as O(output-nodes, output-states) where *output-nodes* is the list of the output nodes of the circuit and *output-states* is the list of the states of these nodes.

4.3   Outcome of an experiment

O is the outcome of the experiment E(I) if I is an input term, O is an output term, and when the inputs nodes of the circuit are set to the states specified in I the output O is observed.

4.4   IO Pairs

(I,O) is an IO pair for the circuit C if I is an input term, O is an output term, and the outcome of the experiment E(I) on the circuit C is O.

4.5   Predicts

The theory T predicts the pair

> (I(input-nodes,input-states),O(output-nodes, output-states)) iff
> T|- PREDICT(input-nodes, input-states, output-nodes, output-states)

4.6   Discriminating Input

I is a discriminating input for the theories T1 and T2 iff:

> T1 predicts (input-nodes,I,output-nodes,O1)
> T2 predicts (input-nodes, I, output-nodes,O2)
> O1 is different from O2 in the state of at least one node.

5   Hypothesizing about the location of faults

One way to view the fault finding process is as a process whereby a theory of the faulty circuit, T', is derived from the known theory of the normal circuit, T. The technique used here to derive T' is a variant of the hypothesize and test paradigm.

Let C be the normal circuit, and T its associated theory. The faulty circuit, C', is identical with C, except for the fault in it. It is required to derive T', which is a theory of C', from T by experimenting on C'.

Let (If,Of) be a known faulty input output pair for C'. By faulty we mean that had the experiment E(If) been conducted on the normal circuit C, the outcome would have been different from Of.

The steps involved in the derivation of T' are as follows:

a.   from T and (If,Of) construct H, the set of hypotheses for the faulty circuit, such that :
   • all the hypotheses in H predict (If,Of);
   • H is guaranteed to include the theory of C'.
   We call H the hypothesis set.
b.   Devise a discriminating input, Id for two elements of H
c.   make the experiment E(Id) on the circuit C' and observe the outcome Od

d. remove from H all the hypotheses that do not predict (Id,Od)
e. repeat from b until the hypothesis set contains just one hypothesis, or a discriminating input can not be found at step b.

Since H is guaranteed to include the theory of the faulty circuit, T', if at the end of this algorithm only one element remains in H, then it must be T'. It is possible, however, that no discriminating input exists for two members of H (i.e., they predict identical outputs for all input combinations). In this case, H will contain two or more hypotheses, which cannot be reduced by experimenting on the circuit.

Example: Assume that C1 develops a fault. Let us call this faulty circuit C1', to distinguish it from the normal circuit.

Assume that when the input nodes of C1' are set to the combination shown in Figure 14.2, we observe the output depicted. In our terminology, we say that the outcome of the experiment

$$E(I(A.B.C.K.NIL, H.H.H.L.NIL))$$

is

$$O(O.NIL,L.NIL),$$

and that

$$(I(A.B.C.K.NIL,H.H.H.L.NIL), O(O.NIL,L.NIL))$$

is a faulty IO pair for the circuit C1'.

The first step in the fault finding process is the construction of the hypothesis set. To do this, we try to predict the output shown above from the input, and analyze the unsuccessful attempt in order to derive the hypothesis set. Thus we run the goal

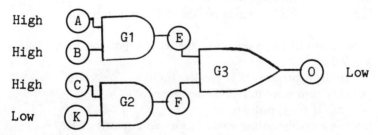

Figure 14.2. The schematic diagram of C1', showing the faulty input output

<-DEMO(D+TB+G, 'PREDICT(A.B.C.K.NIL,H.H.H.L.NIL,O.NIL,L.NIL)' ,**trace**)

and analyze **trace**. [**trace** is the trace of the unsuccessful attempt to prove the above. The form of the trace, and the way it is analyzed, will be discussed in more detail later.]

From this analysis, we conclude that there are two hypotheses which 'explain' the faulty input-output pair observed. These hypotheses are:

a.   The gate G3 is faulty, and its truth table is TABLE(G3,OR,x,L) (i.e. its output is 'stuck' at Low).
b.   The gate G1 is faulty, and its truth table is TABLE(G1,AND,x,L)

Next, a discriminating input is devised. In this case, a discriminating input is

I(A.B.C.K.NIL,L.L.H.H.NIL)

It is a discriminating input because if hypothesis (a) were true, then the application of this input to the circuit would result in the output being low, whereas if the hypothesis (b) were true, then its application would result in the output being high.

The discriminating input is applied to the circuit, and the output observed. We call this experiment a discriminating experiment. Assume that the output terminal is high after the application of the discriminating input.

Following the experiment, all the hypotheses that do not predict its outcome are rejected. Here hypothesis (a) does not predict the observed outcome of the experiment, and it is removed from the hypothesis set. Since only one hypothesis remains in the hypothesis set at this stage, namely hypothesis (b), (b) is the theory of the faulty circuit, $C1'$.

6   Constructing the Hypothesis Set

The hypothesis set contains a set of hypotheses, or prospective theories, of the faulty circuit, C'.

Every element of the hypothesis set must have the following properties:

- It must predict the faulty input-output pair (If,Of);
- It must include the D and G subtheories intact (this is due to the fact that, by assumption, a fault cannot change the structure of the circuit or the general laws of logic circuits)
- It must include a subtheory such as TBf from which the truth tables of all the gates are derivable. Furthermore, since we assume that only one gate is

faulty, the truth tables derived from TBf must be identical with those derived from TB except for the one relating to one of the gates.

The hypothesis set is built in two steps:
Step 1. Try to prove

PREDICT(input-nodes,input-states, output-nodes, faulty-output)

from T and obtain the trace of the unsuccessful attempt,
Step 2. Analyze the trace and propose modifications to T that would make the proof successful. Put the modified instances of T in H.

Explanation of step 1: Step one is straightforward except that to make the analysis at step two possible a particular subgoal selection strategy must be followed. This strategy is:

Never choose a truth table goal for expansion as long as other goals are present in the goal set. [Truth table goals are those whose predicate is TABLE.]

Thus at one stage in the proof, the goal set will contain only truth table goals.

Explanation of step 2: The proof tree is scanned until the point is reached where the goal set contains nothing but truth table goals. Let us call this set of truth table goals B.

Obviously, if B were provable from TB, PREDICT would be provable from T. We know that TB can yield the truth tables of all gates in C' but one. It is the job of the Hypothesizer to find out which gate this one can be, and alter TB in a way that reflects this.

The algorithm for constructing the hypothesis set is as follows:

1. Pick one of the goals in B and call it g. Call B-g B'
2. Prove B' from TB. Call the substitution obtained **alpha**. If proof is unsuccessful skip to 6
3. Apply **alpha** to g. Call the resulting goal g'
4. Modify TB so that g' is provable from it. Call the resulting subtheory TBf. (the way this is done is explained in the subsection 6.1)
5. Add D+G+TBf to the hypothesis set
6. Start from the beginning, picking another goal this time. Continue in this way until all the goals in B have been chosen.

Example: We use the same example as was used in section 4.
When the proof of

<-PREDICT(A.B.C.K.NIL,H.H.H.L.NIL,O.NIL,L.NIL)

from the theory of C1 is attempted, at one stage we will have the goals

<--TABLE(G1,AND,H.H.NIL,x),TABLE(G2,AND,H.L.NIL,y),
TABLE(G3,OR,x.y.NIL,L)

Obviously this set of goals cannot be proved from TB. (Try it if you do not believe this!)

This is how FAULTFINDER produces the hypotheses that were mentioned earlier:

1. select a goal in this set. e.g. TABLE(G1,AND,H.H.NIL,x). Call it g. Call the remaining goals B'.
   [Here B' is TABLE(G2,AND,H.L.NIL,y),TABLE(G3,OR,x.y.NIL,L)]
2. Prove B' from TB. Call the substitution employed **alpha**. Here alpha is (y/L,x/L)
3. apply **alpha** to g. Call the resulting goal g'. Thus we apply (y/L,x/L) to TABLE(G1,AND,H.H.NIL,x) and obtain TABLE(G1,AND,H.H.NIL,L)
4. Modify TB so that g' is provable from it. Add the resulting theory to the hypothesis set. This would be the hypothesis (b) in this example.
5. start from 1 again, this time choosing a different goal, e.g. TABLE-(G2,AND,H.L.NIL,y) etc.

6.1   Deriving the Hypothetical Truth Tables

TB, which is the subtheory that contains the truth tables of the gates, is listed below:

TABLE(g,AND,H.H.NIL,H)<-NORMAL(g)
TABLE(g,AND,H.L.NIL,L)<-NORMAL(g)
TABLE(g,AND,L.H.NIL,L)<-NORMAL(g)
TABLE(g,AND,L.L.NIL,L)<-NORMAL(g)

TABLE(g,OR,H.H.NIL,H)<-NORMAL(g)
TABLE(g,OR,H.L.NIL,H)<-NORMAL(g)
TABLE(g,OR,L.H.NIL,H)<-NORMAL(g)
TABLE(g,OR,L.L.NIL,L)<-NORMAL(g)

and similarly for normal NOT, NAND, NOR gates.

TB contains the following clauses for defining the truth tables of faulty gates:

TABLE (gate,type,input,H)<-STUCK-AT-HIGH(gate);
TABLE (gate,type,input,L)<-STUCK-AT-LOW(gate);

TB also includes assertions about the status of the gates, i.e. whether they are normal, stuck-at-high or stuck-at-low. For the normal circuit, we would have assertions such as

NORMAL(G1);
NORMAL(G2); etc.

for all the gates.

Recall that to generate a hypothesis, we need to modify TB such that a certain truth table goal, as determined by the process described in the previous section, is provable from it. At the same time, we want the truth tables for all the other goals to remain unaltered.

In accordance with the assumption we have made about the nature of the faults occurring in a gate, which limits us to stuck-at faults, to alter TB in the manner described above it is sufficient to delete the normality assertion for the gate concerned, and add either a STUCK-AT-HIGH assertion or a STUCK-AT-LOW assertion for the gate. Which of the above we add depends on whether we have a high or a low in the output of the truth table goal.

Example: Consider the step 4 in the previous example [modify TB such that g' is provable from it etc.]. Here we want to modify TB such that the goal

<-TABLE(G1,AND,H.H.NIL,L)

is provable from it. To do this, we delete the assertion

NORMAL(G1)

and add STUCK-AT-LOW(G1)

7   Devising a Discriminating Input

Take two elements of the hypothesis set, h1 and h2. We want an input term, Id, such that:

h1 predicts (Id, O1), and
h2 predicts (Id, O2),

where O1 and O2 are output terms, and the state of at least one of the output nodes is different in O1 and O2.

The discriminating input for h1 and h2 is devised by running the meta-level goal:

<-- DEMO(h1,'PREDICT(input-nodes,input-states,output-nodes,O1)',trace1),
    DEMO(h2,'PREDICT(input-nodes,input-states,output-nodes,O2)',trace2),
    DIFFERENT('O1','O2', trace1, trace2);

where *input-states* is a variable, and similarly, O1 and O2, which stand for the output states, are variables.

On successful execution of the above goals, the variables in *input-states*, O1 and O2 would get bound. The substitution would be recorded in trace1 and trace2. (note: at the meta-level constants stand for object level variables.)

The bound instance of the *input-states* so attained is a discriminating input for the whole circuit.

In order to speed up the above search, we fail without further computation the cases where both the hypotheses are being invoked in a way that the inputs to the suspect gates are nondiscriminating with respect to the outputs of those gates and the nature of the suspected faults. For example, the input L.H.NIL is non-discriminating for the fault TABLE(G,AND,x,L), because the output that we get for this input is the same as that for a normal AND gate.

8   Conclusion

We have demonstrated how the ideas of meta-level programming, i.e. programs as data structures, proof analysis, control of the proof process, etc., can be used for implementing a nontrivial diagnosis program. As such, FAULTFINDER is a successful instance of the application of the mixed (object-level + meta-level) logic programming method (Kowalski, 1979). Its practical utility, however, is restricted by the range of circuits it can handle, and the assumptions it makes about the nature of the faults.

FAULTFINDER was implemented in Micro-Prolog, running on a CP/M-based microcomputer (Mc.Cabe, 1980). The versatility and power of this language, considering the restricted hardware on which it was run, was surprising indeed.

Since at present no 'proper' amalgamated object-level and meta-level programming system exists, this effect was simulated by using the "meta-variable" facility of Micro-Prolog.

References

Kowalski, R. (1979). *Logic For Problem Solving*. Chapter 12. Artificial Intelligence Series 7 the Computing Science Library, North Holland Inc.

McCabe, F. (1980). *Micro-PROLOG Programmer's Reference Manual*. Imperial College, London, England.

PART V
NATURAL LANGUAGE

Focalizers, the Scoping Problem, and Semantic Interpretation Rules in Logic Grammars

Michael C. McCord

Computer Science Department
University of Kentucky
Lexington, Kentucky 40506*

1   Introduction

The term **grammar** (for natural language) is being used here in the broad sense of a formal system which relates the written or spoken form of a language to its semantic representation. There may or may not be an intermediate level of syntactic representation. If there is, then the grammar has a syntactic component, which relates written or spoken form to syntactic structures, and a semantic interpretation component, which relates syntactic structures to their semantic representations.

A **logic grammar** is a grammar expressed entirely in predicate logic. All the rules of the grammar are logical formulas, and semantic representation is logical form. Logical inference is used to relate textual form to semantic representation. Typically, the grammar rules are expressed in the Horn clause subset of logic (Kowalski, 1979), making the requisite inference more amenable to efficient computer processing. Thus a logic grammar can be viewed as a particular sort of **logic program.**

The work in logic grammars described in this paper is especially related to work by Colmerauer (1978, 1979), Colmerauer and Pique (1980), Kowalski (1979), Dahl (1979, 1980, 1981), and Pereira and Warren (1980). It is used in subsequent joint work with Dahl (Dahl and McCord, 1983). It is implemented in the logic programming language Prolog (Roussel, 1975), specifically, in Prolog-10 (Pereira, Pereira, and Warren, 1978), a very efficient version of Prolog for the DEC-10, with a compiler as well as an interpreter.

This paper deals with certain extensions and improvements of a logic gram-

---

* New address: IBM Thomas J. Watson Research Center, P.O. Box 218, Yorktown Heights, New York 10598.

mar reported on in McCord (1982). This system (both in its earlier and its current form) uses intermediate syntactic representations. The improvements reported on here involve the semantic interpretation rules and the things they relate (syntactic structures and logical forms). The syntactic rules of the system have been modified to some extent, but they will not be dealt with here. The semantic interpretation component can be understood independently; and in fact the current paper can be read more or less independently of the previous one.

A major advantage of separating semantic interpretation rules from syntactic rules is that the difficult problem of **scoping** can be dealt with in a more isolated fashion. It is well known that a sentence like

Somebody loves everybody

can have different readings (different logical forms) depending on whether 'somebody' or 'everybody' is understood as having the wider scope. The view taken here is that the **same** syntactic structure (and the same parsing path) is involved in both of these readings ('somebody' is the subject of 'loves', 'everybody' is the object, etc.); and from this syntactic structure the semantic interpretation rules can produce the most likely reading or even all of the readings. Our rules use heuristics to produce a single, "most likely" reading. (For the above example, 'everybody' is given wider scope in spite of the fact that it occurs last.) The current rules consider only the sentence in isolation: but in a more complete system, the whole discourse structure should be considered. However, a point is that, when considering the various scoping alternatives, one should not have to reparse the sentence for each case.

The problem of scoping involves much more than the quantifiers like 'every', 'some', and 'many' that appear as determiners in noun phrases. In fact, on every level of the sentence, all of the constituents (or **modifiers** as they are called in this system), for example adverbials and adjectivals, enter into the scoping problem, and may have roles in the semantic representation which do not correspond directly to their positions in syntactic structure.

Of special interest for this paper are the scoping problem and semantic representation for a class of modifiers I will call **focalizers.** These include

1. quantificational determiners like 'all', 'some', 'most', 'many', 'few', and 'no'.
2. quantificational adverbs like 'always', 'sometimes', 'usually', 'often', 'seldom', and 'never'.
3. the adverbs 'only', 'just', 'also', 'too', and 'even'.
4. certain discourse-functional modifiers dealing with topic/comment, yes/no questions, contrast, etc.

Section 2 of the paper (**Focalizers**) is devoted to a discussion of these modifiers, their semantic representations, and what they have in common. Briefly, though, the reason for the name 'focalizer' is that the scope of such a modifier involves an element called its **focus,** which is often correlated with sentence stress.

Section 3 deals with the **Semantic interpretation rules,** the form of the syntactic structures they deal with, and the way they handle the scoping problem, especially for focalizers.

An **Appendix** includes a complete listing of the semantic interpretation rules.

2   Focalizers

In the semantic representation proposed in this paper, all of the modifiers called **focalizers,** of the four types listed in the Introduction, will be higher-order predicates with two arguments, called the **base** and the **focus** of the focalizer:

focalizer(Base,Focus).

The base and the focus are open sentences. The pair (Base,Focus) is called the **scope** of the focalizer.

The best examples to begin with are the quantificational adverbs: 'always', 'often', etc. The analysis of these adverbs adopted here is essentially the same as that proposed by David Lewis (1975). (See also the treatment of Aqvist, Hoepelman and Rohrer, 1980.) Lewis argues convincingly that these adverbs are not in general quantifiers over times (as their root meanings suggest), or quantifiers over events, but are quantifiers over **cases,** where cases are tuples of values of the free variables appearing in their scopes. They are **unselective** quantifiers, in that they bind whatever free variables are in their scopes, not just a selected variable.

For example, consider the sentence

Leopards often attack *monkeys* in trees.

Here the focus of 'often' is 'monkeys', as is indicated by the stress. Under one reading, the base comes from the remainder of the sentence, and the quantification is over cases of leopard attacks in trees, with the assertion that in a "large" percentage of these cases, the attack is on a monkey. Our logic grammar can analyze this sentence, and produces essentially the following:

often(leopard(X)&tree(Z)&attack(E,X,Y)&in(E,Z), monkey(Y)).

Here 'often' quantifies over four variables: X, Y, Z, and the event variable E for the verb 'attack'.

Where we write

quantifier(Base,Focus)

Lewis (1975) writes

$$\text{quantifier} + \text{(if Base)} + \text{Focus}$$

but that is only a notational difference. (Lewis intends this as a special three-part form distinct from

$$\text{quantifier} + \text{(if Base then Focus).)}$$

A contribution of the present work is an actual grammar that can deal with an interesting range of sentences involving these adverbs and other focalizers, especially considering the problem of variation of scope.

For the same sequence of words making up a sentence, the focus (and hence the scope) of a quantificational adverb may vary:

> Leopards often attack monkeys in *trees*.
> often(leopard(X)&monkey(Y)&attack(E,X,Y), tree(Z)&in(E,Z))
>
> *Leopards* often attack monkeys in trees.
> often(monkey(Y)&tree(Z)&attack(E,X,Y)&in(E,Z), leopard(X))

In each of these examples, the focus is indicated by stress (underlining in the text) and the base (in the reading given) comes from the remainder of the sentence. In general, though, the focus may be determined in other ways (by our system) and the base may be less than the remainder.

A rough approximation to the meaning of often(Base,Focus) is as follows: Let B be the number of cases where Base is **true** and Focus is **defined** (has no presupposition failures), and assume B is finite. Let BF be the number of cases where Base&Focus is **true.** Then the meaning is that the ratio BF/B is "large." Similar (rough) analyses for the other quantificational adverbs can be given in terms of the ratio BF/B. For instance, 'always' requires that (BF/B)=1. Further comments on the meanings of focalizers will be given at the end of this section.

Let us now turn to the quantificational determiners ('all', 'some', 'most', etc.). In calling these 'focalizers', I am in particular saying that they have *two* arguments, their **base** and their **focus,** and they are unselective quantifiers. For example, my analysis of

> All people like Mary.

is (essentially)

> all(person(X), like(E,X,mary)).

Typically, the base comes from the remainder of the noun phrase in which the determiner appears, and the focus comes from some of the sisters of the noun phrase.

The most standard analysis in the literature (e.g., Woods et al., 1972; Colmerauer, 1979; McCawley, 1981) is with a selective, *three*-place quantifier, e.g.,

$$all(X, person(X), like(X,mary))$$

where the first argument is the selected variable for quantification. (We neglect here the problem of the event variable for 'like'.) Analysis with the classical universal quantifier (a different sort of two-place predicate) is well known to be inadequate.

A compelling reason for the analysis of quantificational determiners as two-place, unselective quantifiers, and more generally for viewing them as focalizers, is that there is a neat correspondence between certain quantificational determiners and certain quantificational adverbs:

all	— always
some	— sometimes
no	— never
many	— often
most	— mostly, usually
few	— seldom

in the sense that all(Base,Focus) means essentially the same thing as always(Base,Focus), etc. This sort of correspondence has been pointed out by Altham and Tennant (1975). Examples of paraphrases are

Leopards seldom attack monkeys in *trees*.
Few leopard attacks on monkeys are in trees.

Leopards always attack *monkeys* in trees.
All leopard attacks in trees are on monkeys.

Leopards often attack monkeys in trees.
Many attacks on monkeys in trees are by leopards.

Now let us look at the focalizers listed as class (3) in the Introduction ('only', 'even', etc.). One might call these **emphatic** adverbs, because they place a special emphasis on their foci (uniqueness, unexpectedness, etc.). They show the same dependence on focus as quantificational adverbs, and our logical forms appear as follows

Leopards only attack monkeys in *trees*.
only(leopard(X)&monkey(Y)&attack(E,X,Y), tree(Z)&in(E,Z))

Leopards even attack monkeys in trees.
even(monkey(Y)&tree(Z)&attack(E,X,Y)&in(E,Z), leopard(X))

John only saw *Mary*.
only(see(E,john,Y), Y=mary)

Note that the arguments (base and focus) of these predicates are taken uniformly here to be open sentences. (In the last example, the focus is not the term 'mary', but the formula Y=mary.) The focus may come from disconnected parts of the sentence, with the resulting formula being a conjunction:

> (Who bought what for the party?)
> *John* only bought *beer*.
> only(buy(E,X,Y), X=john&beer(Y))

This can happen as well for the quantificational adverbs.

The sense of 'only' used in the above examples can be described roughly by saying that only(Base,Focus) presupposes that there is a case for which Base&Focus holds and asserts that for each case for which Base holds, Focus also holds. (Here the term 'case' is being used in the sense of Lewis described above.) This formulation is close to the formulation of Horn (1969) and even closer to a formulation of Bergmann (1981), but it is one sense more general, because of the unselective quantification. (Bergmann has a formal semantic treatment using a two-dimensional logic to handle the presuppositions.) There is another sense of 'only' (appearing in 'John only *likes* Mary'), but I will not comment here on its meaning or the meanings of the other emphatic adverbs.

The discourse-functional focalizers are for the most part **abstract** (in the sense of not corresponding to lexical items), and they are therefore more controversial. The current grammar deals with only three of them, 'dcl', 'yesno', and 'wh', occurring, respectively, in the logical forms of declarative, yes/no, and wh-sentences. I believe, however, that there are more of them, dealing for example with contrast and with abstract versions of 'even' and 'only'.

In a sentence of the form

> dcl(Base, Focus)

the pair Base/Focus is intended to be what is sometimes meant by Topic/Comment. The simplest informal description is that the Topic is a formula identifying what the sentence "is about", and the Comment adds information to this. Examples are

> The King of France is bald.
> dcl(def(X,king(X,france)), bald(X))

> (John visited several people yesterday.)

> At 3:00, he visited Mary.
> dcl(visit(E,john,Y), time(E,3:00)&Y=mary)

The topic (base) of a 'dcl' form is always a presupposition of that form: but it need not exhaust all the presuppositions of the sentence, because there may be other focalizers present. A property shared by all focalizers is that they presuppose their bases (with free variables considered existentially quantified). For example, we have the analysis

> The King of France visited each country.
> dcl(def(X,king(X,france)), all(country(Y), visit(E,X,Y)))

in which the focus of 'dcl' has a further focalization (by 'all') which has its own presupposition (that there exist countries).

In the above examples, we are translating definite noun phrases with the predication def(X,P), which asserts that there is a unique X such that P (and which is considered to bind X to this unique object). We do not view def(X,P) as itself presupposing the existence or uniqueness of X. Such a presupposition can occur, however, if the definite form is within the base of a focalizer, such as 'dcl'. This agrees with (and generalizes) observations by Strawson (1950, 1964) and by McCawley (1981). In the first of the two sentences

> The King of France visited the exhibition.
> The exhibition was visited by the King of France.

the normal reading (with 'the King of France' as topic) does presuppose a (unique) king of France; but the second (with the normal reading, where there is a different topic) does not presuppose this.

The focalizers 'yesno' for yes/no questions and 'wh' for wh-questions have much in common with 'dcl'. For each of these, the base can still be called topic, and the focus is something asked about the topic. Examples are

> Did John see *Mary?*
> yesno(see(E,john,Y), Y=mary)
>
> Is the King of France bald?
> yesno(def(X,king(X,france)), bald(X))
>
> Who did John see?
> wh(see(E,john,X), name(X))

A feature of the system discussed here is that discourse focalizers are treated on a par with other grammatical entities by the semantic interpretation rules, and enter into the determination of scoping by these rules.

The main concern of this paper is the form of the semantic representation language for natural language and the rules for producing semantic representations of English sentences, with special attention to the scoping problem. A complete treatment must of course give a precise specification of the meaning of the semantic representation language itself. In discussing focalizers above, I have given some rough indications of what I have in mind for their meanings, but there are many interesting and difficult problems to solve.

Two of these are the treatments of presuppositions and of fuzziness. For both of these problems (which interact) it may be appropriate to use multivalued logic. In this direction, ideas of Colmerauer (1979), Colmerauer and Pique (1980), Zadeh (1978, 1981), Lakoff (1972) and McCawley (1981) are relevant. However, the successes and promises of multivalued logic are not completely clear; and there are some advantages, in the case of presuppositions, in an approach which manipulates and exhibits presuppositional formulas explicitly. I intend to investigate these alternatives in later work.

3   Semantic interpretation rules

The semantic interpretation rules are used to associate logical forms of sentences with syntactic structures of sentences. Let us look first at the format for syntactic structures. This is a modification of the format used in McCord (1982).

A syntactic structure is a tree, each node of which is represented by a term of the form:

syn(Features,Operator,Marker,Predication,Modifiers).

We call these **syntactic items** ('syn's). Here (1) **Features** is a list of (mainly) syntactic and morphological features of the node. (2) **Operator** is a term used in a crucial way by the semantic interpretation rules for determining how the given syntactic item acts as a modifier of other items. (3) **Marker** is a term which is used only by the syntactic rules and is important in slot-filling. (4) **Predication** is the central predication of the item, associated for example with the head verb in a verb phrase. (5) **Modifiers** is the list of all daughters of the item, given in their textual left-to-right order. (These are again 'syn's.)

The difference between this representation and that of McCord (1982) lies in the two fields Operator and Marker. Previously, these were lumped into a single field called the Determiner. In addition, in the case of noun phrases, the Determiner contained information from the lexical determiner of the noun phrase. For generality, the lexical determiner must be treated as a syntactic item in its own right, because it can be modified by other items (as in 'almost all men').

Since the marker is not used at all by the semantic interpretation rules, we will omit it in most of the following discussion, and pretend that 'syn' structures have only the four other fields.

As an example, the syntactic rules produce the following tree for the sentence 'The man saw John'. (In the display of a 'syn' tree, the Features, Operator, and Predication are printed on one line, and the daughter nodes are displayed below and indented.

```
[s,prop,dcl] | true
    [np,def,sg] num(sg) man(X)
        [detph,nil,sg] @P def(X,P)
    [mood,dcl] Q≪R dcl(Q,R)
    [advc,tense] r past(E)
    [verb,head,fin(sg,past)] | see(E,X,Y)
    [np,def,sg] num(sg) Y=john
```

In this example, the operators are the terms l, num(sg), @P, Q≪R, etc. Currently there are ten different types of operators in the system; they will be discussed below. The logical form produced from this example is

$$dcl(def(X,man(X)), see(E,X,john)\&past(E)).$$

As in McCord (1982), semantic interpretation proceeds in two stages: (I) The syntactic structure tree is **reshaped** into another tree "with the same nodes," but with (possibly) different sister and daughter relationships. More precisely, the nodes in the reshaped tree are again 'syn's and there is a one-to-one correspondence between the node sets of the two trees such that corresponding nodes are the same, except possibly in their last (Modifiers) field. The reshaped tree reflects the proper scoping of all modifiers. (II) To the reshaped tree, a procedure 'translate' is applied, which produces the logical form. As each modifier (node of the reshaped tree) is called upon by 'translate', the Operator field of the modifier, as well as that of the modificand, is used in building a new logical form.

The point of view in these two stages is that the scoping problem is concentrated entirely in the first (reshaping) stage. This stage can be viewed as a sort of "correction" of the scoping which is already implicit in the syntactic structure. For sentences that are "nicely expressed" enough, reshaping makes no changes or few changes. For the example displayed above ('The man saw John'), the only change made is that the 'np' node for 'John' is moved to become a left sister of the 'tense' node, and this actually has no effect in the final logical form. The 'translate' procedure could apply to the original syntactic structure and produce the same result.

Since reshaping is ancillary to 'translate', it will be best to give details of 'translate' first. The main idea is straightforward. Any 'syn' node can be translated to logical form as follows: Its modifiers (daughters) are translated recursively, and these translations then modify its predication, with the leftmost acting as the outermost modifier, etc.

The terms that get built up by this processing of a 'syn' tree are not simply logical forms, but are actually pairs of the form

Operator-LogicalForm.

(We use the infix operator '-' to form the pairs.) These pairs, we call **semantic items.** New operators can get created by old operators during the translation, and these are carried along in these pairs. This is a feature of the current system which is different from that in McCord (1982).

The key work for 'translate' is done by three subprocedures, 'transmod', 'transmods', and 'trans'. Their meanings are as follows:

1. transmod(Syn,Sem1,Sem2) means that when syntactic item Syn is translated and then modifies semantic item Sem1, the result is semantic item Sem2.
2. transmods(Syns,Sem1,Sem2) means that when all syntactic items in the list Syns are translated and then modify semantic item Sem1, the result is semantic item Sem2.
3. trans(Sem0,Sem1,Sem2) means that when semantic item Sem0 modifies semantic item Sem1, the result is semantic item Sem2.

The top-level procedure, 'translate', associates with a syntactic item Syn its logical form LogForm. It does this by calling upon 'transmod' to make Syn modify a trivial top-level semantic item l-true, producing a preliminary logical form LogForm0. Then this is **simplified** to produce LogForm, by removing trivial conjunctions with 'true' and by making substitutions associated with certain predications of the form variable=constant in LogForm0. (Not all of these produce substitutions; for instance, if they are foci, they do not.)

The definitions of these procedures can be seen in the Appendix, which contains the complete listing of the semantic interpretation rules. The heart of the translation method is in the procedure 'trans', which determines the way a single semantic item modifies its parent. If the modifying item is Op0-P0 and the parent is Op1-P1, then 'trans' relates these two items to a third item Op2-P2, which is the "modified version" of the parent. In many cases, Op0 is the key to the operation and Op2 is left the same as Op1. But, in general, the result may depend on both Op0 and Op1, and Op2 can be a newly created operator. Thus, in general one should think of the modifier "combining" with its parent. Let us now discuss the various operators explicitly.

(1) Operator 'l' stands for 'left conjoin'. Its 'trans' clause

trans(l-P,Op-Q,Op-(P&Q))

means that when l-P modifies Op-Q, the result is Op-(P&Q). Note that the result keeps the same operator Op as the modificand. The operator 'l' is associated for example with the main verb of a clause.

(2) 'r' stands for 'right conjoin'. This is the obvious variant of 'l'. It is associated with certain adjectives and adverbs.

(3) num(N), where N=sg or N=pl, is the operator for noun phrase 'syn's. It currently acts the same as 'l', but in future use there may be other rules involving it. If the noun phrase has a determiner, this operator can get replaced by an operator resulting from the determiner's operator.

(4) For subst(X), the result is like the modificand with the modifier's logical form substituted for the variable X. This is used for clause and verb phrase complements.

(5) 'id' is the identity operator. It is used for "empty" items like existential 'there'.

(6) For @P, the result is (normally) Op-Q, where Q is the modifier's logical form, Op is the modificand's operator, and the logical form of the modificand is substituted for the variable P (which normally appears in Q). An example of this is for the determiner 'the', which as a semantic item is @P-def(X,P).

The remaining operators are associated with focalizers.

(7) P/Q is used for quantificational determiners. For example, 'all', as a semantic item, is P/Q-all(Q,P). When P/Q-R operates on Op-S, S gets unified with Q, and the result is @P-R. (Op is lost.) Thus, when P/Q-all(Q,P) operates on num(pl)-man(X), as it would for 'all men', the result is @P-all(man(X),P).

(8) P<Q is used for all the adverbial focalizers. For example, 'often', as a semantic item, is (P<Q)-often(P,Q). The notation P<Q is meant to suggest that the base P lies to the left of the focalizer and the focus Q lies to the right. In fact the focalizer acts somewhat like a left-associative infix operator. The action of this operator is best understood from an example given below (and from the 'trans' clauses that define it).

(9) P≪Q is used for the abstract discourse focalizers. For example, 'dcl', as a semantic item, is (P≪Q)-dcl(P,Q). This is much like P<Q, but it behaves differently when there are other focalizers to the right, acting more like a *right*-associative infix operator. This will appear in the example below.

(10) Finally, base(Op,R,P) is an operator created by the focalizer operators P<Q and P≪Q. It is used to "save" the information in R and P until the base of the creating focalizer has been determined, at which time P is unified with this base. This is also illustrated in the following example.

Let us take the sentence

The man saw only Mary.

Reshaping actually does not change the syntactic structure tree at all. For the sake of brevity, we exhibit this tree with the nodes already expressed as semantic items.

$$l\text{-true} \qquad\qquad (1)$$
$$\text{num(sg)-man(X)}$$
$$@P\text{-def(X,P)}$$
$$(Q \ll R)\text{-dcl(Q,R)}$$
$$r\text{-past(E)}$$
$$l\text{-see(E,X,Y)}$$
$$(S < T)\text{-only(S,T)}$$
$$\text{num(sg)-(Y=mary)}$$

Then, to illustrate the workings of the 'translate' stage, we show successive transformations of this tree, corresponding to the actual succession of calls to 'trans'. The reader should refer to the 'trans' rules in the Appendix, which are numbered for reference in the following.

In the first call, the rightmost modifier of the top node—represented by the last line in (1)—operates on the top node by the twelfth 'trans' rule. This modifier has done its work, and we now display the tree with this modifier removed and the top node modified:

$$l\text{-(Y=mary)\&true} \qquad\qquad (2)$$
$$\text{num(sg)-man(X)}$$
$$@P\text{-def(X,P)}$$
$$(Q \ll R)\text{-dcl(Q,R)}$$
$$r\text{-past(E)}$$
$$l\text{-see(E,X,Y)}$$
$$(S < T)\text{-only(S,T)}$$

Next the 'only' node operates on the top node by the third 'trans' rule, giving:

$$\text{base(l,only(S,Y=mary\&true),S)-true} \qquad\qquad (3)$$
$$\text{num(sg)-man(X)}$$
$$@P\text{-def(X,P)}$$
$$(Q \ll R)\text{-dcl(Q,R)}$$
$$r\text{-past(E)}$$
$$l\text{-see(E,X,Y)}$$

Note that information is saved in the operator ('base') itself. Next the 'see' node operates on the top node by the sixth, and recursively the tenth, 'trans' rules, with the result:

$$\text{base(l,only(S,Y=mary\&true),S)-see(E,X,Y)\&true} \qquad\qquad (4)$$
$$\text{num(sg)-man(X)}$$
$$@P\text{-def(X,P)}$$
$$(Q \ll R)\text{-dcl(Q,R)}$$
$$r\text{-past(E)}$$

By the eleventh rule we get:

$$base(1,only(S,Y=mary\&true),S)-see(E,X,Y)\&true\&past(E) \qquad (5)$$
$$num(sg)-man(X)$$
$$@P-def(X,P)$$
$$(Q\ll R)-dcl(Q,R)$$

The second rule gives:

$$base(l,dcl(Q,only(see(E,X,Y)\&true\&past(E), \quad (top \qquad (6)$$
$$Y=mary\&true)),Q)-true \quad (node$$
$$num(sg)-man(X)$$
$$@P-def(X,P)$$

In the next call, the 'def' node operates on the 'man' node by rule 9, giving:

$$base(l,dcl(Q,only(see(E,X,Y)\&true\&past(E), \qquad (7)$$
$$Y=mary\&true)),Q)-true$$
$$num(sg)-def(X,man(X))$$

Then the single remaining modifier of the top node acts by rules 6 and 12 to give:

$$base(l,dcl(Q,only(see(E,X,Y)\&true\&past(E), \qquad (8)$$
$$Y=mary\&true)),Q)-def(X,man(X))\&true$$

Next, 'translate' lets this node modify a trivial top-level item, l-true. Rules 7 and 10 apply, and the result is

$$l-dcl(def(X,man(X))\&true,only(see(E,X,Y)\&true\&past(E), \qquad (9)$$
$$Y=mary\&true))\&true$$

Finally, 'translate' calls 'simplify', producing the logical form

$$dcl(def(X,man(X)), only(see(E,X,Y)\&past(E),Y=mary)). \qquad (10)$$

Now let us look at the 'reshape' procedure, where the scoping problem is tackled. The overall action of 'reshape' is the same as in McCord (1982) and involves two kinds of movements of nodes: (1) left-right shuffling of sisters, and (2) raising or promotion of some of the daughters of a node to sisters of that node. The recursive relation

$$reshape(Tree,Sisters,Tree1)$$

means that, for a given Tree, Tree1 is the reshaped tree with promoted Sisters. (For the top-level Tree, Sisters will be empty.)

The raising of nodes is needed mainly because some noun complements are "out of place," as in 'the king of each country', where the complement 'each country' needs to be promoted to left sister of 'the king'. This action is essentially the same as in McCord (1982), and will not be discussed in detail here.

As can be seen in the defining clause for 'reshape' in the Appendix, the daughters Daus of the root node of the Tree to be reshaped are themselves reshaped recursively (by 'reshapelist'), giving a modified list of daughters Daus1. Then this list is **reordered** by two procedures 'reorder1' and 'reorder2'. These are the main steps of interest here in the scoping problem and will be discussed below, as will the auxiliary procedure 'flatten'. Then raising is performed on the daughters and the new tree Tree1 is formed.

Reordering of the modifier list depends on two factors. One is the association of (heuristic) **precedence numbers** with modifiers, such that items with higher precedence tend to go to the left. All precedence reordering is done by 'reorder1'. This mechanism is essentially the same as in McCord (1982). The other factor is the notion of **capturing,** whereby one modifier "captures" others, and the group move all the way to the right. This is currently applied only to focalizers; a focalizer can 'capture' its focus elements. Capturing is done by both 'reorder1' and 'reorder2'.

In writing the clauses that determine precedence numbers of 'syn's and the clauses that determine when a 'syn' can capture another 'syn', one would be free to have these clauses look at any aspects of the 'syn's involved—the features, the operator, the marker, the predication, or even the modifiers. However, currently these clauses look only at the features—in fact, only at two particular features. One is the (phrasal) **category** of the 'syn' (such as 'np', 'verbph', etc.); this is picked out by the relation 'cat'. The other feature is the 'stype' (meant to suggest "scoping type"). In fact, all the precedence numbers are determined from the 'stype' by unit clauses for the relation 'prec1', which one can examine in the Appendix.

The focus of a focalizer can be determined either by 'capturing' or by just wherever the focalizer ends up through the action of precedence ordering. For example, for the sentence

Americans often like Venice.

no capturing takes place. The syntactic structure produced by the grammar is the following tree:

```
[s,prop,dcl] | true
   [np,indef,pl] num(pl) american(X1)
   [mood,dcl] X2≪X3 dcl(X2,X3)
```

```
[advc,tense] r present(X4)
[advph,advq(often)] X5<X6 often(X5,X6)
[verb,head,fin(pl,present)] I like(X4,X1,X7)
[np,def,sg] num(sg) X7=venice
```

Thus the order of the top-level syntactic elements is in abbreviated form:

[americans,dcl,present,often,like,venice].

After reshaping due to reordering, the tree becomes

```
[s,prop,dcl] I true
   [mood,dcl] X1≪X2 dcl(X1,X2)
   [np,def,sg] num(sg) X3=venice
   [np,indef,pl] num(pl) american(X4)
   [advph,advq(often)] X5<X6 often(X5,X6)
   [advc,tense] r present(X7)
   [verb,head,fin(pl,present)] I like(X7,X4,X3)
```

Thus the ordering is, in abbreviated form:

[dcl,venice,americans,often,present,like].

The logical form produced from this by 'translate' is

dcl(true,often(american(X),like(E,X,venice)&present(E))).

For the sentence

Often Americans like Venice.

the syntactic structure is of course different, but reordering produces the very same result as it did for the preceding sentence, and hence the same logical form. Again, no capturing takes place.

On the other hand, for the sentence

Only Americans like Venice.

the focalizer 'only' captures 'Americans' as a focus and the pair [focalizer,focus] moves to the end. Combined with other reordering by precedence, this produces the reordering

[dcl,venice,present,like,only,americans].

(Of course the original, correct slot-filler relations are not disturbed by the reordering: 'americans' is still the subject of 'like', etc.) The logical form produced from this is

$$dcl(true,only(like(E,X,venice)\&present(E),american(X))).$$

In the present system, capturing can take place in two ways. One is through the procedure 'lcapture' (the 'l' is for 'left'), whereby certain items (like 'only' and 'even') can capture certain other items (like noun phrases) which are either immediately to the right or possibly follow after some abstract (non-lexical) items. This sort of capturing is tested for by 'reorder1' before any items to the right have been moved by precedence reordering, because "immediately to the right" refers to the original textual order.

The other sort of capturing is of stressed items (indicated by underlining in the text). This sort of capturing is done by 'reorder2', after the precedence reordering. Stressed items are given a very low precedence and they tend to move to the right and get captured by focalizers. In general, rightmost "capturers" get a chance to make captures first. In the present system, the rightmost focalizer (after precedence reordering) that has not made captures will capture all stressed items.

In order to keep track of captures that have already been made (so that the same item will not get captured twice), the list [capturer|capturees] is placed at the end of the list of daughters (as a single list element). The purpose of the procedure 'flatten' is to replace these lists by the elements they contain, after all the reordering and raising of a level has been done.

The scheme for semantic interpretation described here covers a fairly wide range of examples. In general, the grammar is an extension of the grammar in McCord (1982), designed now to include focalizers. Constructions handled by the grammar include a wide variety of verb and noun complements (through slot-filling), adjunct modifiers (like adverbials for verb phrases and relative clauses and participial clauses for noun phrases), possessive noun phrase premodifiers of noun phrases, passivization, and unbounded left-movement for wh-clauses, topicalization, and relative clauses. See McCord (1982) for more details.

However, much research remains to be done on the scoping problem, especially on the question of the choice of foci, and on the use of discourse structure. Hopefully, the present system can serve as a good basis for further work.

References

Altham, J. E. J. and N. W. Tennant. (1975). "Sortal quantification." In E. L. Keenan (Ed.), *Formal Semantics of Natural Language*. Cambridge University Press.

Aqvist, L., J. Hoepelman, and C. Rohrer. (1980). "Adverbs of frequency." In C. Rohrer (Ed.), *Time, Tense, and Quantifiers*. Niemeyer, Tubingen.

Bergmann, M. (1981). "*Only, even*, and clefts in two-dimensional logic." *Proc. Eleventh Int. Symposium on Multiple-Valued Logic*, pp. 117–123. Univ. of Oklahoma.

Colmerauer, A. (1978). "Metamorphosis grammars." In L. Bolc (Ed.), *Natural Language Communication with Computers*. New York: Springer-Verlag.

Colmerauer, A. (1979). "Un sous-ensemble interessant du francais." *R.A.I.R.O., Informatique Theorique, 13*, pp. 309–336.

Colmerauer, A. and J. F. Pique. (1980). "About natural logic." In H. Gallaire, J. Minker and J. M. Nicolas (Eds.), *Theoretical Issues in Data Bases*. New York: Plenum Press.

Dahl, V. (1979). "Quantification in a three-valued logic for natural language question-answering systems." *Proc. Sixth International Joint Conference on Artificial Intelligence*. Tokyo, Japan.

Dahl, V. (1980). "A three-valued logic for natural language computer applications." *Proc. Tenth International Symposium on Multiple-valued Logic*. Univ. of Illinois.

Dahl, V. (1981). "Translating Spanish into logic through logic." *American Journal of Computational Linguistics, 7*, pp. 149–164.

Dahl, V. and M. C. McCord. (1983). "Treating coordination in logic grammars." *American Journal of Computational Linguistics, 9*, 69–91.

Horn, L. R. (1969). "A presuppositional analysis of *only* and *even*." *Papers from the Fifth Regional Meeting, Chicago Linguistic Society*, pp. 98–107.

Kowalski, R. A. (1979). *Logic for Problem Solving*. New York: North Holland.

Lakoff, G. (1972). "Hedges: a study in meaning criteria and the logic of fuzzy concepts." *Papers from the Eighth Regional Meeting, Chicago Linguistic Society*, pp. 183–228.

Lewis, D. (1975). "Adverbs of quantification." In E. L. Keenan (Ed.), *Formal Semantics of Natural Language*. Cambridge University Press, England.

McCawley, J. D. (1981). *Everything that Linguists Have Always Wanted to Know about Logic*. The University of Chicago Press.

McCord, M. C. (1982). "Using slots and modifiers in logic grammars for natural language." *Artificial Intelligence, 18*, pp. 327–367. (Originally Tech. Report, Computer Science Department, University of Kentucky, 1980.)

Pereira, L., F. Pereira, and D. Warren. (1978). *User's guide to DECsystem-10 Prolog*. Dept. of Artificial Intelligence, Univ. of Edinburgh.

Pereira, F. and D. Warren. (1980). "Definite clause grammars for language analysis—a survey of the formalism and a comparison with augmented transition networks." *Artificial Intelligence, 13*, pp. 231–278.

Roussel, P. (1975). *Prolog: manuel de reference et d'utilisation*. Groupe d'Intelligence Artificielle. Univ. d'Aix-Marseille.

Strawson, P. (1950). "On referring." *Mind, 59*, pp. 320–344.

Strawson, P. (1964). "Identifying reference and truth values." *Theoria, 30*, pp. 96–118.

Woods, W. A., R. M. Kaplan, and B. Nash-Webber. (1972). *The Lunar Sciences Natural Language Information System*. BBN Report 2378 and N.T.I.S. N72-28984.

Zadeh, L. A. (1978). "PRUF—a meaning representation language for natural languages." *Int. J. Man-Machine Studies, 10*, pp. 395–460.

Zadeh, L. A. (1981). *Test-score semantics for natural languages and meaning representation via PRUF*. Tech. Report, SRI International, Menlo Park, CA.

Appendix

/* Semantic Interpretation Rules */

```
:- op(800,xfy,&).
:- op(400,fx,@).
```

/* Reshaping Rules */

```
reshape(Tree,Sisters,Tree1) :-
  daughters(Tree,Daus),
  reshapelist(Daus,Daus1),
  reorder1(Daus1,Daus2),
  reorder2(Daus2,Daus3),
  raise(Daus3,Tree,Sisters,Daus4),
  flatten(Daus4,Daus5),
  newdaus(Tree,Daus5,Tree1).

reshapelist([Tree|Trees],Trees2) :-!,
  reshapelist(Trees,Trees1),
  reshape(Tree,Sisters,Tree1),
  concat(Sisters,[Tree1|Trees1],Trees2).
reshapelist([],[]).

reorder1([A|L],M) :-
  lcapture(A,L,B,L1),!,
  reorder1(L1,L2),
  concat(L2,[[A,B]],M).
reorder1([A|L],M) :-
  reorder1(L,L1),
  insert(A,L1,M).
reorder1([],[]).

lcapture(A,[B|L],B,L) :-
  lcapture1(A,B),!.
lcapture(A,[B|L],C,[B|L1]) :-
  abstract(B),
  lcapture(A,L,C,L1).

insert(A,[B|L],[B|L1]) :-
  prec(A,PA),prec(B,PB),PB>PA,!,
  insert(A,L,L1).
insert(A,L,[A|L]).

reorder2([A|L],M2) :-
  reorder2(L,M),
  captures(A,M,Capts,M1),
```

```
      (Capts=[],!,M2=[A|M1] |
       concat(M1,[[A|Capts]],M2)).
   reorder2([],[]).

   captures(A,[B|L],[B|Capts],L1) :-
      capture(A,B),!,
      captures(A,L,Capts,L1).
   captures(A,[B|L],Capts,[B|L1]) :-
      captures(A,L,Capts,L1).
   captures(A,[],[],[]).

   flatten([[A|L]|M],M2) :-!,
      flatten(M,M1),
      concat([A|L],M1,M2).
   flatten([A|M],[A|M1]) :-!,
      flatten(M,M1).
   flatten([],[]).

   raise([Dau|Daus],Tree,[Dau|Sisters],Daus1) :-
      above(Dau,Tree),!,
      raise(Daus,Tree,Sisters,Daus1).
   raise([Dau|Daus],Tree,Sisters,[Dau|Daus1]) :-
      raise(Daus,Tree,Sisters,Daus1).
   raise([],Tree,[],[]).

   newdaus(syn(Feas,Oper,Marker,Pred,_),Daus,
           syn(Feas,Oper,Marker,Pred,Daus)).

   prec(Syn,P) :- stype(Syn,S),prec1(S,P),!.
   prec(_,0).

   prec1(wh,10).
   prec1(indef1,9).
   prec1(no,8).
   prec1(def,6).
   prec1(dcl,6).
   prec1(yesno,6).
   prec1(all,6).
   prec1(indef,4).
   prec1(advq(_),3).
   prec1(advp(_),3).
   prec1(tense,2).
   prec1(head,2).
   prec1(stress(_),-10).

   capture(A,B) :-
      stype(B,stress(_)),
      stype(A,S),
      focal(S).
```

```
focal(advq(_)).    focal(advp(_)).
focal(dcl).    focal(yesno).

lcapture1(A,B) :-
  stype(A,advp(_)),
  cat(B,np).

abstract(A) :- cat(A,mood).
abstract(A) :- stype(A,tense).

above(Syn1,Syn2) :-
  cat(Syn1,np),cat(Syn2,Cat),
  (Cat=np;Cat=verbph;Cat=pp).
```

/* Translation Rules */

```
translate(Syn,LogForm) :-
  transmod(Syn,1-true,1-LogForm0),
  simplify(LogForm0,_,LogForm).

transmods([Mod|Mods],Sem1,Sem3) :-
  transmods(Mods,Sem1,Sem2),
  transmod(Mod,Sem2,Sem3).
transmods([],Sem,Sem).

transmod(syn(_,Oper0,_,Pred0,Mods),Sem1,Sem2) :-
  transmods(Mods,Oper0-Pred0,Sem0),
  trans(Sem0,Sem1,Sem2).


/*  The following rules for 'trans' are
    the heart of translation to logical form
    and are numbered for reference in the text.  */

trans((P<Q)-R,base(Op,S,R)-Q,base(Op,S,P)-true) :-!.      % 1
trans((P<<Q)-R,base(Op,Q,B)-B,base(Op,R,P)-true) :-!.     % 2
trans((P<Q)-R,Op-Q,base(Op,R,P)-true) :-!.                % 3
trans((P<<Q)-R,Op-Q,base(Op,R,P)-true) :-!.               % 4
trans(@P-Q,base(Op,P,B)-B,Op-Q) :-!.                      % 5
trans(Op-P,base(Op1,Q,B)-P1,base(Op2,Q,B)-P2) :-!,        % 6
  trans(Op-P,Op1-P1,Op2-P2).
trans(base(Op,P,B)-B,Sem1,Sem2) :-!,                      % 7
  trans(Op-P,Sem1,Sem2).
trans(P/Q-R,Op-Q,@P-R).                                   % 8
trans(@P-Q,Op-P,Op-Q).                                    % 9
```

```
trans(1-P,Op-Q,Op-(P&Q)).                                    % 10
trans(r-P,Op-Q,Op-(Q&P)).                                    % 11
trans(num(_)-P,Op-Q,Op-(P&Q)).                               % 12
trans(subst(X)-X,Sem,Sem).                                   % 13
trans(id-P,Sem,Sem).                                         % 14
```

/* Simplification Rules */

```
simplify(E,D,E) :- var(E),!,enter(E,D).
simplify(E,_,E) :- atomic(E),!.
simplify(E&true,D,E1) :-!,simplify(E,D,E1).
simplify(true&E,D,E1) :-!,simplify(E,D,E1).
simplify((X=Y)&E,D,E2) :-!,
  (var(X),dmem(X,D),!,simplify(E,D,E1),E2=(X=Y&E1)   |
   X=Y,simplify(E,D,E2)).
simplify(E,D,E1) :-
  E=..[P|Args],
  simplist(Args,D,Args1),
  E1=..[P|Args1].

simplist([E|L],D,[E1|L1]) :-
  simplify(E,D,E1),
  simplist(L,D,L1).
simplist([],_,[]).

dmem(_,D) :- var(D),!,fail.
dmem(X,[Y|_]):- X==Y,!.
dmem(X,[_|D]) :- dmem(X,D).

enter(V,D) :- var(D),!,D=[V|_].
enter(V,[V1|_]) :- V==V1,!.
enter(V,[_|D]) :- enter(V,D).
```

CHAPTER 16

Restriction Grammar: A Prolog Implementation*

Lynette Hirschman
Karl Puder

Research and Development Division
SDC—A Burroughs Company
P.O. Box 517
Paoli, Pennsylvania 19301

1   Introduction

This paper describes the Prolog implementation of Restriction Grammar, a formalism for writing natural language grammars. The term Restriction Grammar (RG) designates a grammar consisting of a set of context-free Backus-Naur Form (BNF) definitions augmented by a set of constraints or *restrictions*. In RG, an automatically generated parse tree records those context-free rules used in constructing the parse. The restrictions are procedures interleaved among the BNF definitions and are stated as

1. constraints on the structure of the existing parse tree, and
2. constraints on the words remaining in the input stream.

Failure of a restriction causes backtracking to the next alternative in the BNF definition. Each restriction has access to the entire previously constructed parse tree; therefore the data structure for a tree must permit free tree traversal. (Several implementations of tree data structure are discussed in section 3.)

Restriction Grammar, as defined here, is derived from the Linguistic String Project (LSP) natural language processing system developed by Naomi Sager at New York University. The current LSP system at NYU is implemented in Fortran (Grishman et al., 1973) and supports a broad-coverage English grammar for processing scientific text (Sager, 1981). The initial motivation for a Prolog implementation of RG was to create an interactive environment for natural lan-

---

*This paper is a revised, expanded version of the paper that appeared in the *Proceedings of the First International Logic Programming Conference*. Karl Puder's current affiliation is: AI Technology Group, Digital Equipment Corp., Hudson, MA.

guage processing which could make use of the existing LSP English grammar. A Prolog implementation for RG also has the additional advantage of providing an integrated logic programming environment for natural language processing, knowledge representation, and inferencing.

In the course of this work, it became clear that the Prolog RG was in itself a useful tool for writing grammars and offered advantages of simplicity, modularity, and ease of modification over other styles of grammar implemented in Prolog, e.g., Metamorphosis Grammars (Colmerauer, 1978: Dahl, 1981), and Definite Clause Grammars (DCG's) (Pereira and Warren, 1980).

2   A Sample Restriction Grammar

In order to illustrate the process of writing a grammar in the RG formalism, we will develop in this section a very small RG to parse a few English sentences. Our initial grammar RG1 (shown in Figure 16.1) contains only the BNF definitions and a few sample dictionary entries.

The grammar RG1 will parse the sentence *Mary likes books* and will produce the parse tree shown in Figure 16.2. The BNF definitions are used to construct a parse tree in the obvious way: for each definition that is applied, the left-hand

```
% BNF DEFINITIONS

sentence ::= subject,predicate,[.].
subject ::= *n.
predicate ::= verb,object.
verb ::= *v.
object ::= *n;nullobj.
nullobj ::= [] .

% * * * * * * * * * * * * * * * * * * * * * * * * * * *
% An asterisk ('*') indicates that the symbol it precedes (e.g., '*n')
% is an atomic symbol; that is, it must be matched by a token of the
% same class from the input word stream.
% Notation:    ,        = concatenation
%              ;        = alternation
%              .        = termination of a rule
%              [...]    = a literal

% DICTIONARY

% Lexical information is organized by word; ':' is an infix operator
% connecting an entry to its attributes (e.g., books is a *n*;
% attributes in turn may have sub-attributes (e.g., the *n* in *books*
% is *plural*.

mary :[n:[singular,nproper]].
likes:[v:[singular,transitive]].
books:[n:[plural]].
reads:[v:[singular,transitive,intransitive]].
```

Figure 16.1. RG1: a Sample Restriction Grammar Without Restrictions

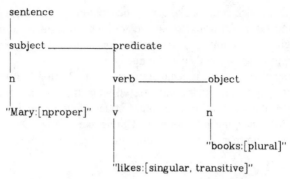

Figure 16.2. Parse Tree for "Mary likes books"

side becomes the parent node; its children are the nodes in the particular alternative chosen. Note that the BNF definitions for RG1 contain no parameters. This is because the tree-building parameters and the word-stream parameters are hidden from the user by an interpreter (described in section 4). When backtracking occurs, the parse tree variables are automatically deinstantiated to reflect backtracking in the tree.

Each atomic BNF definition (indicated by an asterisk, e.g., *n) picks up a word from the input stream. Dictionary look-up precedes the actual parsing; the lexical look-up procedure passes to the parsing procedure an input stream consisting of the list of dictionary entries for the sentence words. The words are shown in quotes in Fig. 16.2. Each attached word is accessible from the parse tree, as are its syntactic attributes (given as a list in the second argument of ":"). The organization of a dictionary by word, and the separation of the lexical look-up procedure from the parsing, are advantageous when using a large dictionary. Several of the LSP dictionaries contain 10,000 or more entries.

The grammar RG1 will also parse the ungrammatical sequence **Mary likes.** However, this can be prevented by adding a verb-object restriction to require that only intransitive verbs can take a null object (nullobj in the BNF definitions). Every restriction must be "housed" with respect to one or more of the BNF definitions. That is, as in DCG, constraints are inserted into the context-free definitions: the constraints do not change the tree structure, but they can either succeed or they can fail, in which case backtracking to the next alternative occurs. Restrictions consist of sequences of movements through the existing parse tree and various tests on any node visited during this movement. In addition, for optimization, a restriction can test whether a given word appears in the input stream of words not yet attached to the parse tree. Therefore, each restriction has two parameters: its starting point in the parse tree (the parent node in the BNF definition in which it appears), from which it can reach any other node in the tree; and the current input stream of words not yet in the parse tree. These parameters are automatically inserted when the BNF definitions are interpreted or translated.

In the definition of a restriction, the parameters for its starting point in the tree and in the word-stream must be stated explicitly, since only the BNF definitions are currently interpreted or translated. (Future plans include adding an interpreter/translator for restrictions.) The restriction consists of a series of movements through the parse tree, coupled with tests for the presence or absence of nodes (via the operator *test*), words (via the operator *word*), or attributes of words "attached" to terminal nodes in the tree (via the operator *attrb*).

The verb-object restriction is inserted after the options of *object*; it tests that if *object* = *n,* the verb has the attribute *transitive,* otherwise if *object* = *nullobj,* the verb has the attribute *intransitive.* RG2, in Figure 16.3 below, shows the modifications to RG1 needed to introduce the restriction *verb_object.*

The movement operators (*up, down, right, left,*) traverse the parse tree; they therefore have two parameters, one corresponding to their starting point in the tree, the second to the position after the movement. The operators *test* and *attrb* have the two position parameters (for uniformity, they are the final two parameters); in addition, they have a parameter to specify what node label or word attribute is being tested for.

The restriction written in this form requires a detailed knowledge of the parse tree. Alternatively, we can define more general-purpose tree-searching routines; these routines are slightly less efficient but easier to use, since they do not require such detailed information about the tree structure. Two useful routines are shown in Figure 16.4, namely the routines for *element* and *coelement*. *Element*

```
% MODIFICATION TO BNF

predicate ::= verb,object,{verb_object}.

% * * * * * * * * * * * * * * * * * * * * * * * *
% R E S T R I C T I O N S
% * * * * * * * * * * * * * * * * * * * * * * * *

% verb_object
%      starting at predicate, checks that if object = n, then
%      v in verb is transitive; if object = nullobj, then v in
%      in verb is intransitive.

verb_object(Predicate,Words) <-
%    locate v in verb, save in V
     down(Predicate,Verb),down(Verb,V),
%    locate n in object and store it in O
     right(Verb,Object),down(Object,O),
%    if O is n, then V must have attribute 'transitive'
     (test(n,O,O) -> attrb(transitive,V,_);
%    otherwise if O is nullobj, V must have attribute 'intransitive'.
     test(nullobj,O,O) -> attrb(intransitive,V,_);
     true).
```

Figure 16.3. RG2: Addition of a Restriction for Verb-Object Agreement

```
% * * * * * * * * * * * * * * * * * * * *
% R O U T I N E S
% * * * * * * * * * * * * * * * * * * * *

% element
%    scans children of node Start for a node X, and returns its
%    location in End.
element(X,Start,End) <-
    down(Start,X1),
    ((test(X,X1,X1),End=X1);
    r(X,X1,End)).

% r
%    iterates moving to the next sib to the right, testing for node X;
%    returns position of X in End.
r(X,Start,End) <-
    right(Start,X1),
    ((test(X,X1,X1),End=X1);
    r(X,X1,End)).

% l
%    iterates moving to the next sib to the left, testing for node X;
%    returns position of X in End.
l(X,Start,End) <-
    left(Start,X1),
    ((test(X,X1,X1),End=X1);
    l(X,X1,End)).

% coelement
%    scans for argument X first in the right sibs, then to the left sibs
coelement(X,Start,End) <-
    r(X,Start,End);l(X,Start,End).

% subject_of
%    starts at Sentence and descends to n of subject, returned in Subj.
subject_of (Sentence,Subj) <-
        element(subject,Sentence,Subject),
        element(n,Subject,Subj).

% verb_of
%    starts at Sentence and descends to v of verb, returned in V.
verb_of (Sentence,V) <-
        element(predicate,Sentence,Pred),
        element(v,Pred,V).
```

Figure 16.4. Routines in a RG

searches the children of the current node left to right for the target node (given in the first parameter). *Coelement* searches the siblings of the current node for the target, first going right, and then left.

These routines can, in turn, be used to define general linguistic operations, such as *host,* which starts at an adjunct and finds the head of the construction. For purposes of illustration, two higher-level routines, *subject_of* and *object_of* are also defined in Figure 16.4 These routines make it possible to extract the head noun of the subject position and the tensed verb respectively, starting at the node *sentence.* Using these routines, we can write a subject-verb agreement restriction, shown in Figure 16.5. Note that because we have used these higher-level routines, the same restriction would apply to subject-verb agreement in, for example, a question, where verb and subject order were reversed. This is because both subject and verb are specified as *elements* of *sentence,* but their exact position within *sentence* is not specified.

Routines allow a more general expression of linguistic constraints, at the expense of efficiency. For example, the LSP English Grammar (Sager, 1981) makes extensive use of very powerful and general routines which cover a variety of tree structures. One routine (*core*) is used to find the head of a variety of constructions, including noun phrases, verb phrases, adverbial and adjectival phrases. Another routine, *deepest-coverb,* finds the "deepest" verb, including embedded constructions; for example, it will return the verb *finished* in the sentence *I was hoping to have finished the book.* The converse routine *ultimate-subject* finds the subject of a verb, climbing through any embeddings. Routines are also used to make the treatment of conjunction transparent to the grammar-writer. In general, the problem of defining adequate constraints is greatly simplified by the existence of these routines which generalize over a variety of tree structures.

Another attractive feature of RG is its ease of modification. In a RG, the context-sensitive information is recorded in the parse tree, rather than being passed by parameter, as in DCG's. As a result, each restriction just checks the parse tree; the grammar-writer does not have to modify the set of parameters that other restrictions or BNF definitions use. For example, if we wish to add the constraint that the subject and the verb must agree in number, we add restriction *subj_verb_agree* in the BNF definition for *verb,* and we define it in the restriction section. However, everything else remains unchanged; it is not neces-

```
% MODIFICATION TO THE BNF

verb ::= *v,{subj_verb_agree}.

% * * * * * * * * * * * * * * * * * * * * * * *
% R E S T R I C T I O N S
% * * * * * * * * * * * * * * * * * * * * * * *

% subj_verb_agree
%     checks that if subject is singular, verb is singular;
%     if subject is plural, verb is plural.

subj_verb_agree(Sentence,Words) <-

% locate subject noun (stored in Subj) and verb (in V):
        subject_of(Sentence,Subj), verb_of(Sentence,V),

% check that attributes of subject, verb correspond:
        (attrb(singular,Subj), attrb(singular,V);
        attrb(plural,Subj),   attrb(plural,V)).
```

Figure 16.5. RG3: RG with an Additional Restriction

sary to change the definition of subject in order to pass the number of the subject to the predicate. This is illustrated in the grammar RG3 (Figure 16.5).

By contrast, DCG's rely on parameters in order to propagate information around a tree. In natural language, there are many constraints that are nonlocal, that is, that involve widely separated parts of the sentence. In this case, parameter-passing becomes cumbersome for the grammar-writer. For example, to express subject-verb agreement, the standard DCG treatment would extract number from the noun phrase in the subject. In order to make this information available to the tensed verb in the predicate, however, the number information must be passed up the tree to the level where the predicate can ''see'' information about the subject, then back down to the tensed verb. This means that every node on the path between the head noun of the subject and the tensed verb in the predicate must contain this parameter. As a result, the context-free definitions in a DCG become difficult to read, because they are cluttered with parameters. This also leads to instability of the grammar. Normally, the context-free portion of a grammar is far more stable than the restrictions. However, the grammar-writer cannot take advantage of this fact if the context-free definitions must constantly be modified to add new parameters for additional restrictions.

RG also differs from DCG in that the output of the parsing process is generated automatically, whereas in a DCG, the output of the parse must be explicitly constructed via parameter instantiation. The RG approach has the advantage that the grammar-writer does not need to construct the tree explicitly while writing the BNF definitions. This makes the BNF much easier to read, and also reduces the likelihood of errors due to inconsistencies of structure. On the other hand, the disadvantage of this approach is that the parse tree reflects the calling sequence of the BNF definitions. If a different structure is desired (for example, when parsing formal languages, or when some regularization of the structure is performed during the parsing phase), then this must be explicitly described by transformations. Alternatively, a small modification to the current RG formalism would allow the passing of arbitrary parameters, as is done for DCG.

It appears that RG pays for the convenience of the grammar-writer mainly in performance: tree-climbing is more time consuming than parameter-passing. It is not clear, however, that there are any other sacrifices, since RG is not incompatible with parameter-passing. Indeed, it might be that one would wish to write a grammar as a RG, but ''compile'' it into a DCG for performance. This may be possible, provided that the kinds of allowed tree movements are reasonably constrained.

3   Data Structures

3.1   The Alternatives

The most interesting part of the implementation of the Restriction Grammar formalism in Prolog is the data structure used to represent the parse tree. From any point in the tree, all of the rest of the tree must be accessible to allow constraints to be applied. We wanted to consider several ways to implement a Prolog structure to allow free tree traversal. Therefore, the implementation of the primitive operations of tree movement and node examination has been kept isolated from the rest of the system, so that various styles of tree can be tried easily. The primitive tree operations are: *up, left, down, right, label, word,* and *attr;* namely, the four basic movements and three node examination primitives. The restriction primitives are written in terms of these tree primitives.

We considered the following alternatives for implementation of the tree:

1. A reference into the tree is actually a pair, consisting of the entire tree (represented as a conventional Prolog term), and a term indicating the path to the intended location.
2. A tree node is just an atom, say an integer, with connections asserted into the database. On backtracking, these assertions must be retracted.
3. Nodes of the tree are represented by tree terms; a tree term has a field for each direction of movement. Doubly linking all connections in this way violates the occurs check, since the parent node references its child, and vice versa.
4. Each tree term contains a field for first child and right sibling; in addition, associated with each node is the path to the root, that is, a list of nodes traversed on the way to the root. This provides free tree movement, but does not require a circular data structure.

The first alternative is the most obvious way to implement the data structure, but has some efficiency problems for moving around the tree. For each move, the path term must be edited. On each examination of a node, the path must be followed to that node. Typically, most of the time in parsing is spent executing restrictions. Since the restrictions do a lot of tree movement interspersed with node examination, and typical trees are large, this method would have been prohibitively slow, and was not further investigated.

The second method relies on side-effecting the database, but this can be masked by defining an assert that retracts when it backtracks. This makes the use of cut (already frowned upon) extremely dangerous, since the retraction of tree connections can be cut away. Moving around the tree is not too bad with this data structure, but the database modification is not as fast as variable instantiation, used in (1), (3) and (4).

The next two subsections discuss the third and fourth alternatives in somewhat greater detail. Both of the these alternatives have been implemented. Alternative (3) is both compact and permits rapid movement through the tree. However, its double linking makes transformations (changes to the tree) prohibitively expensive. Alternative (4) requires more space and also requires a larger number of operations to move about the tree. However, the looser linking makes transformations much cheaper, and for this reason, it is the data structure currently in use.

3.2   A Doubly-Linked Structure

The doubly-linked tree term provides the fastest tree movement, but requires a special printer (implemented through the use of portray) to avoid printing the backward references. In addition, the occurs check is violated, so care must be taken to avoid unbounded recursion in the unification algorithm when giving it infinite terms. Our initial implementation, described in Hirschman and Puder (1982) was based on this structure.

Each node of the tree is represented as a term with six fields:

tt(Label, Parent, LeftSib, FirstChild, RightSib, Attributes).

Note that each field corresponds to one of the primitive operations. The tree movement and node examination operations are implemented as simple field extractions from the *tt* term with the constraint that the field extracted must not be a variable. This prevents restrictions from examining beyond the fringe of a partially instantiated tree (See Figure 16.6).

The main disadvantage of this data structure is that transformations are very costly to perform, due to the double linking. Each node in the tree is linked in both a forward (down, right) direction, as well as a backward (up, left) direction. As a result, a modification to any one node in the tree requires recalculation of the links for every node in the tree.

The connection of nodes into the tree during parsing is interesting. The atom $\sim$ is used to indicate a null connection, that is, that there is no right sibling or no child. Vertical connections are made by *child* and horizontal connections are made by *sib*. Their definitions are:

```
% label extracts the label (grammatical class) associated with the node
label(tt(L, _, _, _, _, _),L).

% up extracts the parent field, checking that it is instantiated.
up(tt( _, P, _, _, _, _), P) <- nonvar(P).

% down extracts the child field, checking that it is instantiated.
down(tt( _, _, _, C, _, _), C) <- nonvar(C).

% left extracts the left sibling field, checking that it is instantiated.
left(tt( _, _, L, _, _, _), L) <- nonvar(L).

% right extracts the right sibling field, checking that it is instantiated.
right(tt( _, _, _, _, R, _), R) <- nonvar(R).

% word extracts the first argument of ':' , namely the word attached to
%       the node, checking that it is instantiated.
word(tt( _, _, _, _, _, W : _), W) <- nonvar(W).

% attrlst extracts the attribute list associated with the word
%       (second argument of ':'), checking that it is instantiated;
%       otherwise the empty list is returned.
attrlst(tt( _, _, _, _, _, _: AL), AL) <- nonvar(AL),!;AL=[].
```

Figure 16.6. Movement Operations for the Doubly-Linked Tree

child(P,C) ←
    C== ~ → P=tt(_,_,_,_,_,_);
    P=tt(_,_,_,C,_,_),C=tt(_,P,_,_,_,_).

sib(S1,S2) ←
    S2== ~ → S1=tt(_,_,_,_,_,_);
    S1=tt(_,P,_,_,S2,_),S2=tt(_,P,S1,_,_,_).

Note that in the case where no connection is made, the right sibling (or first child) field is left as a variable. Terminators for the actual fringe of the tree are not necessary because the tree movement operations will not move to a variable.

3.3   Separating Forward and Backward Links

The fourth alternative is the one currently in use: A node in the tree is made up of two components: the tree term which contains the forward (down, right) links; and a path, consisting of the links back to the root node. Because the tree term structure in this alternative contains only the child and right sibling links, it forms a straightforward representation of a tree in Prolog, with no circularity:

tt(Label , Child , RightSib , Word).

The path containing the backward links provides a set of directions for navigating back to the root node. It consists of a list of terms made up of a functor giving a direction (up or left), and its argument which is the tree term reached by moving in that direction. For example, the representation of the node *verb* in Figure 16.2 is shown in Figure 16.7. Here *verb* has as its child the tree term *Child* with label *v*, and a right sibling *Sib* with label *object*. The path to the root is given by the sequence *up to Parent* (with label *predicate*), *left to Sib* (with label *subject*), *up to Root* (with label *sentence*).

The path back to the root is maintained by the basic movement operators. The operations for *down* and *right,* as before, retrieve the child and right sibling fields respectively; however, in addition, they must also extend the path appropriately by adding to it the node just traversed. *Up* and *left* use the path to find the parent or left sibling; it may be necessary to go left several times until an **up**

[tt(verb , Child , RightSib , Word), up(Parent), left(Sib), up(Root)].

where	Verb	= tt(verb, Child , RightSib , Word),
	Child	= tt(v,_,_,likes:[singular,transitive]),
	RightSib	= tt(object,ONoun,_,_),
	ONoun	= tt(n,_,_,books:[plural]).
	Parent	= tt(predicate, Verb , _, _),
	Sib	= tt(subject, SNoun, Parent, _),
	SNoun	= tt(n,_,_,mary:[nproper]),
	Root	= tt(sentence,Sib, _, _),

Figure 16.7. Separating Up and Down Links: the Representation of a Node

direction is reached. The backwards operations remove the nodes traversed from
the path. These operations are shown in Figure 16.8.

The connection between nodes is done by the procedure *connect,* shown in
Figure 16.9. *Connect* makes use of the fact that every node in the tree is either a
(first) child of the most recently constructed node, or a right sibling of this node.
Connect has three arguments: the most recently constructed node (*Here*), the
previous node (*Prev*), which may be the left sibling or parent of *Here;* and
Parent, the parent of *Here.* If *Here* is the first child of *Parent* (indicated by *Prev*
$==$ *Parent*), *connect* builds a parent-child connection between these two nodes.
Otherwise it builds a sibling connection between *Prev* and *Here.*

4   Implementation

We have implemented both an interpreter and a translator for RG. The interpreter
(described in 4.2) is used for interactive debugging of a grammar. The translator

```
% label returns the name (label) of a node in its second argument.
label([tt(L, _, _, _) | P], L).

% down starts at node Here with path Path, and goes to the child node Child;
%       the starting node is then added to the path associated with Child.
down([Here | Path],[Child, up(Here) | Path]) <-
        Here = tt(_, Child, _, _), nonvar(Child).

% right starts at node Here with path Path, and goes to the right sib Sib;
%       the starting node is then added to the path associated with Sib.
right([Here | Path],[Sib, left(Here) | Path]) :-
        Here = tt(_, _, Sib, _), nonvar(Sib).

% word retrieves the word (first argument of the operator :).
word([tt( _, _, _, W : _) | P], W) <- nonvar(W).

% attrlst retrieves the attribute list (second argument of :).
attrlst([tt( _, _, _, _: AL) | P], AL) <- nonvar(AL),!.

% left starts at node Here, and requires that the first element on
%       its associated path be left(Sib); it returns Sib, and the
%       remainder of the path Path.
left([Here, left(Sib) | Path], [Sib | Path]) <-
        nonvar(Sib).

% up has two cases: either the first node on the path list is the
%       parent P, in which case the pair consisting of P and the
%       remainder of the path Path is returned. Otherwise, the left(Sib)
%       is popped off the path, followed by another call to up.
up([Here, up(P) | Path], [P | Path]) <-
        !, nonvar(P).
up([Here, left(Sib) | Path], P) <-
        nonvar(Sib),
        up([Sib | Path], P).
```

Figure 16.8. Movement Operations for Tree Term + Path

```
% connect
% Makes either the parent-child connection between Parent and
%      Here (child), if the paths from the previous node (PrevPath)
%      and the parent node (PPath) are identical; otherwise makes the
%      sibling connection between the left sibling Prev, and its
%      right sibling Here.
%      If no node is made (Here == ~) then no connection is made.
connect(Here, Prev, [Parent]) <- var(Parent), !.
connect([Here | HerePath], Prev, Parent) <-
      Here == ~, !.
connect([Here , up(Parent) | PPath], [Prev | PrevPath], [Parent | PPath]) <-
      PrevPath == PPath, !,
      Parent = tt( _, Here, _, _).
connect([Here, left(Prev) | PrevPath], [Prev | PrevPath], Parent) <-
      Prev = tt( _, _, Here, _).
```

Figure 16.9. Connection Operation

produces a set of Prolog clauses which can then be compiled. This gives good performance for running debugged grammars. (On the DEC-10, we were able to obtain a five to ten-fold speed-up using the translator followed by compilation.)

4.1   The Translator

The translator is a straightforward extension of the translator for DCG's, although somewhat more complex, due to the additional parameters that are syntactically sugared away. There are two parameters in the outer level translator, and eight parameters in the inner translator. This may seem like a lot of parameters, but they are all necessary, as will be explained below.

The outer translator splits up the head and body of the grammar rule, and makes the proper connections and initialization. The inner translator, which translates the body of the rule, simply recurses through the **and**'s and **or**'s, calling other specialized translators for restrictions and literals.

The two parameters in the outer translator are the grammar rule and the equivalent Prolog rule. Six additional parameters are handed about in the inner translator.

Two parameters in the inner translator are almost the same as for the DCG translator: the before and after versions of the list of word definitions in the sentence. (The dictionary lookup is done for the whole sentence before the parser gets called, and the entire definition of each word is retrieved at once.)

One parameter is the tree node corresponding to the head of the rule being translated. This is the parent of all nodes created in the translation of the body of the rule. It is also the node given to restrictions from which they start their examination of the tree. The most recently created node prior to entering a given sub-translation is also passed around (**Prev**). This information is used in the procedure **connect,** to determine whether to make a parent or a sibling connection. It is also used in those cases where no node is created (restrictions and the null node [].)

Two of the parameters are used to keep track of the chain of siblings in a conjunction. They are called *First* and *Last*. *First* is the first node to be created by the piece of grammar being translated in this call to the translator. *Last* is the last node created in this call to the translator; it is the node that will (possibly) be connected to any following nodes created by adjacent conjoined definitions; i.e., it becomes *Prev* for the next sub-translation. In the case that no nodes are created by this sub-translation (e.g., for restriction), *First* = *Last* = *Prev*. In case exactly one node is created (for atomic nodes and literals), *First* = *Last*.

4.2   The Interpreter

The interpreter is identical to the translator with a few exceptions. The outer interpreter has rather a different form from the translator, since it must be given the word-streams and the root of the parse tree. The inner interpreter is extremely similar to the inner translator.

The main difference is that the interpreter executes the translation, rather than passing it around as a parameter. Therefore the interpreter has one less parameter than the translator. Also, the interpretation of alternatives is more straightforward than their translation: in the interpreter, the bindings are performed as one alternative is pursued, and simply undone on backtracking, if the alternative fails. On the other hand, when translating alternatives, the tree connections must be delayed until a particular alternative has been chosen, causing more bookkeeping to be performed.

The interpreter is decorated with calls to a trace package which resembles that of Prolog itself. All similar commands have been given the same name as in the Prolog trace package. Additional commands have been included to allow perusal of the parse tree and the word-streams.

5   Future Directions

5.1   Enhancement of the Translator and Interpreter

The restrictions are sometimes clumsy to write because of the parameters that need to be connected between the tree movement primitives. We plan to enhance the translator and interpreter to eliminate the need to exhibit these parameters explicitly. This would also fix an unfriendliness in the trace package which is caused by the poor interface between the RG and Prolog trace packages (currently the restrictions use the Prolog trace package).

5.2   Transformational Component

One of the main motivations for having chosen a data structure that separates the down/right connections from that for the up/left connections is that it greatly facilitates transformations of the parse tree. With the original doubly-linked circular data structure, any change in a tree would have required that all tree terms be recalculated. Using the separated up/left and down/right connections, we have recently implemented some of the primitive transformational operators for restriction grammar (*create* a node, *insertafter* and *insertbefore* a given node, *delete* a node, *copy* a node). These operations require that the parent/left sibling links and the associated path be recalculated for all nodes to the left or above the node where the transformation is taking place. However, the tree terms for the nodes below (i.e., to the right or down from the current node) are not affected, since they record only their children and right siblings. The code for some of the transformational primitives is given in Appendix 2. In order to incorporate the transformational operators into the RG framework, both the interpreter and the translator require extra parameters to pass around the changed tree structure; restrictions also require a tree node output parameter, in addition to the current input parameter which is used as a starting position for execution of the restriction.

5.3   Efficiency

The largest RG that we have implemented to date (QRG) consists of approximately 60 BNF definitions and 20 restrictions. However, the full LSP grammar contains approximately 250 BNF definitions and 300 restrictions. So far, the performance of the compiled QRG on a DEC-10 is comparable to the parse times for the Fortran implementation of a similar grammar: a 10-word sentence parsed in 0.4 seconds. It is not clear whether the implementation of the full LSP system will cause a significant degradation in performance. Our experience to this point has been that the interpreted version of the system is significantly slower than the compiled version (by a factor of 5); however, its highly interactive nature makes it very easy to write and debug grammars. Once debugged, the system can be compiled in order to achieve acceptable performance times.

References

Grishman, R., N. Sager, C. Raze, and B. Bookchin. (1973). "The Linguistic String Parser." *AFIPS Conference Proceedings* **43,** AFIPS Press, pp. 427–434.

Sager, N. (1981). *Natural Language Information Processing: A Computer Grammar of English and Its Applications.* Reading, MA.: Addison-Wesley.

Colmerauer, A. (1978). "Metamorphosis Grammars." In *Natural Language Communication with Computers,* L. Bolc (ed.), Springer, pp. 133–189.

Dahl, V. (1981). "Translating Spanish into Logic through Logic." *American Journal of Computational Linguistics* **7**(3), pp. 149–164.

Pereira, F. C. N., and D. H. D. Warren. (1980). "Definite Clause Grammars for Language Analysis—A Survey of the Formalism and a Comparison with Augmented Transition Networks." *Artificial Intelligence* **13,** pp. 231–278.

Hirschman, L., and K. Puder. (1982). "Restriction Grammar in Prolog." In *Proc. of the First International Logic Programming Conference*, M. van Caneghem (ed.), Faculte des Sciences de Luminy, Marseilles, pp. 85–90.

Appendix 1

```
<- op(1200,xfx,::=).
<- op(700,xfx,in).
<- op(700,xfx,notIn).
<- op(600,xfx,:).
<- op(500,fx,*).

translate((X::=Y),
        (A <- label(Parent,X),B)) <- !,
        transPred(X,A,Parent,InList,OutList),
        trans(Y,B,YTree,Last,Parent,Parent,InList,OutList).

transPred(X,A,Here,In,Out) <-
        A=..[X,Here,In,Out].

/* trans(Source,Object,Here,Last,Prev,ParentNode,
        InputTokenStream,RemainingTokenStream)
translates Source to Object.
ParentNode is used by restrictions as a
starting point for parse-tree reference.
Here & Last are the first and last siblings created by Source.
InTok. is the token stream given to the parse, and RemTok. is the
token stream which remains after this parse.
*/

trans((X,Y),
    (A,B),
    First,Last,Prev,R,In,Out) <- !,
        trans(X,A,First,XLast,Prev,R,In,IOtmp),
        trans(Y,B,YFirst,Last,XLast,R,IOtmp,Out).
trans((X;Y),
    ((First=XTrans,Last=XLast,In=InX,Out=OutX,A);
    (First = YTrans,Last=YLast,In=InY,Out=OutY,B)),
    First,Last,Prev,R,In,Out) <- !,
        trans(X,A,XTrans,XLast,Prev,R,InX,OutX),
        trans(Y,B,YTrans,YLast,Prev,R,InY,OutY).
trans({X},A,[~|_],Prev,Prev,R,IO,IO) <- !,
        trans1(X,A,R,IO).
trans(*X,    (connect(Here,Prev,R),
             find(Defns,X,Stuff),label(Here,X),word(Here,W),
             putattr(Here,Stuff)),
        Here,Here,Prev,R,[W:Defns|Out],Out) <- !.
trans([Hd,..Tl],A,First,Last,Prev,R,In,Out) <- !,
        words([Hd|Tl],A,First,Last,Prev,R,In,Out).
trans([],true,[~|FP],Prev,Prev,R,IO,IO) <- !.
trans(X,
    (label(First,X),connect(First,Prev,R),A),
    First,First,Prev,R,In,Out) <-
        transPred(X,A,First,In,Out).


trans1((X,Y),(A,B),T,IO) <- !,trans1(X,A,T,IO),trans1(Y,B,T,IO).
trans1((X;Y),(A;B),T,IO) <- !,trans1(X,A,T,IO),trans1(Y,B,T,IO).
```

```
trans1(X,A,T,IO) <-
        atom(X),A=..[X,T,IO].

words([Hd,Nx|Tl],(connect(HD,Prev,R),A,B),HD,Last,Prev,R,[Head|Tail],Out) <- !,
        tword(Hd,A,HD,Head),
        words([Nx|Tl],B,NX,Last,HD,R,Tail,Out).
words([Hd],(connect(HD,Prev,R),A),
        HD,HD,Prev,R,[Head|Tail],Tail) <-
        tword(Hd,A,HD,Head).

tword(W,(label(Here,W),word(Here,W),putattr(Here,Defns)),
        Here,W:Defns) <- atom(W).


label([tt(L,_,_,_)|P],L).
down([Here|Path],[Child,up(Here)|Path]) <-
        Here=tt(_,Child,_,_),nonvar(Child).
right([Here|Path],[Sib,left(Here)|Path]) <-
        Here=tt(_,_,Sib,_),nonvar(Sib).
word([tt(_,_,_,W:_)|P],W) <- nonvar(W).
attrlst([tt(_,_,_,_:AL)|P],AL) <- nonvar(AL),!.

up([Here, up(P) | Path], [P | Path]) <-
        !, nonvar(P).
up([Here, left(Sib) | Path], P) <-
        nonvar(Sib),
        up([Sib | Path], P).
left([Here, left(Sib) | Path], [Sib | Path]) <-
        nonvar(Sib).


% connect
% Makes either the parent-child connection between Parent and
%       Here (child), if the paths from the previous node (PrevPath)
%       and the parent node (PPath) are identical; otherwise makes the
%       sibling connection between left sib Prev, and its right sib Here.
%       If no node is made (Here == ~) then no connection is made.
%       Also for the root node (path = []) no connection is made.

connect(Here, Prev, [Parent]) <- var(Parent), !.
connect([Here | HerePath], Prev, Parent) <-
        Here == ~, !.
connect([Here | up(Parent) | PPath], [Prev | PrevPath], [Parent | PPath]) <-
        PrevPath == PPath, !,
        Parent = tt( _, Here, _, _).
connect([Here, left(Prev) | PrevPath], [Prev | PrevPath], Parent) <-
        Prev = tt( _, _, Here, _).


% find(A,B,C) = in A, find a place with tag B,
%               and return the stuff at that place in C.
find(Tag,Tag,[]).
find(Tag:Stuff,Tag,Stuff).
find([Tag|_],Tag,[]).
find([Tag:Stuff|_],Tag,Stuff).
find([_|Defns],Tag,Stuff) <- find(Defns,Tag,Stuff).
```

Appendix 2

```
% ***************************
% TRANSFORMATION OPERATORS
% ***************************

%
% Some primitive used to write the transformational operators.
%

% sib(Left, Right) makes the sibling connection
sib([Left | Path], [Right, left(Left) | Path]) <-
        Left = tt(L,C,Right,W).

% child(Parent, Child) makes the parent connection.
child([Parent | Path], [Child, up(Parent) | Path]) <-
        Parent = tt(L,Child,R,W).

% breaksib(Node, NewNode, NewSib) gives NewNode as a copy of
% Node without its right sibling, and NewSib is the detached sibling.
breaksib(Node, NewNode, NewSib) <-
        right(Node, Sib), detach(Sib, NewSib),
        breakcopysib(Node, NewNode, _).

% breakchild(Node, NewNode, NewChild) gives NewNode as a copy of
% Node without its first child, and NewChild is the detached child.
breakchild(Node, NewNode, NewChild) <-
        down(Node, Child), detach(Child, NewChild),
        breakcopychild(Node, NewNode, _).

% detach(Node, NewNode) produces NewNode as a copy of Node with its
% path to the root cleared.
detach([Here | Path], [Here | _]).

breakcopysib([tt(L,C,S,W) | Path], [NHere | NPath], NS) <-
        NHere = tt(L,C,NS,W), breakcopy(Path, NPath, NHere).

breakcopychild([tt(L,C,S,W) | Path], [NHere | NPath], NC) <-
        NHere = tt(L,NC,S,W), breakcopy(Path, NPath, NHere).

breakcopy([], [], Prev).

breakcopy([up(Here) | Path], [up(NHere) | NPath], Prev) <-
        breakcopychild([Here | Path], [NHere | NPath], Prev).

breakcopy([left(Here) | Path], [left(NHere) | NPath], Prev) <-
        breakcopysib([Here | Path], [NHere | NPath], Prev).

% ELEMENTARY TRANSFORMATION OPERATORS

% insertbefore(Here, Insert) puts node Insert before node Here
%       There are two cases, depending on whether Here has a left sib or not.
insertbefore(Sib, Insert) <-
        left(Sib, Left),!,
        insertafter(Left,Insert).

insertbefore(Child, Insert) <-
        up(Child, Par),
        breakchild(Par, NPar, NewCh),
        child(NPar,Insert),
        sib(Insert, NewCh).
```

```
% insertafter(Here, Insert) puts node Insert after node Here.
%       There are two cases, depending on whether it has  right sib or not.
insertafter(Here, Insert) <-
        right(Here, Sib),!,    /* Do we need to breaksib? */
        breaksib(Here, NH, NewSib),
        sib(NH, Insert),
        sib(Insert, NewSib).

insertafter(Here, Insert) <-
        sib(Here, Insert).     /* otherwise just do sib */

% create(Label, Node) creates a new Node with label Label, and variable path.
create(Label,Node) <-
        label(Node,Label).

% copy(Node, Copy) creates a copy of Node without its right sib, and
%       with a variable path.
copy(Node,Copy) <-
        detachsib(Node,Copy).

detachsib([tt(L,C,R,W) | P1], [tt(L,C,New,W) | P2]).

% delete(Node,Prev) deletes Node and returns the previous node (left
%       sibling if there is one, otherwise parent.
delete(Node,NP) <-
        left(Node,Prev),
        breaksib(Prev,NP,_),
        connectsib(Node,NP,~). /* connectsib needs non-variable 3rd arg */

delete(Node,NP) <-
        up(Node,Parent),
        breakchild(Parent,NP,_),
        connectsib(Node,NP,NP).

connectsib(Node,Prev,Parent) <-
        right(Node,Sib),
        connect(Sib,Prev,Parent).
connectsib(Node,Prev,Parent).
```

CHAPTER 17

BUP: A Bottom-Up Parsing System for Natural Languages

Yuji Matsumoto Hozumi Tanaka

Electrotechnical Laboratory
Ibaraki, 305, Japan

Tokyo Institute Of Technology
Tokyo, 152, Japan

Masaki Kiyono

Matsushita Electric Industrial Co., Ltd.
Tokyo, 105, Japan

1   Introduction

For high-quality language analysis it is indispensable to have a flexible and efficient parsing system as well as a powerful descriptive language. Prolog is a language based on first-order predicate logic and has very useful features especially for symbolic manipulation. We have been using DECsystem-10 Prolog (Pereira, Pereira, and Warren, 1978) for our Japanese and English analyzing system. This Prolog provides a grammar formalism called Definite Clause Grammars (DCG's) (Pereira and Warren, 1980). In DCG's, each context-free grammar rule is represented as a Prolog clause and each grammar category in a rule is treated as a predicate in the clause. Therefore, a context-free grammar is translated into a Prolog program in a one-to-one manner. Context-sensitive information can be handled easily in DCG's, since we can use the arguments of predicates to deal with such information. Furthermore, arbitrary Prolog calls can be inserted in a grammar rule. These facilities make it easy to combine the parser with auxiliary routines such as semantic-checking or structure-building. A DCG translated into a Prolog program works as a top-down parsing system. Therefore, they provide not only a clear and powerful formalism but a parsing system. Although they have such advantages, DCG's have some drawbacks. They cannot deal with grammars that include left-recursive rules, because of the top-down processing of Prolog. Top-down parsing mechanisms treat the grammar and the dictionary in the same stage. Hence, it is not easy to determine when the parser should consult the dictionary. That is, grammar rules and the dictionary are not treated separately in the top-down parsing processing. In a large natural language analysis system, the size of the dictionary will be much bigger than that of the grammar. In case a large vocabulary is needed in a system, the dictionary should be handled independently in an efficient way.

We have given DCG's another procedural semantics. This is done by transforming each rule written in DCG format into a certain form of Prolog clause. Our system is called BUP (Bottom-up Parsing) and we implemented a translator, called BUP translator, which translates the grammar rules and the dictionary written in DCG into a set of Prolog clauses. The translated clauses, together with some additional clauses, work as a bottom-up parsing system. The dictionary is automatically separated by the translator. In our bottom-up parsing mechanism, the time when the dictionary is consulted is known easily, and the sole Prolog predicate is defined to look up the dictionary. The parser can deal with any cycle-free context-free grammar without empty-productions. Moreover, BUP can be easily reinforced with some facilities very elegantly, as described in Section 4, while for DCG's this is not so easy and will be very complicated.

The next section briefly introduces DCG's. Some basic concepts are inherited in BUP.

Section 3 explains the basic idea of our parsing system, BUP. In BUP, context-free grammar rules correspond to Prolog clauses just as in DCG's. Some additional clauses are necessary to implement this system in Prolog, however. A simple example is also given.

Section 4 describes some improvements which give BUP system facilities to handle morpheme analysis and make the system more efficient.

2   Definite Clause Grammars (Pereira and Warren, 1980)

Definite clauses are of the form:

$$H :- G1, G2, \ldots, Gn. \text{ or}$$
$$H.$$

where H is the head of the clause and G1, ... ,Gn are goals. A Prolog program consists of a set of definite clauses. Note that the forms of definite clauses are structurally equivalent to those of context-free grammar rules. In DEC-10 Prolog, a context-free grammar rule such as

$$\text{sentence(s(NP,VP))} \text{--> np(NP,N),vp(VP,N).}$$

is translated into a definite clause

$$\text{sentence(s(NP,VP),S0,S)} :- \text{np(NP,N,S0,S1),vp(VP,N,S1,S).}$$

This clause means, "there exists a sentence between the points S0 and S, if there is a noun phrase between S0 and S1, and a verb phrase between S1 and S."

In case a sequence of words is represented by the difference of two lists, for example, "John walks" is expressed as the difference of lists [john,walks] and [], then a rule expanding to a terminal symbol, such as

$$np(np(john),sing) \text{ --> } [john].$$

(where the square brackets specify a terminal symbol) can be translated into the unit clause

$$np(np(john),sing,[john|S],S).$$

This form of grammar rule translation is provided in DEC-10 Prolog.

The parsing algorithm used for DCG's mapped into Prolog is top-down depth-first search, because the underlying strategy of the Prolog implementation is input linear resolution of Horn clauses, which always selects the leftmost goal.

DCG's can be considered to be extended context-free grammars. Non-terminal symbols may have any number of arguments. Extra conditions, in the form of Prolog calls, may be written anywhere in the right-hand side of a grammar rule. Such conditions are written in braces, "{" and "}". These are the main facilities of DCG's for specifying the extra conditions and are also provided in BUP, as described in the next section.

3   Principle of BUP

3.1   Basic form of BUP clauses

This section presents the basic idea of the BUP system. The basic form of the grammar rules must be context-free. Context-sensitivity can be expressed by putting arguments in non-terminal symbols or inserting Prolog calls into clauses. We assume that the given context-free grammar is a cycle-free grammar with no empty-productions (hereafter e-productions).

Context-free grammar rules can be expressed in either of the following forms.

$$C \text{ -> } C1,C2, \dots ,Cn \text{ } (n>=1) \qquad (1)$$

$$C \text{ -> } a \qquad (2)$$

An upper case letter stands for a non-terminal and a lower case letter stands for a terminal. To keep the grammar and the dictionary separate, we consider the case where terminal symbols appear only in rules of type 2. As shown in the next section, terminal symbols can also be put in type 1 rules with a slight modification. The above rules are transformed to the following Prolog clauses. According to DEC-10 Prolog's syntax, lower case and upper case indicate constants and variables, respectively. Non-terminal symbols are expressed in lower case letters. Note that Xn-1 in the following clause does not represent a complex structure but it merely indicates the n-1th variable X. Such notations will be found in the following part.

$$cl(G,X1,X) :- goal(c2,X1,X2), \ldots ,goal(cn,Xn-1,Xn),c(G,Xn,X). \tag{1'}$$

$$dict(c,[a|X],X). \tag{2'}$$

Alternatively, they can be expressed in the syntax of DCG's, as follows:

$$cl(G) --> goal(c2), \ldots ,goal(cn),c(G). \tag{1''}$$

$$dict(c) --> [a]. \tag{2''}$$

The predicate 'goal' in the above clause is defined as follows:

$$goal(G,X,Z) :- \tag{4}$$
$$dict(C,X,Y),P=..[C,G,Y,Z],call(P).$$

'=..' is the built-in operator and P becomes a literal whose predicate symbol is C and whose argument list consists of G, Y, and Z. Therefore, P takes the form $C(G,Y,Z)$ when call(P) is executed, provided that C has been instantiated to a constant.

Another set of clauses to be added to the above clauses are as follows. They are the terminal condition of the call of non-terminal symbol, illustrated later.

$$c(c,X,X). \quad \text{(for every non-terminal symbol C)} \tag{5}$$

To explain how the above set of Prolog clauses works as a parser for context-free grammars, we will show an example.

Example. Suppose that the given grammar rules are 1), 2), and 3) in Figure 17.1. They are translated into BUP clauses as 1'), 2'), and 3'). Clauses from 4) to 7) are the additional clauses.

If the sentence to be parsed is "John walks," then BUP is triggered by the following call.

$$?- goal(s,[john,walks],[]).$$

Figure 17.2 shows the execution flow of the above call. In this figure, "=>" indicates the new body created by the unification of a call, "=" means that the both sides of this symbol are equivalent, and "<->" shows that the both literals indicated by this symbol are resolved upon successfully.

```
1)  s --> np,vp.

2)  np --> [john].
3)  vp --> [walks].

1') np(G,X,Z) :- goal(vp,X,Y),s(G,Y,Z).

2') dict(np,[john|X],X).
3') dict(vp,[walks|X],X).

4) goal(G,X,Z) :-
      dict(C,X,Y),P=..[C,G,Y,Z],call(P).

5) np(np,X,X).
6) vp(vp,X,X).
7) s(s,X,X).
```

Figure 17.1. A Sample Grammar and Corresponding BUP Clauses

The BUP system consists of three parts. They are the goal part, the rule part and the dictionary part. Although the dictionary part may be the largest one, it is called only from the goal part. The parsing algorithm of BUP can be expressed by describing the behavior of the goal part and the rule part. The goal part corresponds to the predicate "goal" and the rule part corresponds to the set of clauses transformed from the grammar rules. The second and the third variables of each predicate work as a d-list (the list which represents a string by the difference of two lists) to represent a substring of the given sentence, like DCG's, as explained in the previous section.

Informal description of BUP parsing algorithm.

Goal part. This part receives a non-terminal symbol and a string to be parsed, and tries to find a prefix string of the given string which belongs to the specified non-terminal symbol. This non-terminal symbol is considered to be a goal.

In practice, it consults the dictionary to get the grammar category (non-terminal symbol name) to which the first word of the string belongs, and calls the rule part having this non-terminal symbol as its head.

```
?- goal(s,[john,walks],[]).
     ⇓
dict(C,[john,walks],X1), ... ,call(C(s,X1,[])).
     ↕
dict(np,[john,walks],[walks])
                                    ‖
                             np(s,[walks],[])
                                    ⇓
                          goal(vp,[walks],X2),s(s,X2,[])
                          ⇓
dict(C1,[walks],X3), ... ,call(C1(vp,X3,X2))
     ↕                            ‖
dict(vp,[walks],[])
                             vp(vp,[],X2)
                                    ↕
                             vp(vp,[],[])

                                                s(s,[],[])
```

Figure 17.2. Execution Flow of BUP Clauses of Figure 17.1

Rule part. This part receives a grammar category, the final goal and a string to be parsed. The role of this part is to find the prefix string of the given string which satisfies the goal, on the assumption that the grammar category it has gotten has already been found.

The practical procedure is:

a. If the given grammar category and the goal are equivalent, then this call terminates successfully. Otherwise, go to (b).
b. Pick up a grammar rule that has the given category as the first element of its right-hand side, then call the goal part for each element of the rest of the right-hand side with its own category name as the goal.
c. If all calls of the goal part in (b) succeed, then call the rule part with the category on the left-hand side of the rule, the original goal, and the rest of the given string.

Steps (b) and (c) are called for every rule that has the given grammar category as the first category of its right-hand side, until the call succeeds.

There are two possibilities of nondeterminism: consulting the dictionary in the goal part, and picking up a grammar rule in the rule part. In the above program, they are done by the backtracking mechanism of Prolog.

The parsing algorithm employed by BUP is the left-corner bottom-up method (Aho and Ullman, 1972), while that of DCG is the top-down method. Therefore, BUP can deal with any left-recursive rules except cycle rules.

3.2   Arguments in non-terminal symbols and extra condition

Non-terminal symbols in a BUP clause may have arguments to convey some information. A non-terminal symbol in a DCG clause also can have any number of arguments, and a non-terminal symbol with n arguments is translated into a predicate of $n+2$ arguments. BUP non-terminals in general may have any number of arguments. However, we have given a restriction on the number, since it is done by the sole predicate 'goal' to search for a substring belonging to a certain grammar category. We have made a translator, which translates a given set of DCG clauses into a set of BUP clauses together with the additional Prolog clauses introduced in the previous subsection. In the translation, the arguments in a non-terminal are gathered into a single list.

The BUP clauses (1′) and (2′) in 3.1 now become

$$cl(G,A1,A,X1,X):- \qquad\qquad (1′)$$
$$goal(c2,A2,X1,X2), \dots ,$$
$$goal(cn,An,Xn\text{-}1,Xn),$$
$$c(G,An+1,A,Xn,X).$$

$$dict(c,A1,[a|X],X). \qquad\qquad (2′)$$

In the above BUP clauses, each of A1,....,An+1 is the list of arguments included in the corresponding DCG non-terminal symbol. Variable A in (1') works as the receiver of the information and is instantiated when the call of (1') succeeds.

Accordingly, the goal clause (4) and the terminate clause (5) are now translated into the following:

goal(G,A,X,Z) :-   (4)
    dict(C,A1,X,Y),
    P=..[C,G,A1,A,Y,Z],call(P).

c(c,A,A,X,X)   (for every non-terminal symbol C)   (5)

Terminate clauses guarantee to pass the information from the second variable to the third variable, which is finally received by the variable A in the goal clause or the variable A in the clause like (1').

For example, the following DCG rules:

sentence(s(NP,VP)) --> np(NP,N),vp(VP,N).   and

np(np(john),sing) --> [john].

are translated to the BUP clauses:

np(G,[NP,N],A) --> goal(vp,[VP,N]),
                sentence(G,[s(NP,VP)],A).   and

dict(np,[np(john),sing]) --> [john].

When the goal G is 'sentence', the call of this clause will succeed with the terminate clause

sentence(sentence,A,A,X,X).

and the variable A in the predicate 'np' will be instantiated to '[s(NP,VP)]' after the success.

In the translation, Prolog calls in a DCG rule are put in the appropriate places in the corresponding BUP clause. The details are discussed elsewhere (Matsumoto et al., 1983).

3.3   Linking Relation

For eliminating useless work in the parsing process and for making our parser more efficient, BUP can be reinforced with the top-down expectation called the 'oracle' in Pratt's algorithm (Pratt, 1975).

The call of a non-terminal symbol in BUP means that a string belonging to the corresponding grammar category has been found. The next work to do is to select a grammar rule whose leftmost element in the right-hand side of the rule is same as that category and to make a call of the predicate 'goal' for each of the remaining grammar categories in the right-hand side. When all of these calls succeed, a string belonging to the category on the left side of the rule has been found. These jobs are done by the selected BUP clause. When a BUP clause is called, it receives the goal G. A rule for which the category on the left-hand side has no possibility of becoming the leftmost son of the received goal in a parse tree need not be selected. Such a possibility can be known by computing the linking relation between grammar categories beforehand.

Let the relation 'link0'' hold between two categories A and B when there is a grammar rule whose form is ''B -> A, ...''. Assume that ''link'' is reflexive transitive closure of ''link0''. This relation can be computed when the grammar rules are read in BUP translator. The only other modification is to transform the clauses like (1') to (i) and the definition of the 'goal' to (ii)

$$cl(G,A1,A,X1,X) :- \qquad\qquad\qquad (i)$$
$$link(c,G),$$
$$goal(c2,A2,X1,X2), \ldots ,goal(cn,An,Xn-1,Xn),$$
$$c(G,An+1,A,Xn,X).$$

$$goal(G,A,X,Z) :- \qquad\qquad\qquad (ii)$$
$$dict(C,A1,X,Y),$$
$$link(C,G),$$
$$P=..[C,G,A1,A,Y,Z],call(P).$$

Clause (i) can be rewritten to the equivalent expression (i') as follows:

$$cl(G,A1,A) \rightarrow \{link(cG)\}, \qquad\qquad\qquad (i')$$
$$goal(c2,A2), \ldots ,goal(cn,An),c(G,An+1,A).$$

This relation 'link' works as the local top-down expectation.

4   Refinements of the BUP system

4.1   Dictionary Look-up

Indo-European languages as well as Japanese are inflectional languages. That is, verbs, nouns, etc. in these languages are inflected in many situations. To analyze such a language, parsing systems must have a facility for so-called morpheme analysis.

In BUP, the dictionary look-up is performed by the predicate 'dict', which is called only from the 'goal' procedure. When a call of 'dict' fails, the parser must detect the possibility of an inflection. If we construct a procedure 'morph' which performs morpheme analysis, it is sufficient to modify the 'goal' predicate as follows:

```
goal(G,A,X,Z) :-
    dictionary(C,A1,X,Y),link(C,G),
    P=..[C,G,A1,A,Y,Z],call(P).

dictionary(C,A1,X,Y) :-
    dict(C,A1,X,Y) ; morph(C,A1,X,Y).
```

In the above definition, the predicate 'dictionary' is called or redone many times and 'dict' is consulted or the morpheme analysis is performed each time. When the dictionary becomes larger and it is put in secondary storage, it is not desirable to do such a time-consuming job repeatedly. In order to avoid useless repetition, we rewrote the predicate 'dictionary' to perform all of these tasks for a word when the dictionary look-up of this word occurs.

```
dictionary(C,A1,X,Y) :-
    wf_dict(_,_,X,_),!,wf_dict(C,A1,X,Y).

dictionary(C,A1,X,Y) :-
    ( dict(C,A1,X,Y) ; morph(C,A1,X,Y) ),
    create_dlist(X,Y,U,V),
    assertz( wf_dict(C,A1,U,V) ),fail.

dictionary(C,A1,X,Y) :-
    wf_dict(C,A1,X,Y).
```

The second definition of the above 'dictionary' is the same as the original definition except that all possible dictionary look-ups and morpheme analyses for the given word are performed at this point and they are asserted with the name 'wf_dict', which stands for a well-formed dictionary entity. The predicate 'create_dlist' creates the pair of lists, U and V that represent the same string that X and Y represent, provided that V is always a variable. This helps to avoid repeated computation when more than one occurrence of the same words are found in a sentence. The third definition is then called to use the results. The first definition indicates that once the 'dictionary' and 'morph' are executed for a word, it is sufficient to use only the information already asserted.

4.2   Keeping Successful Goals and Failed Goals

The BUP system utilizes the backtracking facility of Prolog to search for all of the possible parse trees. Although the backtracking facility makes the description of BUP quite a simple one, it causes inefficiency in the parsing process. The situation is just the same with DCG's. When Prolog backtracks, the corresponding information is forgotten. It happens in many cases that BUP tries to perform the same job it has already done; that is, BUP frequently searches the same goal in the same position of the same sentence.

Since the sole predicate 'goal' in BUP searches for a string belonging to the specified grammar category, we can achieve the improvement only by modifying the 'goal' predicate so as not to do the same process repeatedly. Once a substructure is constructed through the success of a call of 'goal', it should be avoided to compute the same thing again. Moreover, once it is found that a string of a certain grammar category cannot be obtained from the certain position of the sentence, it is no use to try the searching process again.

These things are accomplished simply by modifying 'goal' as follows:

```
goal(G,A,X,Z) :-
    ( wf_goal(G,_,X,_) ;
    fail_goal(G,X),!,fail ),!,
    wf_goal(G,A,X,Z).

goal(G,A,X,Z) :-
    dictionary(C,A1,X,Y),link(C,G),
    P=..[C,G,A1,A,Y,Z],call(P),
    assertz( wf_goal(G,A,X,Z) ).

goal(G,A,X,Z) :-
    ( wf_goal(G,_,X,_) ;
    assertz( fail_goal(G,X) ) ),!,fail.
```

The second definition of the above 'goal' is the same as the original one except that the successful goal is asserted with the name 'wf_goal', which stands for a well-formed goal pattern. There are two cases for the second clause to fail: one is that it fails without finding any well-formed goal pattern, and the other is that it fails after finding at least one successful goal pattern. In the former case, it is no use to call 'goal' in the same situation. The third definition asserts this fact with the name 'fail_goal'. Note that the only information required here is the current goal G and the parsing position of the sentence X. Once 'goal' is executed for a goal G and a certain position of the sentence, it need not be tried again. The first definition checks whether 'goal' is called in just the same situation encountered before. The meaning of this clause is as follows: If successful goals have been found, it is sufficient to use them, else if it is known that the attempt to call 'goal' in the given situation eventually fails, it should be avoided to go further, and else if there is no information about the current call, the second clause must be executed.

The completeness of the above refinement will be convinced by the following two facts, though we do not give a precise proof here. First, when 'goal' is called, it receives merely a non-terminal symbol and a certain position within the given sentence. Secondly, once 'goal' is called at a certain position of a sentence, another 'goal' is never called at the same position unless the computation of the previous 'goal' has been finished completely.

5   Discussions

The reason we have developed BUP is to overcome the defects of DCG's. They are:

1.   DCG's cannot deal with left-recursive rules.
2.   The grammar rules and the dictionary are not independently accessible in DCG's.

BUP does not have these drawbacks, although it requires the grammar to be cycle-free and to have no e-productions.

Cycle grammars must be rewritten to cycle-free grammars beforehand. However, a cycle grammar is a special case of a left-recursive grammar. So, the restriction on grammars in this aspect is less for BUP. We are now trying to write a program to reduce cycles.

Although the current BUP does not accept e-productions, it is easy to augment our system to handle such rules. DEC-10 Prolog can express "logical or" in a body of a clause. If the given grammar includes an e-production, for example, "C -> []", then replace every occurrence of "goal(c)" in BUP clause bodies with "(goal(c);[])". If the head name of a BUP clause is "c," then add another BUP clause that is to be created from the grammar rule whose form is the same as the original one except that the first category in the right-hand side is deleted. Through this modification, we have to check whether it changes the grammar to have cycles or e-productions, again. If so, these processes will be applied repeatedly. Although this procedure may be endless, we are also writing a program to reduce e-productions step-by-step. An English grammar we have been using for a machine translation system is translated into a cycle-free, no e-production grammar by the BUP translator. The sizes of the grammar rules and the dictionary are about 150 and 300, respectively.

The BUP system requires some additional Prolog clauses (goal, link, and terminal condition clauses) that DCG's do not have. Each non-terminal symbol needs some additional variables in BUP. Thus, the total amount of the parsing program is larger for BUP than DCG's. These make BUP less efficient when the parsing process can be done in a deterministic manner. We must note, however, that the advantages of BUP may have a more positive effect on execution time. The bottom-up parsing mechanism together with the top-down expectation,

```
|: BUP analyzes many kinds of phrases and sentences.

GC Time = 0  msec.
989  msec.
No. 1
                                               bun
                                                |
              sentence---------------------------------------------------end
                 |                                                         |
                sdec                                                       |
                 |                                                         |
     subj--------v---------------obj                                       |
      |          |                |                                        |
      np       v----suf          np                                        |
      |          |     |          |                                        |
    nomhd        |     |        det---nomhd--------ncomp                    |
      |          |     |          |     |            |                     |
      n          |     |          |     n            pp                    |
                 |     |          |     |            |                     |
                 |     |          |   n--suf   p--------------obj          |
                 |     |          |     |      |               |          |
                 |     |          |     |      |              np          |
                 |     |          |     |      |               |          |
                 |     |          |     |      |  np-----coconj-------np   |
                 |     |          |     |      |   |             |     |   |
                 |     |          |     |      | nomhd           |   nomhd |
                 |     |          |     |      |   |             |     |   |
                 |     |          |     |      |   n             |     n   |
                 |     |          |     |      |   |             |     |   |
                 |     |          |     |      | n---suf         | n----suf|
                 |     |          |     |      |   |    |        |   |    ||
     BUP   analyze  s  many kind  s  of phrase   s       and sentence  s  .
```

Figure 17.3. Example of Parse Tree

makes the search space smaller, and dictionary look-up can be made more efficient for BUP, since it is done by only one predicate "dict". The refinements introduced in Section 4 have made the above-mentioned grammar about ten times faster. Sample parse trees produced by the refined BUP are shown in Figures 17.3 and 17.4. Although our grammar is written in the DCG format, it is not executable in Prolog because of the left-recursive rules. Our Japanese grammar also has left-recursive rules. To make a comparison of the execution time, we wrote another English grammar without left-recursive rules, which includes 25 grammar rules and 40 dictionary entities. We parse several sentences of ten words or so on this grammar. While the original BUP (BUP without the refinements) consumes twice execution time compared with the DCG, the refined BUP runs twice faster than the DCG.

The refinements described in Section 4 are peculiar to BUP. Morpheme analysis is easily implemented in BUP because dictionary look-up is done by the sole predicate 'dict'. In the same manner, predicates 'wf_goal' and 'fail_goal' guarantee that the task of searching for a string of a given grammar category is not tried repeatedly. This is also easily implemented in BUP because searching for a string is dealt with only by the predicate 'goal'.

Although DCG's can be reinforced with similar ideas, that is, it is possible for DCG's to have a morpheme analysis facility and to avoid the same jobs repeat-

```
GC Time = 0  msec.
490  msec.
No. 2
                                                        bun
                                                         |
                      sentence----------------------------------------------end
                         |                                                    |
                        sdec                                                  |
                         |                                                    |
        subj--------v----------------------------obj                         |
          |         |                              |                          |
         np      v----suf                         np                          |
          |      |     |                           |                          |
        nomhd    |     |            np--------------coconj-------np           |
          |      |     |            |                             |           |
          n      |     |      det---nomhd----ncomp              nomhd         |
          |      |     |       |      |        |                  |           |
          |      |     |       |      n        pp                 n           |
          |      |     |       |      |        |                  |           |
          |      |     |       |    n--suf   p-----obj          n----suf      |
          |      |     |       |      |  |     |     |            |   |        |
          |      |     |       |      |  |     |    np            |   |        |
          |      |     |       |      |  |     |     |            |   |        |
          |      |     |       |      |  |     |   nomhd          |   |        |
          |      |     |       |      |  |     |     |            |   |        |
          |      |     |       |      |  |     |     n            |   |        |
          |      |     |       |      |  |     |     |            |   |        |
          |      |     |       |      |  |     |   n---suf        |   |        |
          |      |     |       |      |  |     |     |   |        |   |        |
        BUP   analyze  s   many kind  s  of phrase   s  and  sentence  s    .

GC Time = 0  msec.
Total Time = 2611  msec.

number of wf_goal was :        26.
number of wf_dict was :         9.
number of fail_goal was :      47.
```

Figure 17.4. Second Example of Parse Tree

edly, it is more complicated in a DCG than in a BUP and efficiency cannot be improved compared with a BUP.

6   Conclusions

BUP, a bottom-up parsing system, has been introduced. In this system, grammar rules are embedded in Prolog, similar to DCG's. It can handle the dictionary independently of grammar rules. The restriction on the form of grammar rules is smaller compared with DCG's. Some modifications make this parsing system quite efficient.

We have developed a BUP translator which produces a BUP system from a grammar and a dictionary written as a DCG.

References

Aho, A. V. and J. D. Ullman. (1972). "The Theory of Parsing, Translation, and Compiling, vol. 1 Parsing," Prentice-Hall.

Earley, J. (1968). *An Efficient Context-free Parsing Algorithm.* Ph.D. Thesis, Carnegie-Mellon University.

Matsumoto, Y., et al. (1983). "BUP: A Bottom-Up Parser Embedded in Prolog," *Journal of New Generation Computing,* vol. 1, no.2.

Pereira, L., F. Pereira, and D. Warren. (1978). *User's Guide to DEC System-10 Prolog.* Department of Artificial Intelligence, University of Edinburgh, Sept.

Pereira, F. and D. Warren. (1980). "Definite Clause Grammars for Language Analysis—A Survey of the Formalism and a Comparison with Augmented Transition Networks." *Artificial Intelligence,* 13, pp. 231–278, May.

Pratt, V. R. (1973). "A Linguistic Oriented Programming Language." *Proc. of 3rd IJCAI,* pp. 372–381, Aug.

Pratt, V. R. (1975). "LINGOL—A Progress Report." *Proc. of 4th IJCAI,* pp. 422–428, Aug.

PART VI
FUTURE DIRECTIONS

CHAPTER 18

Aiming for Knowledge Information Processing Systems[1]

Kazuhiro Fuchi

Director, ICOT Research Center
Institute for New Generation Computer Technology
Tokyo, Japan

1 Introduction

In envisaging the fifth generation of computers, what role should "basic theories" play? If there were already an image, the role would have been to provide the generation with theoretical foundations. However, at the present stage, where an image is still being sought, a more aggressive role may be anticipated.

There can be no doubt that when computers were invented, substantial contributions were made from the theory side. Achievements not only in electronics (in those days called electron tube technology) but also in mathematical logic and neurophysiology were skillfully put to use. Turing's theory of logic contributed to the establishment of an image for universal machines, and McCulloch-Pitts's physiological model was closely associated with the philosophy of logic elements. These were cleverly synthesized by J. von Neumann and others, to form the basis for today's computers.

Since then, however, the development of computers has mainly been technological and autonomous. Automata theory, the theory of formal languages, and others emerged but they have not directly influenced the progress of computers. Rather, computer technology can be said to have created more diverse phenomena than then existing theories could have predicted.

Early in the seventies the phenomena were properly formalized (theorized). This theorization belonged in the field of mathematical theories of programming. This movement is still progressing, and is not as yet complete. It may be described as an intermediate stage in organizing the creations of computer technology. On the other hand, in this an image for new machines (new architecture) seems to be gestating.

---

[1] This is a revised version of an article of the same title which appeared in the *Proceedings of the International Conference on Fifth Generation Computer Systems*, Tokyo, October 19–22, 1981.

Independently (at least on the surface) of mathematical theories of programming, there have been, since the early seventies, gropings toward a new machine architecture. Noteworthy amongst these are research on database machines and dataflow machines. The reason for this particular attention at this time is that such machines have started exhibiting progress that synchronizes with the progress in mathematical programming theories. The synchronization, however, is not necessarily clear under the conventional philosophy on architecture, and perhaps because of this, has led only to spontaneous proposals. It is felt that under a new concept many of the proposals made so far can be integrated.

There is much dissatisfaction with present-day computers. One of the complaints which perhaps calls for introspection on the computer side is that today's technology is far from the ideal of being truly "handy" for users.

One of the factors concerned with "handiness" is the interface between man and machine. Natural media for communication from the human side are primarily graphic communications and conversations in natural languages. To realize these communication objectives calls not only for expansion of input and output media, but also, necessarily, for higher performance capabilities of the system itself.

Meanwhile, another factor involved in "handiness" apart from sophistication of communication media, is that functions inherent to the system need to be upgraded. This may be termed, sloganistically, integration of "knowledge."

With current computer technology, a majority of solutions for a problem must be "programmed." If information relative to the object areas of the problem together, preferably, with laws governing those areas can be integrated, it will distinctly improve the problem-solving capabilities of the computer system. Information of this kind corresponds to "knowledge" on the human side.

Integration of "knowledge" is one way of achieving "handiness." This problem at the same time is bound up with such sophistication of communication media as natural languages. On the human side, too, languages and knowledge are inextricably linked.

Incidentally, the subject of realizing high performance capabilities by way of knowledge and languages was, in the seventies, the main theme of research into so-called "artificial intelligence." Of course, the research has not solved this problem. It is necessary to organize the achievements of research efforts of the past, and to develop them still further. At the same time, here is other material to be added in contemplating fifth generation computers. If basic theories are not limited to "mathematical" theories, this material may be included in generalized basic theories.

Research into artificial intelligence has not been aimed at mere realization of high performance capabilities. Investigation of the mechanisms needed to realize high performance is a necessary part of the research. For instance, take the subject of a "programming language" for artificial intelligence. Its final form has not been established, but proposals made on the basis of such investigations are rich in suggestions for new machine organization.

Of much interest is the fact that such proposals have started resonating with proposals made separately based on mathematical theories of programming. The imminent emergence of a common image, from research efforts thus far promoted in separate fields of activity, seems to portend a new computer image for the future.

Judging from basic research achievements accumulated in the seventies, progress in hardware technologies, and other related fields, the time now seems to be ripe to plan new computers together with a new system of information processing.

If a bold proposal were to be made at this point, it might be summarized as "realization of knowledge information processing and knowledge information processors (inference machines)." This is to collectively pursue the feasibilities of a new (non-von Neumann) architecture, and of the utilization of language information and knowledge information.

Frankly, such a proposal may be entertained at present only as recognition or hypothesis. However, whereas the fourth generation is generally believed to be a continuation of the present generation, in contemplating the forthcoming fifth generation computers, such a discontinuity in ideas appears to be inevitable. In planning for the fifth generation of computers, views based on basic theories may provide the required guidance.

Many stages must be gone through to realize an ideal, but it now appears to be time to take the first step in that direction (as a trial). The currently dwindling optimism for continued progress in present-day technology is believed to signify a certain type of maturity and plateauing of conventional technologies. It is causing some pessimism concerning the advancement of generations, but at the same time it may signify that the opportunity for the next, new generation is ripe.

2   Interrelations Between Various Basic Research Efforts

The seventies may be viewed as an era in which computer-related technologies each exhibited interesting advances. In the latter part of the decade, interrelations between them became more and more apparent. These can be seen as the advance preparations for the overall development to come in the eighties which will eventually bear fruit in the nineties. They permit anticipation today of a new generation of information processing technology and a new image of the computers which will form its core.

Advances in large-scale integration (SI) technology, though perhaps not revolutionary technically, have certainly been outstanding, with their impact expected to be revolutionary in providing the groundwork for the new era. It should be the responsibility of the new era to find out how best to take advantage of such advances.

2.1   Trials for New Computer Architecture

Concerning computer systems as a whole, distributed processing and the building of networks were developed in the seventies as a new direction. Meanwhile, the principles of the internal structure of computers themselves have not changed much since von Neumann's invention. Moreover, various situations have kept computers somewhat tied down to "standard architectures" such as that of the IBM S/370. Changes in the philosophy of system architecture, such as distributed processing, have the potential to affect computer architecture itself, but have not manifested themselves as yet.

The study of computer architecture itself has been going on for a long time. Such proposals as associative processing, parallel processing, and variable structures were made some time ago. Also, proposals of implementation techniques such as stacking, tagging, and hashing, have been numerous. Architecture philosophies based on high-level languages have already been proposed.

However, even though some techniques such as stacking have actually been put into practice, most of these proposals have not as yet borne fruit. Prototype machines designed with this "bottom-up" philosophy have faced programming and other difficulties, and failed to gain favorable evaluation. Meanwhile, high-level language machine philosophies have failed to prove that they are particularly advantageous when implementations were limited to conventional ones, and since the structure of the language employed itself was predicated on a von Neumann architecture, the effort has essentially been circular.

So far, it rather appears that the strength of von Neumann's system has been reconfirmed. Taking this opportunity, let us take a little time to review some features of von Neumann's system that represent the basic principles for all universal computers in use at the present time.

The basic structure of von Neumann's system is in the combination of uniformly structured memory devices and simply structured arithmetic and control units. Realization of complex and sophisticated functions is left to "programs." A program consists of a group of simply structured instructions, and the program itself is stored in uniformly structured memory devices, with its execution being serial and simple.

The essential property of von Neumann's system is the realization of universal machines with simple structures. It was in conformity with the electronics technology levels of those days as well as those available until recently. For instance, if he had started with a machine capable of directly executing lambda calculus, realization of universal computers would have been substantially delayed. Since his days, various extensions have been attempted based on this simple structure.

Both the advantages of von Neumann's system and the complaints against it in some quarters stem from this structure.

The most significant of the latest complaints is the complexity and difficulty in programming (Kowalski, 1974). The difficulty is especially severe in producing large-scale software. The von Neumann system, despite various improvements and extensions, essentially leaves realization of high-performance functions up to software.

With regard to programming, employment of high-level languages has hitherto been promoted as a solution to these problems. Even here however, compilers and other language processing systems are required, inviting cumbersome software.

Meanwhile, parallel processing and associative functions have been considered to provide higher performance functions and more sophisticated functions. Ironically, however, prototypes based on these philosophies invited even worse difficulties in programming. Array architecture and matrix architecture computers were put to experimental use for ultra-high-speed numerical computations (Russell, 1978). Even viewing these as dedicated machines, the difficulties in programming were overwhelming. Regarding associative functions, technical difficulties in realizing associative memory devices for them have helped aggravate the difficulties.

This situation is about to change. On the one hand, the outstanding LSI advances have started to make the realization of complicated hardware feasible. At the same time, in attempting to take full advantage of this, the von Neumann system is beginning to be seen as a bottleneck. On the other hand, new ideas have emerged concerning architecture. And in the area of programming as well, introspection on its styling has recently been going on.

With regard to architecture for parallel computers, dataflow type architecture has lately drawn much attention (see Gurd, Kirkham, & Watson, for example). The dataflow philosophy describes the computing processes via the flow of data rather than centering around controls. Parallel operations are described naturally in terms of the flow of data, and are then to be executed by hardware. However, if this idea is realized, the resulting processor will serve only one purpose. In moving toward the variable architecture, Dennis developed the architecture based on a message-exchanging philosophy (Dennis & Misunas, 1975). Here can be seen a fusion of parallel processing and variable architecture philosophies. In its architecture, it is a totally different system from von Neumann's.

Of particular interest is the recent emergence of yet another fusion with a philosophy from the software engineering side. Dataflow is based on a concept of function. On the other hand, as will be described later, software engineering proposed new-style programming to side-step the difficulties in conventional programming. One of these new styles was Backus's functional programming, which was to become linked with the dataflow machine philosophy (Backus, 1978).

From the conventional fixed idea concerning difficulties in programming for parallel machines, this was an epoch-making change in the situation. Backus's proposal itself, as a non-von Neumann programming system, is not necessarily predicated on the existence of suitable hardware. However, it relates to the hardware architecture represented by dataflow machines.

Actually, as a functional programming language, there is a single assignment language (SAL) that is a natural intermediate language, and this SAL relates naturally to the dataflow language. SAL itself conforms to a language that was proposed as an easy language for verification by software engineering with an entirely different motivation than that for dataflow machines.

SAL, furthermore, resembles what has been derived from research on inference systems (connection graphs) (Jackendoff, 1972; Sickel, 1976; Stickel, 1982). The dataflow machines made by Dennis and others were initially considered for use in numerical computations, but at this point a still greater potential for them has been found. It is feasible to extend dataflow machines to inference machines.

This step, as will be described later, embraces logic programming philosophies and formal specification languages, includes subjects on relational databases (and database machines based on them), and furthermore exhibits a potential for linkage with the semantics of natural languages. Whether such machines will prove themselves remains to be seen, but this concept is an extremely attractive one. If such machines were realized, all kinds of subjects could be integrated and uniformly organized, down to even the machine architecture level.

2.2   New Programming Styles

For computer technology, the issues of software productivity have lately become matters of increasing concern. The contribution of software to the total cost of computers has been increasing and now represents the major part. This is not only due to the increased size of the software component. It is also due to increasingly greater labor required to guarantee program quality.

One requirement is to guarantee the "correctness" of programs and another is to develop procedures to produce correct programs. It is a major problem for software engineering to establish a system for (correctly) producing programs in accordance with the required specifications.

To clearly express "specifications," the problem of specification writing methods (the language for specifications) must be overcome. For this purpose, a language of higher level than programming languages will be required.

Assuming a specification can be clearly expressed, if a correct and efficient program in accordance with it could be automatically synthesized, that would be ideal. However, realization of the ideal is still a long way in the future. Before that, for instance, a procedure will need to be established to build up the program by stages while guaranteeing its correctness. This may be restated as a matter of program manufacturing methods (styles).

Since Dijkstra's proposal for "structured programming," there has been frequent introspection into programming styles (Dahl, Dijkstra, & Hoare, 1972).

Given such awareness of the problem, are the presently-used programming languages appropriate? Introspection into styles is accompanied by examination of how programming languages should behave. Recently, out of this stream of philosophizing, there emerged proposals which could be entitled "logic programming." One is a proposal for predicate calculus programming, and another a proposal for functional programming. As a language, the former employs a predicate calculus form, and the latter is based on function logics. These proposals recommend the use of the logic forms themselves as programming languages.

These correspond to the two streams in formal specification languages (the function and predicate calculus types), while they also urge examination of how specification and programming languages should behave. Formal specifications may be regarded as generalized (highly abstract) programs. These abstract programs are made concrete in accordance with system requirements. If this transformation could be detected in the same language (logic), it would provide many advantages. Research efforts are beginning to get under way along this direction. Such a philosophy may possibly link up in the future with the "data abstraction" philosophy which is also one of the main streams in software engineering (Liskov & Zilles, 1977).

"Program transformations" need to be effected while guaranteeing correctness (identity of meanings retained) (see Pepper, 1984, for example). "Verification" (as a system) is also one of the major subjects of software engineering. However, if, for the programming language, one of the languages normally used is employed, various difficulties will arise. For this reason, easily verifiable programming languages are being proposed, for instance, Lucid by Ashcroft and others (Ashcroft & Wadge, 1982). This is a kind of SAL, described previously.

Functional programming languages and predicate calculus programming differ somewhat in style, but in fact there is a natural relationship between them. Lucid and other SALs (and extensions of them) have emerged as intermediate languages in this correspondence.

SAL links with the dataflow machine philosophy, as stated previously. This leads to the concept of "inference machines" which are extended dataflow machines.

2.3 Semantics of Programming Languages

Verification of the correctness of programs may be restated as confirmation of identical "meanings." Therefore, the "semantics" of programming languages needs to be established.

It may be inferred that with "artificial" languages such as programming languages, the definition of meanings should be simple. In reality, however, considerable difficulties have been encountered, even historically. The syntax of artificial languages can be expressed as "artificial" (simple), but their meanings do not seem to be artificial. The situation parallels the difficulties in the semantics of natural languages.

From the sixties to the seventies, a number of trials in semantics were conducted. One was operational semantics. In it, an abstract machine was imagined, where the meanings of languages were to be provided by descriptions of an interpreter. This was developed in the late sixties as the Vienna definition method (Bjorner & Jones, 1978). Using it for verification, however, presented great difficulties.

In the seventies, axiomatic semantics were started by Hoare and others (Hoare, 1969). This was a development of Floyd's theory concerning flowcharts in the latter part of the sixties (Floyd, 1967). In this case, selection of the language to be axiomatized became a problem. At the same time, the "correctness" of the axiomatic system and inference rules presented a theoretical problem.

In parallel with the above, denotational semantics was developed by Scott and others (Stoy, 1977). This was intended to accurately and mathematically designate language semantics based on a model theory. Scott's theory may also be considered to support axiomatic and operational semantics. With this as a base, the "mathematical theory of programming" recently started developing.

One of the conclusions drawn from these efforts is that the normally-used programming languages are difficult to handle through semantic approaches. Is it because the semantics are constructed inadequately? Particularly interesting is the fact that items for introspection concerning programming styles, which were intuitively pointed out independently of such theoretical approaches, happened to coincide with difficulties in semantics.

In structured programming, for instance, the use of "GO TO" statements was considered to be harmful (Dijkstra, 1968). Similarly, the semantic construction of "GO TO" is also difficult to analyze.

These situations reinforce the directions toward new programming styles and new programming languages to support them. As Backus pointed out, the difficulties found in conventional languages stem from the von Neumann type machines that they are dedicated to. The new direction is a change over to non-von Neumann type languages, which leads to expectations of non-von Neumann type computers.

The semantics of the functional and predicate calculus languages previously described are rather clear-cut. These, furthermore, link with non-von Neumann architecture such as dataflow machines.

2.4   Relational Databases

Development of database systems was one of the central elements in the progress of computer technology in the seventies. How to organize and utilize gigantic volumes of data was the question. Progress was made by accumulating experience. Along with it, efforts to organize such experience theoretically also went on.

Codd's proposal for relational databases was made early in the seventies (Codd, 1970), but is only now about to become a major stream in structuring databases. This is based on a theory of "relations." As query language for databases, both predicate formulas (relational calculus) and functional formulas (relational algebra) have been proposed. These are mutually interchangeable. They can be regarded as certain special kinds of logic, and during the seventies a great deal of theoretical research effort was made in this area.

As described earlier, proposals for logical forms are being made from the standpoint of programming. The philosophy of relational databases is closely linked with this. Relationships between them, and the fusing of the two, are becoming very interesting, as the themes of the latest research.

Research on "database machines" based on relational databases was vigorously carried on in the seventies. None of it, however, seems to have attained a usable level as yet. Though relational databases are theoretically clear-cut, their prototype machines seem to have been structured through ad hoc approaches only.

Database machines, however, are predicted in many quarters to become the buds which will flower as the new architecture machines of the future. However, research on database machines during the eighties will have to be substantially stepped up. Research achievements toward this objective that are worthy of note have been emerging lately (Ottman, Rosenberg, & Stockmeyer, 1982).

As is predictable from the relations with logic programming already pointed out, database machines were expected to be associated with dataflow machines. In fact, a proposal for dataflow type database machines (relational algebraic machines) has quite recently been made (by Y. Tanaka, 1984). This is still at a specialized machine stage, but is promising for future generalization. Its high-order retrievals on databases are just a form of "inference" itself. It can also be said to have pointed out the feasibility of inference machines from the standpoint of database machines.

At present, databases and programming languages are typically separate systems. This is not a desirable situation. Their unification is a subject for the future, but as described in the foregoing, it appears to be quite feasible. This will then become the starting point for a new software system. Simultaneously, we can look forward to organization of the whole based on a unified viewpoint that encompasses even the hardware level.

2.5   Contributions from Linguistics

Expectations are rising that natural languages will be usable in programming and for querying databases. However, this will require a major advance in the way we communicate with computers, and at present few people appear to feel that the theories of natural languages (linguistics) and computer systems will ever merge. Is this so?

Research into the nature of languages surely is the main job of linguistics. At the same time, theoretical linguistics establishes a language model. At this point, let us view theoretical linguistics with regard to its framework.

In the sixties, tremendous developments were made in linguistics based on Chomsky's "generative-transformational grammar" theory (Chomsky, 1957, 1965), which attempted to explain the syntactic phenomena of languages. Its framework defines the basic structures from which, by transformational rules, the surface structures of languages are derived. In the seventies, more emphasis on the analysis of "meanings" subjected the framework of the generative-transformational theory to major changes. The generative-transformational theory then divided into two major streams, generative semantics (Lakoff, 1969) and interpretive semantics (Jackendoff, 1972).

Meanwhile, early in the seventies, Montague's new linguistic theory emerged (Montague, 1973). This came from a branch of philosophical linguistics, and is directly concerned with how to formalize semantic theories. It extended formal semantics contained in philosophical linguistics and applied it to a fragment of English, producing a model that unified syntax and semantics for the first time. This task had been considered a difficult problem since ancient times. Mainstream linguistics had rather side-stepped the issue. The handling of semantics was only partially presented in relation to phenomenal analyses, and no clear presentation was made of the structure of the entire discipline of semantics.

Opinions of linguists vary with regard to the Montague theory. Some have negative opinions. On the other hand, some degree of convergence has begun. This is especially true with generative semantics, owing to the similarity of its model. Meanwhile interpretive semantics, with which Chomsky himself is involved, is also becoming more closely associated with logic, independently of, but in parallel with, the foregoing.

Montague's theory is a logical linguistic theory. In it, "intensional logic" (Gallin, 1975), whose semantics is clear-cut, is introduced as the base logic, and a procedure is given for transforming sentences in natural language into the intensional logic. In this framework, Montague demonstrated a method of applying formal semantics to natural languages, something which had previously been regarded as questionable.

Intensional logic is a kind of modal logic that has been transformed into functional forms. The semantics of modal logic (model theory) was introduced by Kripke (1963). It seeks to define the meanings of logical formulas in terms of "possible worlds."

Then, what is the significance of such developments in linguistics from the standpoint of computer technology? Functional logic is no stranger to the world of computers. The language Lisp is based on such a logic. Functional languages have thus regained prominence because of proposals for functional programming. Intensional logic is an extension of this logic.

The structure of the Montague theory itself closely resembles LINGOL, a parser system created by Pratt from a totally different perspective (Pratt, 1975). Thus, the Montague theory by accident largely overlaps with what has been created from computer technology.

The semantics of programming languages referred to earlier originally stemmed from formal semantics. One of the interesting aspects is that the timing of the breakthroughs made in both fields (again accidentally) roughly coincided.

Furthermore, the model theory of intensional logic (Kripke's possible worlds model) is intuitively easy to grasp if viewed from a database standpoint.

The range of natural language to be handled practically by computers is limited to portions that are logically graspable. Were this limitation to be unnatural, it would support an argument against the original intention behind natural languages. Even with this limitation, the range of natural language that can be used adequately will still be wide enough to be able to say natural language is indeed handled. From this viewpoint, progress in logical linguistics will be highly welcome to the computer side. In the course of this progress, it is conceivable that logical linguistics and computer technology will tend to merge as many overlapping phenomena are observed. To make this happen will be far from easy, but its potential for the future is believed to be almost unlimited (Barwise & Perry, 1983).

2.6   Developments in Artificial Intelligence

Research in artificial intelligence goes back a long way (McCorduck, 1979). Also, there have been many different approaches to it. Artificial intelligence research reached a turning point in the early seventies, with its awareness of the problem of "languages and knowledge." Such awareness was considered too highbrow by ordinary computer engineers. At that time, the philosophies of software engineering, database methodology, and the like, were against it. Lately, however, these movements have begun to overlap to a large extent, and to become fused together.

The maturing of artificial intelligence in the seventies is symbolized by the emergence of Winograd's question-answering system (Winograd, 1972). This had as its object a limited world of toy building blocks, but with a knowledge model in its background: it handled questions and answers in natural language.

Since then, a wider awareness of the central problems in artificial intelligence research, such as how to represent and use knowledge, has emerged. Because of this, discussion among linguistics and psychology became active.

At the same time, practical research has been conducted on the problem of determining programming languages for artificial intelligence. Planner and other similar proposals (Hewitt, Bishop, & Steiger, 1973; Sussman & McDermott, 1973) may be regarded, not only as programming languages for artificial intelligence, but also as representing the direction of evolution of programming languages themselves.

Planner was an attempt at converting an inference system into a programming language. In it were included concepts for pattern-matching, nondeterministic computation, and multiple databases. On the other hand, subsequent progress in research on theorem-proving (or inference) systems has shown that it is feasible to directly convert the Planner concept back into an inference system. This is represented by the predicate calculus programming proposal described earlier. Prolog, and other languages based on the predicate calculus programming philosophy (Clocksin & Mellish, 1981; Malachi, Manna, & Waldinger, 1984; Weyhrauch, 1977), may be regarded as a logically reorganized Planner. This development also makes sense from the viewpoint of programming language semantics. The formal semantics of Planner is not clear, which is probably one reason why it did not last.

Planner itself subsequently progressed to an actor model (Plasma) (Hewitt, Bishop, & Steiger, 1973). Plasma models processes using a philosophy of message exchanges. This scheme can be regarded as being an extended form of the dataflow philosophy. Actors and dataflow, however, have different motivations. In reviewing the research endeavors of the seventies, a number of phenomena have emerged from research efforts which started from independent motives and later linked with each other, of which the above is one example.

Research into knowledge representation is a major theme of artificial intelligence, but here, too, links with research on databases have become increasingly evident (Gallaire & Minker, 1978). Knowledge representation has come to be associated with an awareness of the problems of making databases more sophisticated. Previously these were concerns of separate research groups, but now there are noticeable efforts to integrate the two together (Tsichritzis & Lochousky, 1982). The task of giving higher-order structure to databases is believed to be also deeply interrelated with intensional logic and its possible world model referred to earlier.

Another notable aspect of artificial intelligence research is that in the latter half of the seventies, applications of artificial intelligence techniques actually started taking place. This applied artificial intelligence is called "knowledge engineering" (Feigenbaum, 1977). Consultation systems integrating specialized knowledge in medicine, chemistry, and other professional fields have been built and are attracting attention. For knowledge engineering, an image, "knowledge base plus inference engine," is being proposed as the system framework (Davis, Buchanan, & Shortliffe, 1977).

Although present-day knowledge engineering may be able to realize part of the goals of artificial intelligence, it is better thought of as the basis for future information processing. As has already been made clear, it is acquiring ever closer links with software engineering and other research efforts. Judging from the closeness of these links, knowledge engineering will probably be able to absorb this other research into a unified form in a natural manner.

At this time, we would like to call such an extended form of knowledge engineering "knowledge information processing." This, we believe, will represent the form of information processing in the nineties.

In artificial intelligence research, there is a concern with the problems of explaining human intelligence, which at present has led to proposals for cognitive sciences. At the same time, artificial intelligence research has also played the role of precipitator of advances in computer technology.

Reviewing the seventies, research efforts in computer technology may be said to have been split into a number of branches or streams, and to have progressed through mutual competition. At the same time, interrelationships between them grew in the latter half of the decade, and a trend towards mutual fusion emerged. This may be regarded as an important legacy from the seventies and a valuable bud which will blossom in the eighties and nineties.

3   Development Steps

For the advanced information processing systems of the 1990s, a "knowledge information processing system" is postulated, and steps for its development will be considered (Figure 18.1).

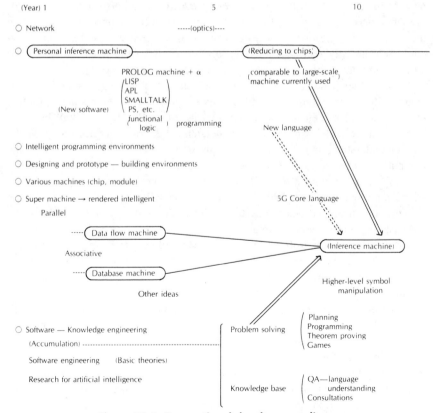

Figure 18.1. Conceptional development diagram

This is an image for the future, and also our hope as an objective. Would such an objective be adequate? Some prefer to remain conservative. Further discussion will be needed to solidify the image. Also, if the objective is accepted, how should the development steps be planned? A number of requirements come to mind.

3.1   Functional Images

Functional images for knowledge information processing systems can be viewed as having two facets, man-machine interfacing and problem-solving capabilities.

Concerning man-machine interface, a function is conceivable which would permit a natural mode of communication with the computer via natural language, graphics and the like. For natural language input, besides a keyboard, written and spoken input will be required. For graphic input, hand-drawn and pictorial input will be desirable. To enable communication using this kind of input, the system will have to extract "meaning" from the input.

In addition to understanding the meaning of input messages, the system will need to have the capabilities of answering questions and also, occasionally, of giving advice. Furthermore, the abiity to give indirect responses after digesting the intent of the questions, and to give summarized answers, will also be desirable. Successively realizing these capabilities will be the most likely way to endow computers with truly intelligent communicative powers.

On the other hand, answering questions and adequately accommodating requests will require internal "problem-solving functions." At this point, mutual understanding between man and machine regarding "problems" will be vital. The computer will be required to understand the problems according to the human understanding. This is just a question of the "knowledge" that the computer possesses concerning the problem area. This type of mutual understanding (even though at a low level initially) is the basis for cooperation between man and machine. This kind of function will be required of advanced CAD (computer-aided design) systems. Such common knowledge will also be the basis for more fluent communication.

Even systems such as those described above will need to be instructed by man to do high-level problem-solving. In decision-making, when multiple solution strategies are presented, augmented by examinations and hypothetical approvals by the computer, man's high-level judgment will be effective.

Functions for describing hypotheses, and examining and approving them will be important, but at the same time, this poses a difficult research problem concerning how to handle incomplete knowledge.

Also important will be functions for acquiring new information and adding to the memory bank's knowledge on the problem area. This is primarily a matter of integrity, i.e., the problem of fusing the additions with the existing knowledge without contradiction and integrating them. Second, there is the question of "inductive inference," or the problem of extracting rules from a set of data. These may be restated as learning problems. There is also the problem of accepting knowledge from man himself. People do not necessarily understand things in a well-organized form. This resembles the problem of requirement analysis in software engineering.

The above may be regarded as auxiliary systems for knowledge information processing system, but can also be viewed as higher-order knowledge (meta-knowledge) systems.

In knowledge information systems, the volume of accumulated software will become vast indeed. For this reason, too, flexible capabilities such as learning functions will be required. Regarding the nature of the processing, there will be a requirement for sophisticated processing of nonnumeric (symbolic) data. This is "inference," and consists essentially of nondeterministic algorithms. To efficiently execute these algorithms will require assistance from hardware, but will also largely depend on the structure and quality of software. Techniques to deal with this are emerging in the field of software engineering. One is the philosophy of data abstraction and the step-by-step programming methodology based on it. This will substantially alleviate the complexity of problems. The second philosophy is the technique of program transformation based on certain rules. This provides a way of transforming the abstract to the concrete. These philosophies will be integrated in a natural manner into the framework of knowledge information processing.

As to hardware requirements, there will be a need for sophisticated "symbol processing machines" that execute inferences at high speed. The requirements here will include pattern-matching functions, nondeterministic processing functions, and associated garbage collection functions (memory control functions). Nondeterministic processing includes not only backtracking but also other possible parallel processing styles. Machines of this kind may be termed inference machines.

The second important hardware element will be a database machine. For better compatibility with inference systems, relational database machines are the most promising. Regarding their retrieval functions, relational algebra machines are conceivable that directly execute relational algebra operations. These are also a kind of inference machine.

Fifth generation computers can be imagined as an extension of the foregoing hardware. They will be knowledge information processors, and as systems, knowledge information processing systems.

3.2   Inference Systems

Universal knowledge information processors may be considered to be problem-solving machines comprising knowledge bases and inference machines. Inference systems are discussed below in terms of their functions.

The degree of difficulty in problem-solving varies widely with the nature of the problem at hand. With regard to the factors affecting the degree of difficulty, those related to logic include completeness and invariance of the knowledge base. Physically, there is the problem of the volume of knowledge to be handled.

3.2.1 Inferences on Databases. Normal databases are theoretically supposed to be invariable in their structure and complete in their knowledge at each respective point in time. Much research work has already been done concerning this, and a technical level has been reached at which retrievals and control can be efficiently performed. Inferences are based on the "closed world assumption," and can be reduced to operations on relational algebra (Reiter, 1978).

Based on the above, various hardware experiments have been described so far in research on database machines. Conceivable for their future direction are relational algebra processors that, as hardware, would execute the relational algebra operations mentioned above. If these were realized, such operations could be executed at high speed. A number of processor proposals exist, of which the most promising probably is the one proposed by Tanaka (1984). This is a proposal for a dataflow type processor operating in parallel in a pipeline mode. It is an inference machine for a limited logic, but it is thought that it could lead to greater sophistication and greater efficiency for commercial databases.

3.2.2 Inferences in Predicate Calculus. When a set of knowledge is incomplete but static (invariable), it can be expressed by normal (not including temporal variables) first-order predicate calculus.

Inference in first-order predicate calculus includes the well-known resolution method. Resolution has simple propositional rules, but involves certain disadvantages in efficiency. Recent achievements, including the connection graphs created by Kowalski (1974) and Sickel (1976), and others where propositional and variable portions are separated, however, constitute efficient procedures for this method.

Also, pertaining to the Horn clause subset of first-order predicate calculus, Prolog, a programming language based on this subset, has been proposed, and at the same time excellent implementation techniques have been developed permitting its efficient execution (Campbell, 1984). This language is based on non-determinism and pattern-matching functions, and has functions similar to Planner, but is superior since it is based on logic. Extensions to it also are being studied (Chikayama, 1984; Clark & Gregory, 1984; Shapiro, 1983).

3.2.3 Metaknowledge and Inference Process Control. A disadvantage of first-order predicate calculus is its inability to handle knowledge about utilization of knowledge (i.e., metaknowledge). In other words, such knowledge generally consists of information for controlling inference processes themselves, and cannot be expressed in first-order logic; on the other hand, if utilization of such knowledge were feasible, one would be able to avoid unnecessary search.

Concerning Prolog, trials are being made to integrate metaknowledge (Bundy & Welham, 1981; Gallaire & Lasserre, 1982).

3.2.4 Truth Maintenance. When the knowledge base is incomplete and dynamic, it becomes necessary to realize inference functions based on hypotheses, and functions to do revision of hypotheses based on new knowledge. This was shown by Doyle (1978) and others to be realizable by problem-solving machines consisting of two subsystems: an inference system and a truth maintenance system. The truth maintenance part is the metasystem for the inference part, and can be used to control the inference part. Using this philosophy, Doyle developed a backtracking control system that is theoretically efficient. When an inconsistency is found, the system backtracks directly to the point where the inconsistency occurred, rather than to the selection point immediately prior to it, as in the case of normal backtracking. As the truth maintenance part is separate, inferences performed so far, except the erroneous portion, remain valid in subsequent inferences. This provides extensions over previous logical systems, and can perform exception-handling inferences.

This system can also be used, when updating databases, as a control procedure to constantly maintain database consistency. It can be also used for step-by-step learning of knowledge. Systems of this kind possess functions desirable for knowledge information processing, but are as yet at the research stage, and their progress is eagerly awaited.

3.3 Intelligent Programming Systems

The theme "intelligent programming" is considered important in pursuit of knowledge information processing technology for two reasons. One is that intelligent programming is indispensable as a tool for developing knowledge information processing systems. With knowledge-based information systems, the software will be on a large scale, and the functions will be sophisticated and complex. Development of these will be accomplished in an evolutionary manner. For this purpose, advanced, well-structured processors will be desirable, but at the same time, a sophisticated development support system will also be required.

The second reason is that intelligent programming systems themselves will have to be developed as knowledge-based information systems. In this sense, they will represent a specimen application of, and prototypes for, knowledge information systems themselves.

Systems such as the above, therefore, will come into being in parallel with research on knowledge information processing systems. As a starting point, they will probably materialize on top of the high-performance personal Prolog machine described later on, and be formed into a network through full utilization of conventional technology. Useful software tools developed beforehand will probably be integrated in these systems from the start. With this kind of accumulation as its basis, progress will probably be toward knowledge-based processing.

Turning to past technology, the following techniques are considered useful:

1. Interactive processing: Interactive processing environments developed on timesharing systems will be further developed. Utilization of editors, graphics terminals, and the like.
2. Structured programming: Structured programming which employs interactive processing.
3. System description languages and specification languages (e.g. the Iota-system of R. Nakajima & Yuasa, 1983).
4. Graphic languages: There are fewer technical difficulties in using graphic languages than in using natural languages. Furthermore, there are advantages in graphic languages themselves. It will be necessary to reconsider graphic (iconic) programming. Structured displays of programs, and others. Techniques will be required for inputting, outputting, editing and controlling graphic data.
5. Data abstraction.
6. Requirement specifications and specification descriptions: Transformation from formal specifications to programs. Various experiments on informal specifications. Experiments on verification methods.
7. Algorithm banks: Program libraries will have to be reorganized in a more versatile manner. For this purpose, description in better languages will be required. Such banks will constitute one kind of knowledge base.
8. Programming in a natural language (Japanese): Intelligent programming systems integrating all of the above techniques will provide, on the one hand, opportunities to review and revise existing technology, and on the other, opportunities for new experiments. The systems are themselves tools with which new products can be constructed. And these constructed products can again work as tools.

So far we have concentrated mainly on programming, but in such systems it should also be feasible to develop intelligent hardware design systems. While these latter have certain unique aspects, many aspects remain that are shared with software design systems. Such systems will facilitate design, not only of software, but also of a great variety of things to enable LSI devices to exhibit their full capabilities. LSI devices are themselves a major theme for the future. At the same time, they also represent tools indispensable for building knowledge information systems up into a new total organization that includes hardware.

3.4   Inference Machines

3.4.1 Prolog Machines and Local Networks. Described below are Prolog machines and the networks that connect them, which are treated here as a starting point for building up knowledge information processing systems.

It goes without saying that appropriate "symbol processing machines" are desirable in knowledge information processing. The recent development of Lisp machines seems to have been aimed towards this same objective.

The reason for our proposal for using Prolog as the starting point rather than Lisp is primarily that Prolog can be seen as an extension of Lisp. Though Prolog systems currently in use still have some flaws, they are considered capable of integrating all the advantageous features of Lisp systems. In addition, Prolog systems provide pattern-matching functions, nondeterministic functions, and other extensions over Lisp. They will also be capable of integrating interesting features of languages other than Lisp, such as Smalltalk, PS (Production System), and APL. Prolog seems to be best viewed as the starting point for foundation of a new base language for knowledge information processing.

Prolog is a programming language based on logic. Its foundation is the same as that of formal specification languages that are also based on logic, thus facilitating transformation of formal specifications to programs. Prolog also has the same logical foundation as relational databases, and is suited as a basis for integrating programming and database query languages. Prolog is also intrinsically suited as a basis for realizing natural language processing and higher level inference functions.

Then will Prolog machines be feasible? If they follow the same line as current Lisp machines, yes, they are technically feasible even now. They will represent somewhat extended Lisp machines. Since Prolog is a language based on elementary inference operations, Prolog machines could represent the first step towards inference machines.

It should in the near future be technically possible to achieve conversational Prolog machines, equipped with for instance, 1M byte or more of main memory, disks of 40M bytes or more, a high quality graphics display, etc., and to create environments so that they can be used as personal machines. A system integrating these in a network would be useful, if not indispensable, for the future development of high-level information processing techniques.

By adding Kanji input and output functions, these machines would also be able to provide a testbed for Japanese language machines. Machines such as the above can be considered as technically belonging to the fourth generation.

Pondering over the above systems provides a starting point towards the knowledge information processing systems we propose, and also a shortcut to them. Technologies accumulated so far may provide the route for successful continuation into future technologies.

3.4.2 New Architecture Machines. Research has progressed on inference systems that could form the basis of knowledge information processing. In the light of such inference systems, how will inference processor hardware emerge? Then, where and how will such hardware be related to a new architecture?

Research is about to be promoted to consider a new architecture based on the Prolog language mentioned earlier and connection graph inference systems. If we attempt to predict the new architecture, it will be an extended and developed form of the dataflow machines and database machines that have recently been the subject of intensive research efforts.

Dataflow machines are currently regarded mainly as one possible configuration of parallel processors intended for ultra-high-speed numerical computation. That they are considered more promising than past approaches is due to expectations that the type of programming difficulties inherent in conventional parallel processors will be eliminated by adopting the functional programming styles of Backus (1978) and others.

Meanwhile, thinking about Prolog and related languages, and certain restrictions to them, you have dataflow architecture. Stated backwards, this means that Prolog machine architecture could take the form of an extension of dataflow machines. Methods for the extension, however, are not clear at present. All the same, such methods are feasible, given that Dennis' dataflow machines can be considered as essentially message flow machines, and extended on that basis.

As for database machines, relational algebra processors are a special kind of inference machine. As stated earlier, proposals have been made to construct such processors in a dataflow style. These would represent dataflow type inference machines, albeit in a specialized form.

When dataflow machines themselves are still at the research stage and even their structure has yet to be established, discussing their extensions may sound like jumping the gun, but various indications of the feasibility of extensions are apparent.

Nondeterminism in inference systems, (though efforts must, of course, be made to reduce it by analysis of problems and by adequate algorithms), is essentially unavoidable. With current serial machines, such efforts are accomplished by backtracking control, which lowers efficiency. This control essentially belongs in the realm of parallel operations. How to achieve parallelism is a problem, and research on dataflow machines as parallel processors has become focused on two main streams of architecture research. If inference machines are to come out of extending dataflow machines, then research should indicate how to achieve inference machines with a revolutionary architecture.

3.5   System Applications

In the foregoing sections, we have described images and the constituent elements for knowledge information processing, and these will now be reviewed from the viewpoint of systems application.

First, let us take the application field, design systems. Design is generally an intellectual activity, and computer assistance is as yet limited to low levels. Design operations vary with the objective.

Mechanical designs (CAD/CAM), for instance, require input and output of graphic information (Maruyama et al., 1984). This, however, is a minimum requirement, and to step up computer assistance, it will be necessary to accumulate numerous models relating to object worlds and to utilize them. Such information may be termed "knowledge." Furthermore, to utilize this knowledge, "problem-solving" functions intended to achieve specific designs from given specifications will be required. Aside from CAD systems expected to be coming out in the near future, the highly functional CADs of the future will require knowledge-based processing. Here, smooth communications and knowledge utilization will be essential, and "knowledge information processors" such as are described will constitute their basis.

Design objectives are various. In a separate field from mechanical designs, there is, "material design." In order to "invent" a new material with required characteristics, fundamental knowledge (knowledge base) relating to materials is required, to discover the desired characteristics from among a variety of combinations. To aid computers, knowledge-based information processing techniques will also be desirable.

In the meantime, "programming" and "chip design" also belong in a design field closely related to computers. For improving these, too, knowledge-based processing is anticipated. These are themselves also tools for developing knowledge information processing systems.

As a second application field, let us take "consultation." As an example already in use, there is a system named MYCIN in the medical field (Shortliffe, 1976).

This system has knowledge on a multitude of new drugs, and makes "suggestions" to doctors for medication according to symptoms. To produce the suggestions, diagnostic rules need to be integrated. These are systematization of the (partial) knowledge that doctors have. The system also has a subsystem to "explain" on what basis it makes its suggestions.

To perform such functions, the system has a knowledge base of facts and rules, together with an "inference system" to make it work. The inference system has, of course, been simulated on a current computer, and to attain a reasonable performance, the number of utilizable rules is limited to a level of a few hundred. If knowledge information processors as proposed here become a reality, the performance of such systems' capabilities will be vastly improved.

The philosophy of systems such as MYCIN is useful not only in medicine but also in fields such as education. Computer-aided instruction (CAI) has for some time been up against a brick wall. To develop it further into a true CAI, knowledge information processing through conversion of knowledge to rules will be exactly what is needed. A similar situation has applied to management information systems for some time also. This proposal was ahead of its time. To perfect it, a sophisticated knowledge information processing system integrating a variety of economic models and system models is a necessary first step.

Similar comments apply to office automation using the fifth generation computers, which is supposed to follow the fourth generation office automation.

In these systems, knowledge, and inference based on that knowledge, will be central. At the same time, as a medium of communication and knowledge representation, "natural language" will inevitably be required. This, in our case, will be Japanese.

This relates to the question of the problem of "Japanese language machines." Here, in addition to surface structure processing of the Japanese language, more advanced processing will be required.

Input and output centered around character systems such as Kanji and Kana, are currently being energetically developed as "Japanese language information processing." This will spread and become established in the very near future. As the next step, processing techniques that extend into "meaning" will be called for, for true Japanese language information processing. Such techniques will be essential for natural communications, and, at the same time, "understanding" of meaning will itself take place, with knowledge bases and the associated inference playing a central rule.

In the field of natural language processing, there is also the problem of machine translation. Translation systems are again beginning to attract attention. In the background are the needs brought about by advanced internationalization, but at the same time, the attention is motivated by awareness of the need to take advantage of the advances of computer technology in the last twenty years. It is now time to pursue the feasibility of machine translation. Explanation of techniques accumulated over the years is feasible, useful, and meaningful. At the same time, their limitations are also apparent. To reach a good translation level, translation techniques encompassing processing of meaning will be required. Toward this end, further research in linguistics will be necessary, and, at the same time, the creation of a technological system integrating knowledge information processing as described here will also be needed.

The application fields described so far are hardly exhaustive, but through the examples given it should be apparent that knowledge information processing is exactly the kind of information processing that the new age will require. For its realization, precise images and precise development steps are necessary. In addition, a great many research questions will need to be solved in the process.

4   Summary

To construct images for fifth generation computers, and a system for the new age of information processing technology, one of the necessary conditions will be a survey of basic theoretical research. "Basic Theories" here is used, not in a narrow sense, covering just mathematics say, but in a wider sense to include research into the mathematical theory of programming, artificial intelligence, and pattern information processing.

A mere survey of the fields mentioned will not itself provide a definitive image for fifth generation computers, but it is now felt to be time for the survey to at least contribute to the establishment of the image. No conventional definition exists of fifth generation computers.

The Fifth Generation computers will not be an extension of gradual improvements over current computers. There is a feeling that the next stage will be a leap forward rather than just an extension. The background for this feeling is primarily the dissatisfaction with current computers which may loosely be expressed as that they are "hard to use."

This stigma applies to contemporary technology as far as end users and the public at large are concerned. The dissatisfaction surely stems from the immaturity of the current technology, but will it disappear if the current system of technology is improved step by step? Or has it been caused by defects in the basic structure of current computers?

Similar dissatisfaction is also emanating from within computer technology. It may be summarized as difficulties in manufacturing large-scale software. Is this latter due to the immaturity of the software engineering? Partially, yes. Elsewhere, introspection into the current (von Neumann) architecture computers has also been noticeable.

The first problem to be aware of, then, is: *handy computers.*

There are many aspects to handiness. There are a number of ways to describe it in terms of functions. Needs from the user side include the problem of "Japanese language machines." The current situation is far from the ideal of free usage of the Japanese language. Use of Japanese for database queries, programming, questions and answers, and suggestions, is still at a preliminary research stage. For free usage, handling of "meanings" has to be possible, for which, however, much further research will be necessary.

The Japanese language represents one natural form for communication with computers, but from the viewpoint of handiness, graphic communication must also be included in the natural modes of communications. In order to input and output words, voice (audio) input and output is also desirable. To achieve these will require highly sophisticated functions.

Thus, *sophisticated and comprehensive functions, and high performance capabilities* represent some of the requirements for handiness.

From the viewpoint of sophisticated and comprehensive functions, not only will numerical computations be required but also a wider range of "symbol processing" functions that need to be made more sophisticated and efficient. These will be needed for the processing of languages and the manufacture of software.

The viewpoint that will later on prove to be important for sophisticated functions is: *knowledge information processing.*

With current computer technology, most problem-solving must be converted to "programs." This relates to the lack of handiness in computers. On the one hand, further research in the mathematical theory of programming will be required. On the other, integrating "knowledge" will become necessary. It will be necessary to substantially upgrade the problem-solving capabilities of computers in the direction of integrating information concerning the problem domain, plus information on the rules. These kinds of information correspond to what is called "knowledge."

The above is equivalent to extending the range of mutual understanding between man and computers. Not only will it upgrade the problem-solving capabilities of computers, it will also represent capabilities that are essential for natural communication, besides being the basis for realizing true "handiness."

Achieving sophisticated functions through languages and knowledge was a main theme in the seventies for research into "artificial intelligence." Numerous research problems remain to be resolved, and here, too, is grist for the mill in considering fifth generation computers.

Also from the viewpoint of sophisticated functions in the above direction, there emerged demands for a new computer structure (architecture), and suggestions as to what it should be like. To summarize the following are the issues needing to be considered:

New computer architecture.
Withdrawal from conventional systems.
A new system of information processing technology to
represent the ultimate goal for easy-to-use. And,
Whether support by basic theories is feasible.

In this paper I have tried to review trends in the various fields of basic research on information processing. Notable is the fact that these individual research activities now show one direction to converge on, though those activities are being promoted independently.

Judging from this phenomenon, it appears highly probable that during the eighties, basic theories in a wider sense will contribute to new systems of information processing technology, and consequently to the new architecture of fifth generation computers.

Considering the above issues on fifth generation computers, images of the following emerged:

Knowledge information processing systems, and *knowledge*
information processors as their cores, which may be considered as
inference machines (inference engines).

Moreover, in attempting to pursue these images, an essential is: *Sophisticated research environment.*

The excellent research tools and environment must be considered important not only as the means to attain the goal, but also as one of the examples toward the aimed for knowledge information processing systems rather than mere supporting systems. This means that research tools themselves can also be prototypes of knowledge information processing. They will, furthermore, provide the environments for training computer scientists and engineers in this field as well as the ground to establish knowledge information processing as a well-staffed technology.

The research themes to be covered in the research and development of fifth generation computers and the related information processing are summarized below in terms of basic research:

1. Research on natural languages including Japanese: Research on language structure, understanding processes, conversation models, etc.
2. Research on the representation of knowledge and inference: Relations between databases and logics, the handling of large volumes of knowledge, handling of complex (small volumes of) knowledge, and the development of new logics to accompany these.
3. Research in software engineering: Research on specification descriptions, verifications, and program transformations. Development and application of semantics. The state of software in the fifth generation.
4. Research on new computer architecture: Further development of schemes for dataflow machines and database machines (relational algebra machines). Study of architecture for inference-based machines (inference machines, inference engines). Research on parallel algorithms and architectures.

The various research themes described above must be aggressively carried forward. These are intended for development during the eighties and for perfection in the nineties, but at the same time it must be remembered that their basic components were developed during the seventies. While the route to knowledge information processing is an advance to a new age, it can also be viewed as representing the inheritance and development of the legacies of the past from the viewpoint of research efforts. In this sense, the route to knowledge information processing represents a practical philosophy and an inevitable direction for the development of information processing technology. The only question is whether to stand still or proceed, as there are no other paths to choose from.

References

Ashcroft, E. A. and Wadge, W. W., "A Summary of Lucid for Programmers (1981 Version)", Univ. of Waterloo, CS-82-57 (1982).

Backus, J., "Can Programming Be Liberated from the von Neumann Style? A Functional Style and Its Algebra of Programs", CACM, Vol. 21, No. 8, pp. 613–641 (Aug. 1978).

Barwise, J. and Perry, J. "Situations and Attitudes", Bradford Books/MIT Press, Cambridge Mass. (1983).

Bjorner, D. and Jones, C. B. (eds.) "The Vienna Development Method: The Meta-Language", LNCS-61, Springer-Verlag (1978).

Bundy, A. and Welham, B., "Using Meta-level Inference for Selective Application of Multiple Rewrite Rule Sets in Algebraic Manipulation", Artificial Intelligence, Vol. 16, pp. 189–212 (1981).

Campbell, J. A., (ed.) "Implementations of PROLOG", Ellis Horwood (1984).

Chikayama, T. "ESP Reference Manual", ICOT TR-044 (Feb. 1984).

Chomsky, N., "Syntactic Structures", The Hague (1957).

Chomsky, N., "Aspects of the Theory of Syntax", MIT Press (1965).

Clark, K. L. and Gregory, S. "PARLOG: PARALLEL PROGRAMMING in LOGIC", RR DOC 84/4, Imperial College (Apr. 1984).

Clocksin, W. F. and Mellish, C. S., "Programming in Prolog", Springer-Verlag (1981).

Codd, E. F., "A Relational Model of Data for Large Shared Data Banks", CACM, Vol. 13, No. 6, pp. 377–387 (Jun. 1970).

Dahl, O-J., Dijkstra, E. W., Hoare, C. A. R., "Structured Programming" A.P.I.C. Studies in Data Processing, Academic Press (1972).

Davis, R., Buchanan, B. and Shortliffe, E., "Production Rules as a Representation for a Knowledge-Based Consultation Program", Artificial Intelligence, Vol. 8, pp. 15–45 (1977).

Dennis, J. B. and Misunas, D. P., "A Preliminary Architecture for a Basic Data-flow Processor", 2nd Annual Symposium on Computer Architecture, pp. 126–132 (1975).

Dijkstra, E. W., "Go to statement considered harmful", CACM, Vol. 11, No. 3, pp. 147–148 (Mar. 1968).

Doyle, J., "Truth Maintenance Systems for Problem Solving", MIT AI-TR-419 (Jan. 1978).

Feigenbaum, E. A., "The Art of Artificial Intelligence - Themes and Case Studies of Knowledge Engineering", IJCAI 77 (Aug. 1977).

Floyd, R., "Assigning meaning to programs", in "Mathematical Aspects of Computer Science", Vol. XIX, pp. 19–32, American Mathematical Society (1967).

Gallaire, H., and Lasserre, C., "Metalevel control for logic programs", in 'Logic Programming', Academic Press, pp. 173–185 (1982).

Gallaire, H., and Minker, J., (eds.) "Logic and Data Bases", Plenum Press, New York (1978).

Gallin, D., "Intensional and Higher-order Modal Logic - With Applications to Montague Semantics", North-Holland Mathematics Studies 19 (1975).

Gurd, J. R., Kirkham C. C. and Watson, I. "The Manchester prototype dataflow computer", CACM, Vol. 28, No. 1, pp. 34–52 (Jan. 1985).

Hewitt, C., Bishop, P., and Steiger, R., "A Universal Modular ACTOR Formalism for Artificial Intelligence", Proc 3rd IJCAI, pp. 235–245 (1973).

Hoare, C. A. R., "An axiomatic basis for computer programming", CACM, Vol. 12, No. 10, pp. 576–580, and p. 583 (Oct. 1969).

Jackendoff, R. S., "Semantic Interpretation in Generative Grammar", MIT Press, Cambridge Mass. (1972).

Kowalski, R. "A proof procedure using connection graphs", JACM, Vol. 22, pp. 572–595 (1974).

Kripke, S. A., "Semantical analysis of modal logic I", Zeitschrift für mathematische logik und Grundlagen der Mathematik Vol. 9, pp. 67–96 (1963).

Lakoff, G., "On Generative Semantics", in Steinberg and Lakobovits (eds.), 'Semantics: An Interdisciplinary Reader in Philosophy, Linguistics, Anthropology and Psychology', Cambridge Univ. Press, London (1969).

Liskov, B. and Zilles, S. "AN INTRODUCTION TO FORMAL SPECIFICATIONS OF DATA ABSTRACTIONS", in R. Yeh (ed.) "Current Trends in Programming Methodology", Vol. I, Prentice-Hall, pp. 1–32 (1977).

Malachi, Y., Manna, Z., and Waldinger, R. "TABLOG: The Deductive-Tableau Programming Language", in Conf. Rec. of 1984 ACM Symp. of Lisp and Functional Programming, pp. 323–330 (Aug. 1984).

Maruyama, F., Mano, T., Hayashi, K., Kakuda, T., Kawato, N., and Uehara, T. "Prolog-Based Expert System for Logic Design", FGCS'84, p. 563–571 (Nov. 1984).

McCorduck, P., "Machines Who Think", Freeman (1979).

Montague, R. "The Proper Treatment of Quantification in Ordinary English" in Hintikka et al. (eds.) 'Approaches to Natural Language' pp. 221–242, Reidel Dordrecht (1973).

Nakajima, R. and Yuasa, T., (eds.) "The IOTA Programming System" LNCS Vol. 160, Springer-Verlag (1983).

Ottman, T. A., Rosenberg, A. L., and Stockmeyer, L. J. "A Dictionary Machine (for VLSI)", IEEE, Vol. C-31, No. 9, pp. 892–897 (Sep. 1982).

Pepper, P. (ed.) "Program Transformation and Programming Environments - Report on a workshop directed by F. L. Bauer and H. Remus", NATO ASI Series, Springer-Verlag (1984).

Pratt, V. R., "Lingol-A progress report", The fourth IJCAI (1975).

Reiter, R., "On Closed World Data Bases", in Gallaire, H. and Minker, J. (eds.) 'Logic and Data Bases', Plenum Press, pp. 55–76 (1978).

Russell, R. M. "The CRAY-1 Computing System" CACM, Vol. 21, No. 1, pp. 63–72 (Jan. 1978).

Shapiro, E. Y. "A Subset of Concurrent Prolog and Its Interpreter", ICOT TR-003 (Jan. 1983).

Shortliffe, E. H., "MYCIN: Computer-based Medical Consultations", Elsevier (1976).

Sickel, S., "A search technique for clause interconnectivity graphs", IEEE Trans. Comp., Special Issue on Automatic Theorem Proving, Vol. C-25, No. 8, pp. 823–835 (Aug. 1976).

Stickel, M. E. "A NONCLAUSAL CONNECTION-GRAPH RESOLUTION THEOREM-PROVING PROGRAM", AAAI-82, pp. 229–233 (Oct. 1982).

Stoy, J. E., "Denotational Semantics: The Scott-Strachey Approach to Programming Language Theory", MIT Press (1977).

Sussman, G. J., McDermott, D. V., "From PLANNER to CONNIVER - a genetic approach", Proc. FJCC, pp. 1171–1179 (1973).

Tanaka, Y. "MPDC: MASSIVE PARALLEL ARCHITECTURE FOR VERY LARGE DATABASE", Proc. FGCS'84, pp. 113–137 (Nov. 1984).

Tsichritzis, D. C. and Lochousky, F. H., "Data Models", Prentice-Hall (1982).

Weyhrauch, R. W., "A Users Manual for FOL", Stanford AI Lab. AIM-235.1, Computer Science Dept. Stanford Univ. (Jul. 1977).

Winograd, T., "Understanding natural language", Academic Press (1972).

Author Index

Italics indicate bibliographic citations.

Subject Index